Digital Forensics and Incident Response

An intelligent way to respond to attacks

Gerard Johansen

BIRMINGHAM - MUMBAI

Digital Forensics and Incident Response

First published: July 2017

Production reference: 1210717

Published by Packt Publishing Ltd.
Livery Place
35 Livery Street
Birmingham
B3 2PB, UK.

ISBN 978-1-78728-868-3

www.packtpub.com

Credits

Author
Gerard Johansen

Reviewer
Nicole L. Stoneman

Acquisition Editor
Rahul Nair

Content Development Editor
Abhishek Jadhav

Technical Editor
Manish D Shanbhag

Production Coordinator
Aparna Bhagat

Copy Editor
Safis Editing

Project Coordinator
Judie Jose

Proofreader
Safis Editing

Indexer
Aishwarya Gangawane

Graphics
Kirk D'Penha

About the Author

Gerard Johansen is an information security professional with over a decade of experience in such areas as penetration testing, vulnerability management, threat assessment modeling, and incident response. Beginning his information security career while a cybercrime investigator, Gerard has built on that experience while working as a consultant and security analyst for clients and organizations ranging from healthcare to finance. Gerard is a graduate of Norwich University's Masters of Science in Information Assurance and a Certified Information Systems Security Professional.

Gerard is currently employed as an Enterprise Security Manager with a large retailer with a focus on incident detection, response and threat intelligence integration. He has also contributed to several online publications focused on various aspects of penetration testing.

About the Reviewer

Nicole L. Stoneman is the Director of Digital of Forensics at Vestigant. Ms. Stoneman has been conducting computer forensic exams since 2005 and has been involved in thousands of forensic investigations. Ms. Stoneman is a Certified Computer Examiner (CCE) through The International Society of Forensic Computer Examiners.

www.PacktPub.com

For support files and downloads related to your book, please visit www.PacktPub.com.

Did you know that Packt offers eBook versions of every book published, with PDF and ePub files available? You can upgrade to the eBook version at www.PacktPub.com and as a print book customer, you are entitled to a discount on the eBook copy. Get in touch with us at service@packtpub.com for more details.

At www.PacktPub.com, you can also read a collection of free technical articles, sign up for a range of free newsletters and receive exclusive discounts and offers on Packt books and eBooks.

https://www.packtpub.com/mapt

Get the most in-demand software skills with Mapt. Mapt gives you full access to all Packt books and video courses, as well as industry-leading tools to help you plan your personal development and advance your career.

Why subscribe?

- Fully searchable across every book published by Packt
- Copy and paste, print, and bookmark content
- On demand and accessible via a web browser

Customer Feedback

Thanks for purchasing this Packt book. At Packt, quality is at the heart of our editorial process. To help us improve, please leave us an honest review on this book's Amazon page at https://www.amazon.com/dp/1787288684/.

If you'd like to join our team of regular reviewers, you can e-mail us at customerreviews@packtpub.com. We award our regular reviewers with free eBooks and videos in exchange for their valuable feedback. Help us be relentless in improving our products!

Table of Contents

Preface

Digital Forensics and Incident Response will guide you through the entire spectrum of tasks associated with incident response, starting with preparatory activities associated with creating an incident response plan and creating a digital forensics capability within your own organization. You will then begin a detailed examination of digital forensic techniques including acquiring evidence, examining volatile memory, hard drive assessment, and network-based evidence. You will also explore the role that threat intelligence plays in the incident response process. Finally, a detailed section on preparing reports will help you prepare a written report for use either internally or in a courtroom.

By the end of the book, you will have mastered forensic techniques and incident response and you will have a solid foundation on which to increase your ability to investigate such incidents in your organization.

What this book covers

Chapter 1, *Incident Response*, addresses the incident response process and how to create an incident response framework for use within an enterprise, which allows for an orderly investigation and remediation of a cyber security incident.

Chapter 2, *Forensics Fundamentals*, focuses on the fundamental aspects of digital forensics. This includes a brief history of digital forensics, the basic elements of forensic science, and integrating these techniques into the incident response framework.

Chapter 3, *Network Evidence Collection*, focuses on the network-based evidence. This includes logs from network devices such as firewalls, routers, proxy servers, and other layer 2 and 3 devices. The chapter also focuses on acquiring network-based evidence from these sources.

Chapter 4, *Host-Based Evidence*, compromised hosts contain a good deal of forensically valuable information. In this chapter, the reader guided through the process of using free tools to acquire the running volatile memory, log files, and other evidence on a running system.

Chapter 5, *Understanding Forensics Imaging*, hard disk drives from compromised systems may contain a great deal of evidence. Furthermore, in cases of fraud or other cybercrimes, most of the evidence that is valuable is obtained from the HDD. As a result, the proper acquisition of this evidence is critical. To do this requires a forensically sound process. This chapter details the steps necessary to properly image a suspect HDD.

Chapter 6, *Network Evidence Analysis*, using free tools such as tcpdump and Wireshark, the reader is guided through the analysis process to identify evidence such as command and control traffic or data exfiltration. Readers are also be guided through correlating firewall and proxy logs with packet captures.

Chapter 7, *Analyzing System Memory*, explores the methods for identifying potential malicious code present within the memory of a compromised system. This includes using commonly available tools and methods to identify processes, network connections, and registry key settings associated with potentially malicious software.

Chapter 8, *Analyzing System Storage*, consists of an overview of several tools and methods available for extracting potential evidence from previously imaged HDDs. An examination of tools and methods is undertaken, but it should be noted that, due to the complexity and depth of digital forensic examination, this will serve only to highlight specific areas.

Chapter 9, *Forensic Reporting*, reporting the findings from an incident is a critical step that is often overlooked. In this chapter, the reader is guided through preparing a report for use by internal stakeholders and potential external legal entities. The end goal is to have a report prepared that can stand the scrutiny of a court of law.

Chapter 10, *Malware Analysis*, will provide an overview of the methods that can be deployed for examining malware in a sandbox environment. This provides incident responders with reverse engineering skills an environment to deploy a suspected piece of malware for investigation.

Chapter 11, *Threat Intelligence*, threat intelligence is a relatively new concept in the information security space, and in particular to the incident response field. In this chapter, the reader will be guided through a review of threat intelligence and how to incorporate that into their incident response framework and processes.

What you need for this book

The following software is required for this book:

- EnCase Imager
- F-Response
- Rekal
- Madiant Redline
- Autopsy

- Wireshark
- tcpdump
- Volatility
- Security Onion
- FTK Imager
- Winpmem
- Eraser
- CAINE OS, a Linux distribution for forensics purposes
- Xplico and CapAnalysis
- ELK stack
- **Fast Incident Response (FIR)** platform
- Pestudio
- Remnux
- Cuckoo Sandbox
- Yara and Loki

The hardware and system requirements for these can be found at there respective websites. Most of this softwares are free, but F-Response is paid.

Who this book is for

This book is targeted at information security professionals, forensics practitioners, and students with knowledge of and experience in the use of software applications and basic command-line experience. It will also help professionals who are new to the incident response/digital forensics role within their organization.

Conventions

In this book, you will find a number of text styles that distinguish between different kinds of information. Here are some examples of these styles and an explanation of their meaning. Code words in text, database table names, folder names, filenames, file extensions, pathnames, dummy URLs, user input, and Twitter handles are shown as follows: The constituency can be defined either as a domain such as `local.example.com` or an organization name such as Acme Inc. and associated subsidiary organizations.

A block of code is set as follows:

```
rule PoisonIvy_Generic_3 {
        meta:
            description = "PoisonIvy RAT Generic Rule"
            author = "Florian Roth"
            date = "2015-05-14"
            hash = "e1cbdf740785f97c93a0a7a01ef2614be792afcd"
        strings:
            $k1 = "Tiger324{" fullword ascii
```

Any command-line input or output is written as follows:

```
caine@caine~$ tcpdump -D
caine@caine~$ sudotcpdump -i ens33 -v
```

New terms and **important words** are shown in bold. Words that you see on the screen, for example, in menus or dialog boxes, appear in the text like this: "In order for F-Response to be able to acquire the necessary evidence, an agent has to be installed.by right-clicking on the system and choosing **Install/Start F-Response**"

Warnings or important notes appear like this

Tips and tricks appear like this

Reader feedback

Feedback from our readers is always welcome. Let us know what you think about this book-what you liked or disliked. Reader feedback is important for us as it helps us develop titles that you will really get the most out of. To send us general feedback, simply e-mail feedback@packtpub.com, and mention the book's title in the subject of your message. If there is a topic that you have expertise in and you are interested in either writing or contributing to a book, see our author guide at www.packtpub.com/authors.

Customer support

Now that you are the proud owner of a Packt book, we have a number of things to help you to get the most from your purchase.

Downloading the color images of this book

We also provide you with a PDF file that has color images of the screenshots/diagrams used in this book. The color images will help you better understand the changes in the output. You can download this file from `https://www.packtpub.com/sites/default/files/down loads/DigitalForensicsandIncidentResponse_ColorImages.pdf`.

Errata

Although we have taken every care to ensure the accuracy of our content, mistakes do happen. If you find a mistake in one of our books-maybe a mistake in the text or the code-we would be grateful if you could report this to us. By doing so, you can save other readers from frustration and help us improve subsequent versions of this book. If you find any errata, please report them by visiting `http://www.packtpub.com/submit-errata`, selecting your book, clicking on the **Errata Submission Form** link, and entering the details of your errata. Once your errata are verified, your submission will be accepted and the errata will be uploaded to our website or added to any list of existing errata under the Errata section of that title. To view the previously submitted errata, go to `https://www.packtpub.com/book s/content/support`and enter the name of the book in the search field. The required information will appear under the **Errata** section.

Piracy

Piracy of copyrighted material on the Internet is an ongoing problem across all media. At Packt, we take the protection of our copyright and licenses very seriously. If you come across any illegal copies of our works in any form on the Internet, please provide us with the location address or website name immediately so that we can pursue a remedy. Please contact us at `copyright@packtpub.com` with a link to the suspected pirated material. We appreciate your help in protecting our authors and our ability to bring you valuable content.

Questions

If you have a problem with any aspect of this book, you can contact us at `questions@packtpub.com`, and we will do our best to address the problem.

1
Incident Response

There are a number of threats to today's complex information systems. An internal employee can download a single instance of ransomware and can have a significant impact on an organization. More complex attacks such as a network exploitation attempt or targeted data breach increases the chaos that a security incident causes. Technical personnel will have their hands full, attempting to determine what systems have been impacted and how they are being manipulated. They will also have to possibly contend with addressing the possible loss of data through compromised systems. Adding to this chaotic situation is senior managers haranguing them for updates and an answer to the central questions of *how did this happen?* and *how bad is it?*

Having the ability to properly respond to security incidents in an orderly and efficient manner allows organizations to both limit the damage of a potential cyber attack, but also recover from the associated damage that is caused. To facilitate this orderly response, organizations of all sizes have looked at adding an **incident response** capability to their existing policies and procedures.

In order to build this capability within the organization, several key components must be addressed. First, organizations need to have a working knowledge of the incident response process. This process outlines the general flow of an incident and the general actions that are taken at each stage. Second, organizations need to have access to personnel who form the nucleus of any incident response capability. Once a team is organized, a formalized plan and associated processes need to be created. This written plan and processes form the orderly structure that an organization can follow during an incident. Finally, with this framework in place, the plan has to be continually evaluated, tested, and improved as new threats immerge. Utilizing this framework will position organizations to be prepared for the unfortunate reality that many organizations have already faced, an incident that compromises their security.

The incident response process

There is a general path that cyber security incidents follow during their lifetime. If the organization has a mature incident response capability, they will have taken measures to ensure they are prepared to address an incident at each stage of the process. Each incident starts with the first time the organization becomes aware of an event or series of events indicative of malicious activity. This detection can come in the form of a security control alert or external party informing the organization of a potential security issue. Once alerted, the organization moves through analyzing the incident through containment measures to bring the information system back to normal operations. The following figure shows how these flow in a cycle with **Preparation** as the starting point. Closer examination reveals that every incident is used to better prepare the organization for future incidents as the **Post Incident Activity** and is utilized in the preparation for the next incident:

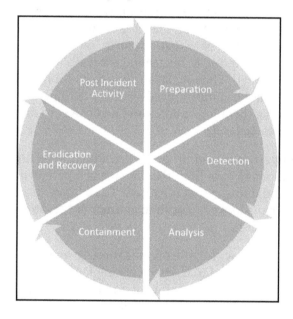

The incident response process can be broken down into six distinct phases, each with a set of actions the organization can take to address the incident:

1. **Preparation:** Without good preparation, any subsequent incident response is going to be disorganized and has the potential to make the incident worse. Some of the critical components of preparation are the creation of an incident response plan. Once a plan is in place with the necessary staffing, ensure that personnel detailed with incident response duties are properly trained. This includes both processes, procedures, and any additional tools necessary for the investigation of an incident. In addition to the plan, tools such as forensics hardware and software should be acquired and incorporated into the overall process. Finally, regular exercises should be conducted to ensure that the organization is trained and familiar with the process.

2. **Detection:** The detection of potential incidents is a complex endeavor. Depending on the size of the organization, they may have over 100 million separate events per day. Couple this mountain of events with other security controls constantly alerting to activity and you have a situation where analysts are inundated with data and have to subsequently sift out the valuable pieces of signal from the vastness of network noise. Even today's cutting edge **Security Incident and Event Management (SIEM)** tools lose their effectiveness if they are not properly maintained with regular updates of rule sets that identify what events classify as a potential incident. The detection phase is that part of the incident response process where the organization first becomes aware of a set of events that possibly indicates malicious activity. This can be from the SIEM technology or other security controls. For example, a security analyst may receive an alert that a particular administrator account was in use during a period of time where the user was on vacation. Detection may also come from external sources. An ISP or law enforcement agency may detect malicious activity originating in an organization's network and contact them and advise them of the situation.
   In other instances, users may be the first to indicate a potential security incident. This may be as simple as an employee contacting the help desk and informing a help desk technician that they received an Excel spreadsheet from an unknown source and opened it. They are now complaining that their files on the local system are being encrypted. In each case, an organization would have to escalate each of these events to the level of an incident (which we will cover a little later in this chapter) and begin the reactive process to investigate and remediate.

3. **Analysis:** Once an incident has been detected, personnel from the organization or a trusted third party will begin the analysis phase. In this phase, personnel begin the task of collecting evidence from systems such as running memory, log files, network connections, and running software processes. Depending on the type of incident, this collection can take as little as a few hours to several days.

   Once the evidence is collected, it then has to be examined. There are a variety of tools to conduct this analysis, many of which are explored in this book. With these tools, analysts are attempting to ascertain what happened, what it affected, whether any other systems were involved, and whether any confidential data was removed. The ultimate goal of the analysis is to determine the root cause of the incident and reconstruct the actions of the threat actor from initial compromise to detection.

4. **Containment:** Once there is a solid understanding of what the incident is and what systems are involved, organizations can then move into the containment phase. In this phase, organizations take measures to limit the ability for threat actors to continue compromising other network resources, communicating with command and control infrastructures, or exfiltrating confidential data. Containment strategies can range from locking down ports and IP address on a firewall to simply removing the network cable from the back of an infected machine. Each type of incident involves its own containment strategy, but having several options allows personnel to stop the bleeding at the source if they are able to detect a security incident before or during the time when threat actors are pilfering data.

5. **Eradication and recovery:** During the eradication phase, the organization removes the threat actor from the impacted network. In the case of a malware infection, the organization may run an enhanced anti-malware solution. Other times, infected machines have to be wiped and reimaged. Other activities include removing or changing compromised user accounts. If an organization has identified a vulnerability that was exploited, vendor patches are applied or software updates are made. Recovery activities are very closely aligned with those that may be found in an organization's *business continuity or disaster recovery* plans. In this phase of the process, organizations reinstall fresh operating systems or applications. They will also restore data on local systems from backups. As a due diligence step, organizations will also audit their existing user and administrator accounts to ensure that there are no accounts that have been enabled by threat actors. Finally, a comprehensive vulnerability scan is conducted so that the organization is confident that any exploitable vulnerabilities have been removed.

6. **Post-incident activity:** At the conclusion of the incident process is a complete review of the incident with all the principle stakeholders. Post-incident activity includes a complete review of all the actions taken during the incident. What worked and more importantly, what did not work are important topics for discussion. These reviews are important because they may highlight specific tasks and actions that had either a positive or negative impact on the outcome of the incident response. It is during this phase of the process that a written report is completed. Documenting the actions taken during the incident is critical to capture both what occurred and also whether the incident will ever see the inside of a courtroom. For documentation to be effective, it should be detailed and show a clear chain of events with a focus on the root cause if it was determined. Personnel involved in the preparation of this report should realize that stakeholders outside of information technology might read this report. As a result, technical jargon or concepts should be explained.

Finally, the organizational personnel should update their own incident response processes with any new information developed during the post-incident debrief and reporting. This incorporation of *lessons learned* is important as it makes future responses to incidents more effective.

The role of digital forensics

There is a misconception that is often held by people unfamiliar with the realm of incident response. This misconception is that incident response is merely a digital forensics issue. As a result, they will often conflate the two terms. While digital forensics is a critical component to incident response (and this is why we have included a number of chapters in this book to address digital forensics), there is more to addressing an incident than examining hard drives. It is best to think of forensics as a supporting function of the overall incident response process. For example, some incidents such as **Denial of Service** attacks will require little to no forensic work. On the other hand, a network intrusion involving the compromise of an internal server and **Command and Control (C2)** traffic leaving the network will require extensive examination of logs, traffic analysis, and examination of memory. From this analysis may be derived the root cause. In both cases, the impacted organization would be able to connect with the incident, but forensics played a much more important role in the latter case.

The incident response framework

When examining the incident response process, it is not ad hoc. Undefined processes or procedures will leave an organization unable to both identify the extent of the incident and be able to stop the bleeding in sufficient time to limit damage. Having an understanding of the incident response process is just the first step to building this capability within an organization. What is needed is a framework that puts that process to work utilizing the organization's available resources. The incident response framework describes the components of a functional incident response capability within an organization. This framework is made up of elements such as personnel, policies, and procedures. It is through these elements that an organization builds its capability to respond to incidents.

The incident response charter

The first step to building this capability is the decision by senior leadership that the risk to the organization is too significant not to address the possibility of a potential security incident. Once that point is reached, a senior member of the organization will serve as a project sponsor and craft the incident response charter. This charter outlines key elements that will drive the creation of a **Computer Security Incident Response Team (CSIRT)**.

 While there are a good deal of titles for incident response teams, the term **Computer Emergency Response Team (CERT)** is often associated with the US-CERT through the **United States Department of Homeland Security** or the **Computer Emergency Response Team Coordination Center (CERT/CC)** through the Carnegie Mellon Software Engineering Institute. For our purposes, we will use the more generic CSIRT.

The incident response charter should be a written document that addresses the following:

- **Obtain senior leadership support**: In order to be a viable part of the organization, the CSIRT requires the support of the senior leadership within the organization. In a private sector institution, it may be difficult to obtain the necessary support and funding, as the CSIRT itself does not provide value in the same way marketing or sales does. What should be understood is that the CSIRT acts as an insurance policy in the event the worse happens. In this manner, a CSRIT can justify its existence by reducing the impact of incidents and thereby reducing the costs associated with a security breach or other malicious activity.

- **Define the constituency**: The constituency clearly defines which organizational elements and domains the CSIRT has responsibility for. Some organizations have several divisions or subsidiaries that for whatever reason may not be part of the CSIRT's responsibility. The constituency can be defined either as a domain such as `local.example.com` or an organization name such as Acme Inc. and associated subsidiary organizations.
- **Create a mission statement**: Mission creep or the gradual expansion of the CSIRT's responsibilities can occur without clear definition of what the defined purpose of the CSIRT is. In order to counter this, a clearly defined mission statement should be included with the written information security plan. For example, *The mission of the Acme Inc. CSIRT is to provide timely analysis and actions to security incidents that impact the Confidentiality, Integrity, and Availability of ACME Inc. information systems and personnel.*
- **Determine service delivery**: Along with a mission statement, a clearly defined list of services can also counter the risk of mission creep of the CSIRT. Services are usually divided into two separate categories, proactive and reactive services:
    - **Proactive services:** These includes providing training for non-CSIRT staff, providing summaries on emerging security threats, testing and deployment of security tools, and assisting security operations with crafting IDS/IPS alerting rules.
    - **Reactive services:** These primarily revolve around responding to incidents as they occur. For the most part, reactive services address the entire incident response process. This includes the acquisition and examination of evidence, assisting in containment, eradication, and recovery efforts, and finally documenting the incident.

CSIRT

Once the incident response charter is completed, the next stage is to start staffing the CSIRT. Larger organizations with sufficient resources may be able to task personnel with incident response duties full-time. More often than not though, organizations will have to utilize personnel who have other duties outside incident response. Personnel who comprise the internal CSIRT can be divided into three categories: core team, technical support, and organizational support. Each individual within the CSIRT fulfills a specific task. Building this capability into an organization takes more than just assigning personnel and creating a policy and procedure document. Like any major project initiative, there is a good deal of effort required in order to create a functional CSIRT.

For each of the CSIRT categories, there are specific roles and responsibilities. This wide range of personnel is designed to provide guidance and support through a wide range of incidents ranging from the minor to the catastrophic.

CSIRT core team

The CSIRT core team consists of personnel who have incident response duties as their full-time job or assume incident response activities when needed. In many instances, the core team is often made up of personnel assigned to the information security team. Other organizations can leverage personnel with expertise in incident response activities. The following are some of the roles that can be incorporated into the core team:

- **Incident response coordinator**: This is a critical component of any CSIRT. Without clear leadership, the response to a potential incident may be disorganized or with multiple individuals via for control during an incident, a chaotic situation that can make the incident worse. In many instances, the incident response coordinator is often the **chief security officer (CSO)**, **chief information security officer (CISO)**, or the **information security officer (ISO)** as that individual often has overall responsibility for the security of the organization's information. Other organizations may name a single individual who serves as the incident response coordinator.

  The incident response coordinator is responsible for management of the CSIRT prior to, during, and after an incident. In terms of preparation, the incident response coordinator will ensure that any plans or policies concerning the CSIRT are reviewed periodically and updated as needed. In addition, the incident response coordinator is responsible for ensuring that the CSIRT team is appropriately trained and oversees testing and training for CSIRT personnel. During an incident, the incident response coordinator is responsible for ensuring the proper response and remediation of an incident and guides the team through the entire incident response process. One of the most important of these tasks during an incident is coordination of the CSIRT with senior leadership. With the stakes of a data breach high, senior leadership such as the Chief Executive Officer will want to be informed of the critical information concerning an incident. It is the responsibility of the incident response coordinator to ensure that the senior leadership is fully informed of the activities associated with an incident. Finally, at the conclusion of an incident, the incident response coordinator is responsible for ensuring that the incident is properly documented and that reports of the CSIRT activity are delivered to the appropriate internal and external stakeholders. In addition, a full debrief of all CSIRT activities is conducted and lessons learned are incorporated into the CSIRT Plan.

- **CSIRT Senior Analyst(s)**: CSIRT Senior Analysts are personnel with extensive training and experience in incident response and associated skills such as digital forensics or network data examination. They often have several years of experience conducting incident response activities as either a consultant or as part of an enterprise CSIRT.

  During the preparation phase of the incident response process, they are involved in ensuring that they have the necessary skills and training to address their specific role in the CSIRT. They are also often directed to assist in the incident response plan review and modification. Finally, senior analysts will often take part in training junior members of the team.

  Once an incident has been identified, the senior analysts will engage with other CSIRT members to acquire and analyze evidence, direct containment activities, and assist other personnel with remediation.

  At the conclusion of an incident, the senior analysts will ensure that both they and other personnel appropriately document the incident. This will include the preparation of reports to internal and external stakeholders. They will also ensure that any evidence is appropriately archived or destroyed depending on the incident response plan.

- **CSIRT Analyst(s)**: The CSIRT Analysts are personnel with CSIRT responsibilities that have less exposure or experience in incident response activities. Oftentimes, they have only one or two years of responding to incidents. As a result, they can perform a variety of activities with some of those under the direction of senior analysts.

  In terms of preparation phase activities, analysts will develop their skills via training and exercises. They may also take part in reviews and updates to the incident response plan. During an incident, they will be tasked with gathering evidence from potentially compromised hosts, from network devices, or from various log sources. Analysts will also take part in the analysis of evidence and assist other team members in remediation activities.

- **Security operations center analyst**: Larger enterprises may have an in-house or contracted 24/7 **Security Operations Center (SOC)** monitoring capability. Analysts assigned to the SOC will often serve as the point person when it comes to incident detection and alerting. As a result, having an SOC analyst as part of the team allows them to be trained on techniques and serve as an almost immediate response to a potential security incident.

- **IT Security Engineer / Analyst(s)**: Depending on the size of the organization, there may be personnel specifically tasked with the deployment, maintenance, and monitoring of security-related software such as anti-virus or hardware such as firewalls or SIEM systems. Having direct access to these devices is critical when an incident has been identified. The personnel assigned these duties will often have a direct role in the entire incident response process.

  The IT Security Engineer or Analyst will often have a large piece of the preparation component of the incident response process. They will be the primary resource to ensure that security applications and devices are properly configured to alert to possible incidents and to ensure that the devices properly log events so that a reconstruction of events can take place.

  During an incident, they will be tasked with monitoring security systems for other indicators of malicious behavior. They will also assist the other CSIRT personnel with obtaining evidence from the security devices. Finally, after an incident, these personnel will be tasked with configuring security devices to monitor for suspected behavior to ensure that remediation activities have eradicated the malicious activity on impacted systems.

Technical support personnel

Technical support personnel are those individuals within the organization who do not have CSIRT activities as part of their day-to-day operations, but rather have expertise or access to systems and processes that may be affected by an incident. For example, the CSIRT may need to engage a server administrator to assist the core team with acquiring evidence from servers such as memory captures or logs. Once completed, the server administrator's role is finished and they may have no further involvement in the incident. The following are some of the personnel that can be of assistance to the CSIRT during an incident:

- **Network Architect/Administrator**: Often, incidents involve the network infrastructure. This includes attacks on routers, switches, and other network hardware and software. The Network Architect or Administrator is vital for insight into what is normal and abnormal behavior of these devices as well as identifying anomalous network traffic. In incidents where the network infrastructure is involved, these support personnel can assist with obtaining network evidence such as access logs or packet captures.

- **Server Administrator**: Threat actors often target systems within the network where critical or sensitive data is stored. These high-value targets often include domain controllers, file servers, or database servers. Server Administrators can aid in acquiring log files from these systems. If the server administrator(s) are also responsible for the maintenance of the active directory structure, they may be able to assist with identifying new user accounts or changes to existing user or administrator accounts.

- **Application support**: Web applications are a prime target for threat actors. Flaws in coding that allow for attacks such as SQL injection or security misconfigurations are responsible for some security breaches. As a result, having application support personnel as part of the CSIRT allows for direct information related to application attacks. These individuals will often be able to identify code changes or to confirm vulnerabilities discovered during an investigation into a potential attack against an application.

- **Desktop support**: Desktop Support personnel are often involved in maintaining controls such as data loss prevention and anti-virus on desktop systems. In the event of an incident, they can assist in providing the CSIRT with log files and other evidence. They may also be responsible for cleaning up infected systems during the remediation phase of an incident.

- **Help Desk**: Depending on the organization, help desk personnel are the proverbial *canary in the coal mine* when it comes to identifying an incident. They are often the first individuals contacted when a user experiences the first signs of a malware infection or other malicious activity. Thus, help desk personnel should be involved in training of the CSIRT responses and their role in the incident identification and escalation procedures. They may also assist with identifying additional affected personnel in the event of a widespread incident.

Organizational support personnel

Outside of the technical realm, there are still other organizational members that should be included within the CSIRT. Organizational personnel can assist with a number of non-technical issues that fall outside those that addressed by the CSIRT core and technical support personnel. These include navigating the internal and external legal environment, assisting with customer communications, or supporting CSIRT personnel while onsite.

The following are some of the organizational support personnel that should be included in a CSIRT Plan:

- **Legal**: Data breaches and other incidents carry a variety of legal issues along with them. Many countries now have breach notification laws where organizations are required to notify customers that their information was put at risk. Other compliance requirements such as HIPAA and the PCI DSS require the impacted organization to make contact with various external bodies and notify them of a suspected breach. Including legal representation early in the incident response process will ensure that these notifications and any other legal requirements are addressed in a timely fashion. In the event that a breach has been caused by an internal source such as an employee or contractor, the impacted organization may want to recoup losses through civil action. Including legal representation early in the process will allow for a more informed decision as to what legal process should be followed.

- **Human resources**: A good deal of incidents that occur in organizations are perpetrated by employees or contractors. The investigation of actions such as fraud all the way to massive data theft may have to be investigated by the CSIRT. In the event that the target of the investigation is an employee or contractor, the human resources department can assist with ensuring that the CSIRT's actions are in compliance with applicable labor laws and company policies. If an employee or contractor is to be terminated, the CSIRT can coordinate with the human resources personnel so that all proper documentation concerning the incident is complete to reduce the potential of a wrongful termination suit.

- **Marketing/communications**: If external clients or customers may be adversely impacted by an incident such as a Denial of Service attack or data breach, the marketing or communications department can assist in crafting the appropriate message to assuage fears and ensure that those external entities are receiving the best information possible. When looking back at past data breaches where organizations attempted to keep the details to themselves and customers were not informed, there was a backlash against those organizations. Having a solid communications plan that is put into action early will go a long way to soothing any potential customer or client adverse reactions.

- **Facilities**: The CSIRT may need access to areas after hours or for a prolonged time. The facilities department can assist the CSIRT in obtaining the necessary access in a timely manner. Facilities also may have access to additional meeting spaces for the CSIRT to utilize in the event of a prolonged incident that requires dedicated workspace and infrastructure.

- **Corporate security**: The CSIRT may be called in to deal with the theft of network resources or other technology from the organization. Laptop and digital media theft is very common. Corporate security will often have access to surveillance footage from entrances and exits. They may also maintain access badge and visitor logs for the CSIRT to track movement of employees and other personnel within the facility. This can allow for a reconstruction of events leading up to a theft or other circumstances that led up to the incident.

External resources

Many industries have professional organizations where practitioners, regardless of their employer, can come together to share information. CSIRT personnel may also be tasked with interfacing with law enforcement and government agencies at times, especially if they are targeted as part of a larger attack perpetrated against a number of similar organizations. Having relationships with external organizations and agencies can assist the CSIRT with intelligence sharing and resources in the event of an incident. These resources include the following:

- **High Technology Crime Investigation Association (HTCIA)**: The HTCIA is an international group of professionals and students with a focus on high-tech crime. Resources include everything from digital forensics techniques to wider enterprise-level information that could aid CSIRT personnel with new techniques and methods. For more information visit the official website: `https://htcia.org/`
- **Infragard**: For those CSIRT and information security practitioners in the United States, the Federal Bureau of Investigation has created a private-public partnership geared toward networking and information sharing. This partnership allows CSIRT members to share information about trends or discuss past investigations. We can find more information on the website: `https://www.infragard.org/`
- **Law enforcement**: Law enforcement has seen an explosive growth in cyber-related criminal activity. In response, a great many law enforcement organizations have increased their capacity to investigate cybercrime. CSIRT leadership should cultivate a relationship with agencies that have cybercrime investigative capabilities. Law enforcement agencies can provide insight into specific threats or crimes being committed and provide CSIRTs with any specific information that concerns them.

- **Vendors**: External vendors can be leveraged in the event of an incident and what they can provide is often dependent on the specific line of business the organization has engaged them in. For example, an organization's IPS/IDS solution provider could assist with crafting custom alerting and blocking rules to assist in the detection and containment of malicious activity. Vendors with a threat intelligence capability can also provide guidance on malicious activity indicators. Finally, some organizations will need to engage vendors who have a particular incident response specialty such as reverse engineering malware when those skills fall outside an organization's capability.

Depending on the size of the organization, it is easy to see how the CSIRT can involve a number of people. It is critical to putting together the entire CSIRT that each member is aware of their roles and responsibilities. Each member should also be asked for specific guidance on what expertise can be leveraged during the entire incident response process. This becomes more important in the next part of the incident response framework, which is the creation of an incident response plan.

The incident response plan

With the incident response charter written and the CSIRT formed, the next step is to craft the incident response plan. The incident response plan is the document that outlines the high-level structure of an organization's response capability. This is a high-level document that serves as the foundation of the CSIRT. The major components to the incident response plan are:

- **Incident response charter**: The incident response plan should include the mission statement and constituency from the incident response charter. This gives the plan continuity between the inception of the incident response capability and the incident response plan.
- **Expanded services catalog**: The initial incident response charter had general service categories with no real detail. The incident response plan should include specific details of what services the CSIRT will be offering. For example, if forensic services are listed as part of the service offering, the incident response plan may state that forensic services include the evidence recovery from hard drives, memory forensics, and reverse engineering potentially malicious code in support of an incident. This allows for the CSIRT to clearly delineate between a normal request, say for the searching of a hard drive for an accidentally deleted document not related to an incident, and the imaging of a hard drive in connection with a declared incident.

- **CSIRT personnel**: As was outlined before, there are a great many individuals who comprise the CSIRT. The incident response plan will clearly define these roles and responsibilities. Organizations should expand out from just a name and title and define exactly the roles and responsibilities of each individual. It is not advisable to have a turf war during an incident and having the roles and responsibilities of the CSIRT personnel clearly defined goes a long way to reducing this possibility.

- **Contact list**: An up- to- date contact list should be part of the Incident Response Plan. Depending on the organization, the CSIRT may have to respond to an incident 24 hours a day. In this case, the Incident Response Plan should have primary and secondary contact information. Organizations can also make use of a rotating *on-call* CSIRT member who could serve as the first contact in the event of an incident.

- **Internal communication plan**: Incidents can produce a good deal of chaos as personnel attempt to ascertain what is happening, what resources they need, and who to engage to address the incident. The incident response plan internal communication guidance can address this chaos. This portion of the plan addresses the flow of information upward and downward between senior leadership and the CSIRT. Communications sideways between the CSIRT core and support personnel should also be addressed. This limits the individuals who are communicating with each other and cuts down on potentially conflicting instructions.

Incident classification

Not all incidents are equal in their severity and threat to the organization. For example, a virus that infects several computers in a support area of the organization will dictate a different level of response than an active compromise of a critical server. As a result, it is important to define within the incident response plan an incident classification schema. The following is a sample classification schema:

- **High-level incident**: A high-level incident is an incident that is expected to cause significant damage, corruption, or loss of critical and/or strategic company or customer information. A high-level incident may involve widespread or extended loss of system or network resources. The event can have potential damage and liability to the organization and to the corporate public image. Examples of high-level incidents include, but are not limited to, the following:
    - Network intrusion
    - Physical compromise of information systems
    - Compromise of critical information

- Loss of computer system or removable media containing un-encrypted confidential information
- Widespread and growing malware infection (more than 25% of hosts)
- Targeted attacks against the IT infrastructure
- Phishing attacks using the organization's domain and branding

- **Moderate-level incident**: A moderate-level incident is an incident that may cause damage, corruption, or loss of replaceable information without compromise (there has been no misuse of sensitive customer information). A moderate-level event may involve significant disruption to a system or network resource. It also may have an impact to the mission of a business unit within the corporation:
  - Anticipated or ongoing Denial of Service attack
  - Loss of computer system or removable media containing un-encrypted confidential information
  - Misuse or abuse of authorized access
  - Automated intrusion
  - Confined malware infection
  - Unusual system performance or behavior
  - Installation of malicious software
  - Suspicious changes or computer activity
  - Playbooks can be configured in a number of ways. For example, a written document can be added to the Incident Response Plan for specific types of incidents. Other times, organizations can use a flow diagram utilizing software such as iStudio or Visio. Depending on how the organization chooses to document the playbook, they should create 10-20 that address the range of potential incidents.

- **Low-level incident**: A low-level incident is an incident that causes inconvenience and/or unintentional damage or loss of recoverable information. The incident will have little impact to the corporation:
  - Policy or procedural violations detected through compliance reviews or log reviews
  - Lost or stolen laptop or other mobile equipment containing encrypted confidential information
  - Installation of unauthorized software
  - Malware infection of a single PC

- **Incident tracking**: Tracking incidents are a critical responsibility of the CSIRT. During an incident, all actions taken by the CSIRT and other personnel during an incident should be noted. These actions should be recorded under a unique incident identifier.

  For organizations that have limited resources and experience a limited number of incidents per year, most IT ticketing systems are sufficient for tracking incidents. The drawback to this method is that these systems generally lack an incident response focus and do not have additional features that are designed to support incident response activities. Larger organizations that have a higher frequency of incidents may be best served by implementing a purpose-designed incident response tracking system. These systems allow for integration of evidence collection and incident playbooks.

- **Training**: The incident response plan should also indicate the frequency of training for CSIRT personnel. At a minimum, the entire CSIRT should be put through a tabletop exercise at least annually. In the event that an incident post-mortem analysis indicates a gap in training, that should also be addressed within a reasonable time after conclusion of the incident.
- **Maintenance**: Organizations of every size continually change. This can include changes to infrastructure, threats, and personnel. The incident response plan should address the frequency of reviews and updates to the incident response plan. For example, if the organization acquires another organization, the CSIRT may have to adjust service offerings or incorporate specific individuals and their roles. At a minimum, the incident response plan should be updated at least annually. Individual team members should also supplement their skills through individual training and certifications through such organizations as SANS or on specific digital forensic tools. Organizations can incorporate lessons learned from any exercises conducted into this update.

The incident response playbook

One key aspect of the incident response plan is the use of playbooks. An Incident Response Playbook is a set of instructions and actions to be performed at every step in the incident response process. The playbooks are created to give organizations a clear path through the process, but with a degree of flexibility in the event that the incident under investigation does not fit neatly into the box.

A good indicator of which playbooks are critical is the organization's risk assessment. Examining the risk assessment for any threat rated critical or high will indicate which scenarios need to be addressed via an incident response playbook. Most organizations would identify a number of threats, such as a network intrusion via a zero-day exploit, ransomware, or phishing as critical, requiring preventive and detective controls. As the risk assessment has identified those as critical risks, it is best to start the playbooks with those threats.

For example, let's examine the breakdown of a playbook for a common threat, social engineering. For this playbook, we are going to divide it out into the incident response process that was previously discussed.

- **Preparation**: In this section, the organization will highlight the preparation that is undertaken. In the case of phishing, this can include employee awareness to identify potential phishing email or the use of an email appliance that scans attachments for malware.
- **Detection**: For phishing attacks, organizations are often alerted by aware employees or through email security controls. Organizations should also plan on receiving alerts via malware prevention or **Host Intrusion Prevention System (HIPS)** controls.
- **Analysis**: If an event is detected, analyzing any evidence available will be critical to classifying and appropriately responding to an incident. In this case, analysis may include examining the compromised host's memory, examining event logs for suspicious entries, and reviewing any network traffic going to and from the host.
- **Containment**: If a host has been identified as compromised, it should be isolated from the network.
- **Eradication**: In the event that malware has been identified, it should be removed. If not, the playbook should have an alternative such as reimaging with a known good image.
- **Recovery**: The recovery stage includes scanning the host for potential vulnerabilities and monitoring the system for any anomalous traffic.
- **Post-incident activity**: The playbook should also give guidance on what actions should take place after an incident. Many of these actions will be the same across the catalog of playbooks, but are important to include, ensuring that they are completed in full.

Playbooks are designed to give the CSIRT and any other personnel a set of instructions to follow in an incident. This allows for less time wasted if a course of action is planned out. Playbooks serve as a guide and they should be updated regularly, especially if they are used in an incident and any key pieces or steps are identified. It should be noted that playbooks are not written in stone and not a checklist. CSIRT personnel are not bound to the playbook in terms of actions and should be free to undertake additional actions if the incident requires it.

Escalation procedures

A critical component of the incident response plan is the escalation procedures. Escalation procedures outline who is responsible from moving an event or series of events from just anomalies in the information system to an incident. The CSIRT will become burned out if they are sent to investigate too many false positives. The escalation procedures ensure that the CSIRT is effectively utilized and that personnel are only contacted if their particular expertise is required.

The procedures start with the parties who are most likely to observe anomalies or events in the system that may be indicative of a larger incident. For example, the help desk may receive a number of calls that indicate a potential malware infection. The escalation procedures may indicate that if malware is detected and cannot be removed via malware prevention controls, they are to contact the CSIRT member on call. That CSIRT member will then take control. If they are able to contain the malware to that single system, they will attempt to remove the malware and, barring that, have the system reimaged and redeployed. At that point, the incident has been successfully concluded. The CSIRT member can document the incident and close it out without having to engage any other resources.

Another example where the escalation moves farther up into an all-out CSIRT response can start very simply with an audit of active directory credentials. In this case, a server administrator with access management responsibilities is conducting a semi-annual audit of administrator credentials. During the audit, they identify three new administrator user accounts that do not tie to any known access rights. After further digging, they determine that these user accounts were created within several hours of each other and were created over a weekend. The server administrator contacts the CSIRT for investigation.

The CSIRT analyst looks at the situation and determines that a compromise may have happened. The CSIRT member directs the server administrator to check event logs for any logins using those administrator accounts. The server administrator identifies two logins, one on a database server and another on a web server in the DMZ. The CSIRT analyst then directs the network administrator assigned to the CSIRT to examine network traffic between the SQL database and the web server. Also, based on the circumstances, the CSIRT analyst escalates this to the CSIRT coordinator and informs them of the situation. The CSIRT coordinator then begins the process of engaging other CSIRT core team and technical support members to assist.

After examining the network traffic, it is determined that an external threat actor has compromised both systems and is in the process of exfiltrating the customer database from the internal network. At this point, the CSIRT coordinator identifies this as a high-level incident and begins the process of bringing support personnel into a briefing. As this incident has involved the compromise of customer data, the CSIRT support personnel such as marketing or communications and legal need to become involved. If more resources are required, the CSIRT coordinator will take the lead on making that decision.

The escalation procedures are created to ensure that the appropriate individuals have the proper authority and training to call upon resources when needed. The escalation procedures should also address the involvement of other personnel outside the core CSIRT members based on the severity of the incident. One of the critical functions of the escalation procedures is to clearly define what individuals have the authority to declare anomalous activity an incident. The escalation procedures should also address the involvement of other personnel outside the core CSIRT members, based on the severity of the incident.

Maintaining the incident response capability

So far, there have been a number of areas that have been addressed in terms of preparing for an incident. From an initial understanding of the process involved in incident response, we moved through the creation of an incident response plan and associated playbooks. Once the capability has been created, it should be run through a tabletop exercise to flush out any gaps or deficiencies. This tabletop should include a high-level incident that involves the entire team and one of the associated playbooks. A report that details the results of the tabletop exercise and any gaps, corrections, or modifications should also be prepared and forwarded to the senior leadership. Once leadership has been informed and acknowledges that the CSIRT is ready to deploy, it is now operational.

Another critical component of the initial deployment is to socialize the CSIRT with the entire organization. This is done to remove any rumors or innuendo about the purpose of the team. Employees of the organization may hear words such as digital investigations or incident response team and believe the organization is preparing a *secret police* specifically designed to ferret out employee misconduct. To counter this, a short statement that includes the mission statement of the CSIRT can be made available to all employees. The CSIRT can also provide periodic updates to senior leadership on incidents handled to demonstrate the purpose of the team.

Regardless of the makeup of the team, another key component of CSIRT deployment is the inclusion of regular training. For CSIRT core members, specific training on emerging threats, forensic techniques, and tools should be ongoing. This can be facilitated through third-party training providers or, if available, in-house training. The technical support members of the CSIRT should receive regular training on techniques and tools available. This is especially important if these members may be called upon during an incident to assist with evidence collection or remediation activities. Finally, the other support members should be included in the annual test of the incident response plan. Just as with the inaugural test, the organization should pick a high-level incident and work through it using a tabletop exercise. Another option for the organization is to marry up the test of their incident response plan with a penetration test. If the organization is able to detect the presence of the penetration test, they have the ability to run through the first phases of the incident and craft a tabletop for the remaining portions.

One final component to the ongoing maintenance of the incident response plan is a complete annual review. This annual review is conducted to ensure that any changes in personnel, constituency, or mission that may impact other components of the plan are addressed. In addition to a review of the plan, a complete review of the playbooks is conducted as well. As threats change, it may be necessary to change existing playbooks or add new ones. The CSIRT personnel should also feel free to create a new playbook in the event that a new threat emerges. In this way, the CSIRT will be in a better position to address incidents that may impact their organization.

Summary

Benjamin Franklin is quoted as saying *by failing to prepare, you are preparing to fail*. In many ways, this sentiment is quite accurate when it comes to organizations and the threat of cyber attacks. Preparing for a cyber attack is a critical function that must be taken as seriously as any other aspect of cyber security. Having a solid understanding of the Incident Response Process to build on with an incident response capability can provide organizations with a measure of preparation so that in the event of an incident, they can respond. Keep in mind as we move forward that the forensic techniques, threat intelligence, and reverse engineering are there to assist an organization to get to the end, that is, back up and running. This chapter explored some of the preparation that goes into building an incident response capability. Selecting a team, creating a plan and building the playbooks and the escalation procedures allows an CSIRT to effectively address an incident. The CSIRT and associated plans give structure to the digital forensic techniques to be discussed. This discussion begins with the next chapter where proper evidence handling and documentation is the critical first step in investigating an incident.

2
Forensic Fundamentals

Forensic science can be defined as the application of scientific principles to legal matters. In an incident, CSIRT members may be called upon to perform analysis on digital evidence acquired during the incident, utilizing digital forensics tools, techniques, and knowledge. To make certain that the evidence is processed correctly and can subsequently be admitted into a courtroom, digital forensic examiners need to understand the legal issues along with the fine points of the digital forensic process.

In this chapter, we will examine the legal statutes that impact the CSIRT and digital forensics examiners as well as the rules that govern how evidence is admitted into court. To give context to actions taken, we will also explore the digital forensic process and finally address the infrastructure necessary to incorporate a digital forensics capability within a CSIRT.

Legal aspects

As we saw in the first chapter, a proper incident response involves a number of individuals from a variety of disciplines. This highlights one of the key misconceptions often held, that incident response is strictly a technology matter. One realm that incident response falls heavily into is the legal arena. There are a number of laws and regulations that directly impact an organization's incident response capability ranging from breach notification to privacy. These laws both provide a framework for governments to prosecute offenders as well as providing strict rules concerning such topics as how evidence is handled and presented in court.

Laws and regulations

In the middle of the 1980s, as computer crime started to become more prevalent, jurisdictions began crafting laws to address the ever-increasing instances of cyber-crime. In the United States, for example, federal criminal law has specific statutes that deal directly with criminal activity utilizing a computer:

- **18 USC § 1029**: Fraud and related activity in connection with access devices. This statute addresses the use of a computer to commit fraud. This is most often utilized by prosecutors in connection with cases where cyber criminals use a computer or computers to commit identify theft or other fraud-related activities.
- **18 USC § 1030 - Computer Fraud and Abuse Act**: Among the number of provisions within this law, the one most commonly associated with incident response is the unauthorized access to a computer system. This law also addresses the illegality of denial of service attacks.
- **Electronic Communications Privacy Act (ECPA)**: This amendment to the federal wiretap statute was enacted in 1986. It makes illegal the unauthorized interception of communications through electronic means such as telecommunications and the internet. The **ECPA** was further amended by the **Communications Assistance for Law Enforcement Act (CALEA)**. CALEA set the requirement on ISPs to ensure that their networks could be made available to law enforcement agencies to conduct lawfully authorized surveillance.
  Having knowledge of the ECPA is critical. Provisions of the law make it a crime for an organization to conduct surveillance and capture traffic on networks, even those under their control, if the users have a reasonable expectation of privacy. This can lead to an organization being held liable for sniffing traffic on its own network if in fact the users have a reasonable expectation of privacy. For the CSIRT, this creates potential legal problems if they have to access network resources or other systems. This can be easily remedied by having all system users acknowledge that they understand their communications can be monitored by the organization, and that they have no reasonable expectation of privacy in regards to their communications when using that particular network.
- **Economic Espionage Act of 1996**: This law contained several provisions found in *18 USC § 1831-1839* and made economic espionage and the theft of trade secrets a crime. This act went further than previous espionage legislation as it dealt directly with commercial enterprises and not just national security or government information.

Rules of evidence

The federal rules of evidence serve as the basis by which evidence can be admitted or excluded during a criminal or civil proceeding. Having knowledge of these rules is important for the CSIRT so that any evidence collected is handled in a manner that prevents contamination and the possibility that the evidence will be barred from being seen in court:

- **Rule 402: Test for relevant evidence** - This rule has two parts. First, the evidence to be admitted into the proceedings would have a tendency to make the fact more or less probable than it would be without the evidence. Second, that the evidence or the facts the evidence proves is of consequence to the proceeding. This makes clear that not only the evidence should be relevant to the proceeding, but also it has the value to prove or disapprove a facet of the case.

- **Rule 502: Attorney-Client privilege and work product** - One of the most sacrosanct tenets of modern law is the relationship between a client and their attorney. One of the provisions of the attorney-client privilege is that what is said between the two is not admissible in court. This not only applies to spoken communications, but written communications as well. In the world of digital forensics, reports are often written concerning actions taken and information obtained. Many times, incident responders will be working directly for attorneys on behalf of their clients. As a result, these reports prepared in conjunction with an incident may fall under attorney work product rules. It is important to have an understanding of when you may be working under an attorney, and when these rules may apply to your work.

- **Rule 702: Testimony by expert witnesses** - Through the acquisition of experience and knowledge in digital forensics, an analyst may be allowed to testify as an expert witness. This rule of evidence outlines the specifics concerning expert witness testimony.

- **Rule 902: Evidence that is self -authenticating** - This rule has recently undergone a revision in regards to digital forensics. A new subpart will be added and will take effect on December 1, 2017. This new subpart will allow verification of digital evidence integrity through hashing (we will discuss the role that hashing has in later chapters). Furthermore, this rule requires that a *qualified person* and that evidence being presented having been collected according to best practices.

- **Rule 1002:Best evidence rule** - In civil or criminal proceedings, the original writings, recordings, or photographs need to be offered up as evidence unless there is a reasonable exception that can be made. In the physical realm, this is fairly easy. Parties to a case can easily present a knife used in an assault. It becomes a bit more complex when the evidence is essentially magnetic polarity on a hard drive or log files that came from a router. In this case, courts have held that a forensically sound image of a hard drive is a reasonable substitute to the actual hard drive that was examined.

- **Rule 1003: Admissibility of duplicates** - One of the most critical steps when conducting a forensic examine of digital media is to make an image or forensic copy of the media. This rule of evidence allows for such an image to be admitted into court. It is important to note that if an image or forensic copy is to be admitted, the analyst who performed that action will most likely have to testify to performing the action correctly.

Digital forensic fundamentals

As it was stated in the previous chapter, digital forensics is an important component of incident response. It is often the application of digital forensic methods that allows incident responders to gain a clear understanding of the chain of events that led to a malicious action, such as a server compromise or other data breach. For other incidents such as internal fraud or malicious insider activity, digital forensics may provide the proverbial *smoking gun* that points to the guilty party. Before a detailed examination of the tools and techniques available to incident responders, it is critical to address the foundational elements of digital forensics. These elements provide not only context to specific actions, but also a method to ensure that the evidence made part of an incident investigation has utility.

A brief history

Law enforcement first started to pay attention to the role that computers play in criminal activity in the middle of the 1980s. Prior to that, existing laws and law enforcement techniques were not adept at identifying and prosecuting computer criminals. As the use of computers by criminals began to gain more prominence, agencies such as the United State **Federal Bureau of Investigation (FBI)** decided to incorporate a dedicated digital and forensic investigations capability. This led to the creation of the FBI **Computer Analysis and Response Team (CART)**. Other agencies such as the Metropolitan Police Service started to build a capability for investigating cyber crime.

A good historical document that addresses the FBI - CART is a short article in the US Dept. of Justice Crime Laboratory Digest dated January 1992.
https://www.ncjrs.gov/pdffiles1/Digitization/137561NCJRS.pdf

Two other seminal events brought the need for cyber investigations and forensics into the minds of many. The first was the break in of the Lawrence Berkeley National Laboratory by the hacker **Markus Hess**. This break-in might have gone undetected if not for the efforts of **Clifford Stoll** who hatched a plan to trap the attacker long enough to trace the connection. These efforts paid off and Stoll along with other authorities were able to trace the hacker and eventually prosecute him for espionage. This entire episode is recorded in Stoll's book, the cuckoo's egg.

The second high profile event was the **Morris Worm** that was unleashed on the fledgeling internet in 1988. The worm created and released by **Robert Morris** caused a denial of service on a number of systems, subsequently causing damage in excess of $100,000. A post incident investigation by a number of individuals, including Clifford Stoll found at least 6000 systems were infected. The rapid spread of the worm and the damage associated with it led to the creation of the Carnegie Mellon CERT/CC.

Throughout the 1990s, as more law enforcement agencies began to incorporate digital forensics into their investigative capabilities, the need for standardization of forensic processes became more apparent. It was in 1993, that an international conference was held to specifically address the role of computer evidence. Shortly thereafter in 1995, the **International Organization on Computer Evidence (IOCE)** was formed. This body was created to develop guidelines and standards around the various phases of the digital forensic examination process. In 1998, in conjunction with the IOCE, the federal crime laboratory directors created the **Scientific Working Group on Digital Evidence (SWGDE)**. This group represented the United States component of the IOCE's attempt to standardize digital forensic practices.

As organizations continued to standardize practices, law enforcement agencies continued to implement digital forensics into their overall forensic capabilities. In 2000, the FBI established the first **Regional Computer Forensic Laboratory(RCFL)**. These laboratories were established to serve law enforcement at various levels in a number of cyber-criminal investigations. The RCFL capability has grown over the last 15 years with 15 separate RCFLs spread across the United States. In addition, other federal, state, and local police agencies have formed task forces and standalone digital forensics capabilites. With the continual increase in computer-related crime, these agencies will continue to perform their critical work.

The digital forensic process

Much like the incident response process, the digital forensic process defines the flow of digital evidence related to an incident from when it is first identified to when it is presented to either the senior leadership or to a trier of fact such as a civil or criminal court. There are a number of schemas that define this process and, for the most part they generally follow a similar path. In this case, we will be utilizing the **Digital Forensics Research Workshop (DFRWS)** Digital Investigate Framework. This framework contains six elements:

1. Identification.
2. Preservation.
3. Collection.
4. Examination.
5. Analysis.
6. Presentation.

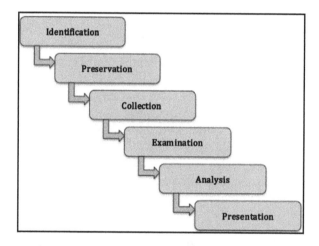

From an incident response standpoint, will not normally seize network components or critical systems and take them offline unless there is a compelling reason to do so. This is one of the balancing acts in regards to digital forensics and incident response. A purely digital forensic approach will take all relevant evidence, secure it, and process it. This process can take months depending on the type of incident. This approach, while thorough and detailed, can leave an organization without critical components. The CSIRT may be able to tell the leadership after a month long analysis what chain of events lead to a breach, but that would do them no good if they have lost a month's of revenue. The examiners assigned to a CSIRT must be ready to balance out the need for thoroughness with the need to resume or continue normal operations.

Identification

One principle that is often discussed in forensic science is the Locard's exchange principle. This principle postulates that when two objects come into contact, they leave a trace on each other. For example, if you walk into a house with carpeting, dirt from your shoes is left on the carpet and the carpet leaves fibers on the soles of your shoes. These traces that are exchanged form the bases of the science of trace evidence in the physical forensics world. In the digital world, we often have very similar trace evidence when two systems come into contact with each other. For example, if an individual browses to a website, the web server or web application firewall may record the individual's IP address within a collection log. The website may also deposit a cookie on the individual's laptop. Just as in the physical world, evidence exchanged in this manner may be temporary and our ability to observe it may be limited to the tools and knowledge we currently have.

This principle can guide the identification of potential sources of evidence during an incident. For example, if a CSIRT is attempting to determine the root cause of a malware infection on a system, they would start by analyzing the infected system. As some malware requires access to a C2 server, analysts can search firewall connection or proxy logs for any outbound traffic from the infected system to external IP addresses. A review of those connection IP addresses may reveal the C2 server, and potentially more details about the particular malware that has infected the system.

It should be noted though, that threat actors very easily manipulate digital evidence, so reliance on a single piece of digital evidence without other corroborating evidence should always be tempered with caution and should be verified before it can be trusted.

Preservation

Once evidence is identified, it is important to safeguard it from any type of modification or deletion. For evidence such as log files, it may become necessary to enable controls that protect log files from removal or modification. In terms of host systems such as desktops, it may become necessary to isolate the system from the rest of the network through either physical or logical controls, network access controls or perimeter controls. It is also critical that any users not be allowed to access a suspect system. This ensures that users do not deliberately or inadvertently taint the evidence. Another facet of preservation measures has been the increased reliance on virtual platforms. Preservation of these systems can be achieved through the snapshotting systems and saving to non-volatile storage.

Collection

The collection element is where digital forensic examiners begin the process of acquiring the digital evidence. When examining digital evidence, it is important to understand the volatile nature of some of the evidence that an examiner will want to look at. Volatile evidence is evidence that can be lost when a system is powered down. For network equipment this could include active connections or log data that is stored on the device. For laptops and desktops, volatile data includes running memory or the Address Resolution Protocol cache. The **Internet Engineering Task Force (IETF)** has put together a document titled **Guidelines for Evidence Collection and Archiving (RFC 3227)** that addresses the order of volatility of digital evidence:

- Registers, cache
- Routing Table, ARP Cache, process table, kernel statistics, Memory (RAM)
- Temporary filesystems
- Disk
- Remote logging and monitoring data
- Physical configuration, network topology
- Archival media

It is imperative that digital forensic examiners take this volatility into account when starting the process of evidence collection. Methods should be employed where volatile evidence will be collected and moved to a non-volatile medium such as an external hard drive.

Proper evidence handling

The proper handling and securing of evidence is critical. Mistakes in how evidence is acquired can lead to that evidence being tainted and subsequently not forensically sound. In addition, if an incident involves potential legal issues, critical evidence can be excluded from being admitted in a criminal or civil proceeding. There are several key tenets of evidence handling that need to be followed:

- **Altering the original evidence**: Actions taken by digital forensic examiners should not alter the original evidence. For example, a forensic analyst should not access a running system if they do not have to. It should be noted that some of the tasks that will be explored have the potential to alter some of the evidence. By incorporating proper documentation and having a justifiable reason, digital forensic examiners can reduce the chance that evidence will be deemed tainted.

- **Document**: One central theme you will often hear in law enforcement is the phrase *if you didn't write it down, it didn't happen*. This is especially true when discussing digital forensics. Every action that is taken should be documented in one way or another. This includes detailed notes and diagrams. Another way to document is photographs. Proper documentation allows for examiners to reconstruct the chain of events if ever the integrity of evidence is called into question.

There are a number of resources available from various law enforcement agencies on proper evidence handling in the field. You should become familiar with these procedures.The following guides are utilized by law enforcement agencies:

`http://www.crime-scene-investigator.net/SeizingElectronicEvidenc`
`e.pdf`
`https://www.ncjrs.gov/pdffiles1/nij/219941.pdf`
`http://www.iacpcybercenter.org/wp-content/uploads/2015/04/digita`
`levidence-booklet-051215.pdf`

Chain of custody

Chain of custody describes the documentation of a piece of evidence through its life cycle. This life cycle begins when an individual first takes custody of the piece of evidence to when the incident is finally disposed of and the evidence can either be returned or destroyed. Maintaining a proper chain of custody is critical. In the event that a piece of evidence has to be brought into a courtroom, any break in the chain of custody can lead to the piece of evidence being excluded from ever being admitted into the proceedings. It is critical, therefore, to ensure that the entire life cycle of the piece of evidence is recorded.

There are two primary ways that a CSIRT can record and maintain the chain of custody of a piece of evidence. The first is electronically. There are a number of software manufacturers that provide organizations such as forensic laboratories or law enforcement agencies with hardware and software that automates the chain of custody process for evidence. These systems utilize unique bar coded stickers for each piece of evidence. A scanner then creates an electronic trail as it reads these bar codes. The second method for creating and maintaining a chain of custody is a paper and pen method. This method makes use of paper forms that contain the necessary information to start and maintain a chain of custody. While the paper and pen method can be a bit cumbersome and requires more due diligence to ensure that the form is safeguarded from destruction or manipulation, it is a much more cost effective solution for smaller CSIRTs that may not have the resources necessary to implement an automated solution.

In terms of what a proper chain of custody contains, there are several sections each with its own details that need to be provided. The following screenshot is a template chain of a custody form that is provided by e-Fense, which contains the necessary pieces of information:

ELECTRONIC EVIDENCE CHAIN OF CUSTODY FORM

Case No: **Page:**   **of:**

ELECTRONIC MEDIA/COMPUTER DETAILS

Item No:	Description:		
Manufacturer:	Model No:		Serial No:

IMAGE DETAILS

Date/Time:	Created By:	Method Used:	Image Name:	Segments:
Storage Drive:		HASH:		

CHAIN OF CUSTODY

Tracking No:	Date/Time:	FROM:	TO:	Reason:
	Date:	Name/Org:	Name/Org:	
	Time:	Signature:	Signature:	
	Date:	Name/Org:	Name/Org:	
	Time:	Signature:	Signature:	
	Date:	Name/Org:	Name/Org:	
	Time:	Signature:	Signature:	
	Date:	Name/Org:	Name/Org:	
	Time:	Signature:	Signature:	
	Date:	Name/Org:	Name/Org:	
	Time:	Signature:	Signature:	
	Date:	Name/Org:	Name/Org:	
	Time:	Signature:	Signature:	
	Date:	Name/Org:	Name/Org:	
	Time:	Signature:	Signature:	

The first of these sections is a detailed description of the item. It may seem redundant to include a number of the different elements, but digital forensics is about details. Having the information recorded leaves no doubt as to its authenticity. This description should contain the following elements:

- **Item number**: A unique item number should be included on the form. In the cases of multiple pieces of evidence, a separate chain of custody form will be completed.
- **Description**: This should be a general description of the item. This can be a simple statement such as **500 GB SATA HDD**.
- **Manufacturer**: This detail assists in the case of multiple pieces of evidence with potentially different manufacturers.
- **Model**: This further details the specific piece of evidence for later separation if needed.
- **Serial number**: This is a critical piece in the event that an incident involves a number of systems with exactly the same configuration. Imagine attempting to reconstruct which chain of custody goes with which HDD if six were all seized together and they had the same make and model number.

A completed first section for the chain of custody form will look like this:

ELECTRONIC MEDIA/COMPUTER DETAILS		
Item No: 1	Description: Western Digital WD0LEURS Hard drive	
Manufacturer: Western Digital	Model No: WD0LEURS	Serial No: WAAV1234567

The next section details the specific steps that the piece of evidence took while in the life cycle. For each stage, the following details should be captured:

- **Tracking number**: This number indicates the step in the life cycle that the piece of evidence took.
- **Date and time**: This is a critical piece of information in any chain of custody and applies equally to each step that evidence took. This allows anyone that views the chain of custody to be able to reconstruct down to each minute each step in the chain of custody life cycle.

- **To and from**: These fields can either be a person or a storage place. For example, if an analyst has seized a hard drive and is moving it to a secure storage locker, they would note that as the "To" location. It is critical to have those individuals named within the chain of custody sign the form when applicable to enforce accountability.
- **Reason**: Moving a piece of evidence should never be done without a reason. In this portion of the chain of custody, the reason is completed.

The following screenshot is a sample of the movement of the hard drive recorded in the previous screenshot. Each move of the individual piece of evidence is recorded here. The first move is the actual seizure of the drive from the system. In this case, there is no individual custodian as the drive has been taken from the data center. What is critical is that the individual **John Smith of ACME Corp**. is the custodian of the drive until he is able to transfer the drive to secure storage as noted in the following screenshot:

Tracking No:	Date/Time:	FROM:	TO:	Reason:
CHAIN OF CUSTODY				
1	Date: 1-21-07 Time: 12:07pm	Name/Org: Acme Comp Data Center Signature: N/A	Name/Org: John Smith /ACME Signature: John Smith	Seizure
2	Date: 1-21-07 Time: 12:33pm	Name/Org: John Smith /ACME Signature: John Smith	Name/Org: Evidence Locker /ACME Signature: N/A	Secure Storage

The chain of custody is maintained throughout the life of the piece of evidence. Even when the evidence is destroyed or returned, an entry is made in the chain of custody form. These forms should be maintained with any other material generated by the incident and also made part of any reporting that is created.

Examination

The examination phase details the specific tools and forensic techniques that are utilized to discover and extract data from the evidence that is seized as part of the incident. For example, in a case where malware is suspected of infecting a desktop system as part of a larger attack, the extraction of specific information from an acquired memory image would take part in this stage. In other cases, digital forensic examiners may need to extract **Secure Shell (SSH)** traffic from a network capture. The examination of digital evidence also continues the process of proper preservation in that examiners maintain the utmost care with the evidence during the examination. If the digital forensic examiner does not take care in the preservation of the evidence in this stage, there is the possibility of contamination that would result in the evidence being unreliable or unusable.

Analysis

Once the Examination phase has extracted the potentially relevant pieces of data, the digital forensic examiner then analyzes the data in light of any other relevant data obtained. For example, if the digital forensic analyst has discovered that a compromised host has on open connection to an external IP address, they would then correlate that information with an analysis of the packet capture taken from the network. Using the IP address as a starting point, the analyst would be able to isolate the particular traffic. From here, the analyst may be able to determine that the compromised host is sending out a beacon to a C2 server. From here, using additional sources, the analyst may be able to determine what the particular attack vector is tied with that IP address.

Presentation

The reporting of facts related to digital forensics needs to be clear, concise, and with or without objectivity. In nearly all instances, a forensic examiner will be required to prepare a detailed written report, which addresses every action and captures the critical data required. This report should be thorough, accurate, and without opinion or bias. This report will often be made part of a larger incident investigation and aids in determining the root cause of an incident.

Another aspect of presentation is the role that the forensic examiner might play in a criminal or civil proceeding. Testifying in court may be required if the incident under investigation has yielded a suspect or other responsible party. It is during this testimony that the forensic examiner will be required to present the facts of the forensic examination in much the same dispassionate manner as the report. The examiner will be required to present the facts and conclusions without bias and may be limited as to what opinions they testify to. How an examiner will be allowed to testify is often dependent on their training and experience. Some may be limited to presenting the facts of the examination. Other times, as examiners acquire skills and have been deemed an *expert witness*, they may be able to offer an opinion.

Digital forensic lab

Digital forensics is an exacting process that involves the use of proper tools, techniques, and knowledge in order to extract potential evidence from systems. It is imperative that forensic examiners have a location that is separate from normal business operations. The best approach to achieving this separation is to provide CSIRT members that are directly involved in the examination of digital evidence, with a location that is completely separate from the rest of the organization. A digital forensics lab should have several key features to both ensure that examiners have the necessary privacy, but to also to ensure the integrity of the evidence while it is being examined.

Physical security

Access to the forensic lab needs to be strictly controlled. In order to maintain a chain of custody, only those with a justifiable need should be allowed access to the lab. This limitation is necessary to remove any chance that the evidence can be tampered with or destroyed. The lab therefore should be locked at all times. Ideally, access should be granted via access cards or fobs with a central management system granting access. This allows for a complete reconstruction of all personnel who access the laboratory within a specific time period.

The laboratory should also contain evidence lockers so that evidence can be properly stored while not being examined. Lockers should be secured either through an onboard lock or through the use of a combination lock. The keys to these lockers should be secured within the laboratory and access given to examiners. If the organization has adequate resources, each specific incident should have its own locker with all the evidence contained within a single locker. This reduces the chance of digital evidence becoming comingled.

Climate should be controlled in much the same way as in any data center. Climate and humidity should be set to the appropriate levels.

Tools

Depending on the specific examinations to be performed, it may become necessary to remove screws or cut wires. Having a small set of hand tools will provide some convenience to the examiners. The laboratory should also be stocked with boxes for securing evidence. If potential exists for the examiners having to process smart phones or tablets, faraday bags should be available. These bags allow examiners to isolate the smart phone or tablet from the cellular network, but still maintain a power source.

Hardware

The laboratory should have sufficient computers and other hardware to perform the variety of functions necessary. Examiners will be tasked with imaging hard drives and processing gigabytes of data. As a result, a forensic computer with sufficient RAM is necessary. While there are personal preferences for the amount, a minimum of 32 GB of RAM is recommended. In addition to memory and processing power, examiners will often be looking at a large amount of data. Forensic workstations should have a primary OS drive that can contain forensic software and a secondary drive to hold evidence. The secondary drive should contain 2 TB or greater of storage.

In addition to a forensic workstation, the examiner should also be provided an internet connected computer. The forensic workstation should have no internet connection to maintain security, but also to guard against possible corruption of evidence during an examination. A secondary machine would be utilized for conducting research or writing reports.

Another piece of critical information is a physical write blocker. This device allows for a connection between a hard drive seized as evidence and the forensic imaging machine. The critical difference between this physical write blocker and a USB or Thunderbolt connection is that the digital forensic examiner can be sure that there is no data written to the evidence drive.

The following image is the **Tableau eSATA Forensic Bridge**physical write blocker:

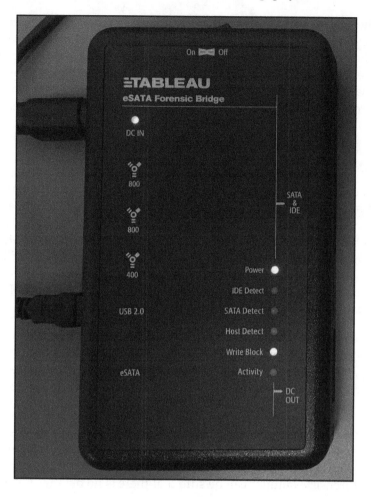

For digital forensic laboratories that conduct a higher number of imaging tasks there is the option of including a dedicated forensic imaging station. This allows for quicker imaging of evidence drives and does not tie up a forensic workstation for proper imaging. The drawback is the expense and, if the CSIRT does not see a performance drop without it, it may be hard to justify the expense.

The CSIRT should also invest in a number of high capacity external USB drives. These are much easier to work with and use in the imaging process than traditional SATA or IDE drives. These drives are utilized to store an evidence drive image for further analysis. The CSIRT should have at least six of these high capacity drives available. Drives that have two to three terabytes of storage space can possibly store several images at a time. Smaller USB drives are also useful to have on hand to capture log files and memory images for later processing. With any of these USB drives, having the latest 3.0 version allows for faster processing as well.

Finally, digital forensic examiners that support a CSIRT should have a durable case to transport all of the necessary hardware, in the eventuality that they must conduct an offsite examination. Many of these tools are fragile and would not stand the pounding delivered by baggage handlers at the local airport. The CSIRT should invest in at least two hard sided cases like those in the following image. One case can transport hardware such as external hard drives and the second can transport a forensics laptop and minimize potential damage through rough handling:

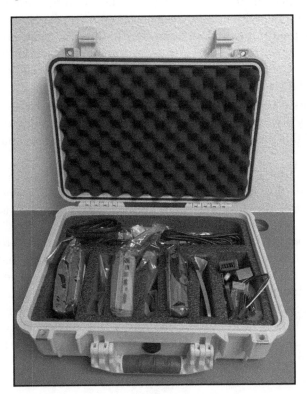

Software

There are a number of software tools on the commercial and freeware market today. The digital forensics laboratory should have access to several tools to perform similar functions. At a minimum, the lab should have software that can perform imaging of evidence drives, examine images, analyze memory captures, and report findings.

There are several different types of forensic software that a digital forensic analyst can utilize. The first of these are forensic applications. These applications are purpose designed to perform a variety of digital forensic tasks. They are often commercially available and are in wide use in the law enforcement and government communities as well as private industry. The following three forensic applications are the most common and widely deployed:

- **EnCase**: Developed by Guidance Software, EnCase is a full spectrum digital forensic application performing the entire rainbow of tasks in examination of digital evidence, primarily from hard drives and other storage media. Besides analyzing digital evidence, EnCase has a reporting capability that allows examiners to output case data in an easy to digest format. EnCase is widely deployed in government and law enforcement agencies. One drawback is the cost associated with the application. Some CSIRTs and forensic examiners on a limited budget will have trouble justifying the cost.
- **FTK: Forensic Tool Kit** (**FTK**) is another full service forensic application that is in wide use by government and law enforcement. With many of the same features as EnCase, this may be an alternative that digital forensic analysts will want to explore.
- **X-Ways**: Another option is the application X-Ways forensics. With similar functionality, this is a great lower-cost option for CSIRTs who may not have need for the functionality found in other applications. Linux forensic tools.

There are also a number of Linux distributions that have been created for digital forensic purposes. These distributions, often provided for free, provide tools that can aid a digital forensics investigator. These tools are divided into two main types. The first of these are distributions that are indented as boot CD/DVD or USBs. These are useful for conducting triage or to obtain access to files without having to image the drive. These distributions can be placed onto a CD/DVD or more commonly now, a USB device. The examiner then boots the system under investigation into the Linux distribution. There are a number of these distributions available.

The following are two that are popular with digital forensic examiners:

- **Deft 8.2**: **Digital Evidence and Forensic Toolkit** (DEFT) is based upon the GNU Linux platform. DEFT can be booted off of a USB or CD/DVD. Once booted, the DEFT platform includes a number of tools that can be utilized by a digital forensic examiner to perform such functions as the acquisition of mass storage such as the hard drive on the system being booted from. DEFT minimizes the risk of altering the data on the system by not booting into the swap partition and does not use automated mounting scripts, thereby ensuring the integrity of the system's storage:

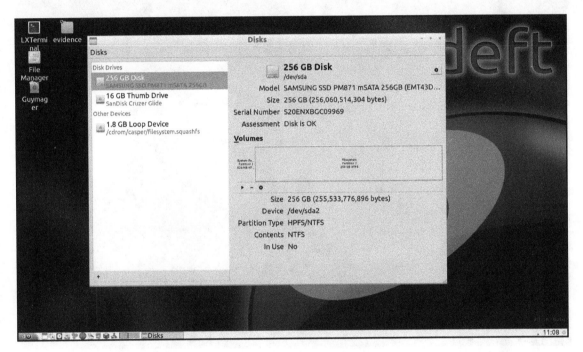

- **Paladin**: Paladin is another Live Linux distribution based on the Ubuntu OS. Paladin has a number of tools that aid in digital forensic tasks such as malware analysis, hashing, and imaging. The forensic toolset includes a number of packages that can be utilized for a wide range of different operating systems:

Another category of Linux distributions are those designed as platforms for conducting examination of evidence such as RAM captures and network evidence. There are several distributions available, but, in this book, we will be using two of these:

- **SANS SIFT**: The SANS Investigate Forensic Toolkit is a comprehensive forensic tool set based upon the Ubuntu 14.04 platform. Tools are included for imaging, memory analysis, timeline creation, and a host of other digital forensics tasks. The SIFT is provided for free by SANS as a standalone virtual machine provided at `https://digital-forensics.sans.org/community/downloads`. Alternatively, the SIFT can be installed onto an existing Ubuntu 14.04 installation. Once Ubuntu has fully installed, run the following command:

  ```
  wget --quiet -O - https://raw.github.com/sans-dfir/sift-
  bootstrap/master/bootstrap.sh | sudo bash -s -- -i -s -y
  ```

Once installed, there is a desktop based upon the Ubuntu distribution with additional tools run from the command line or through a GUI:

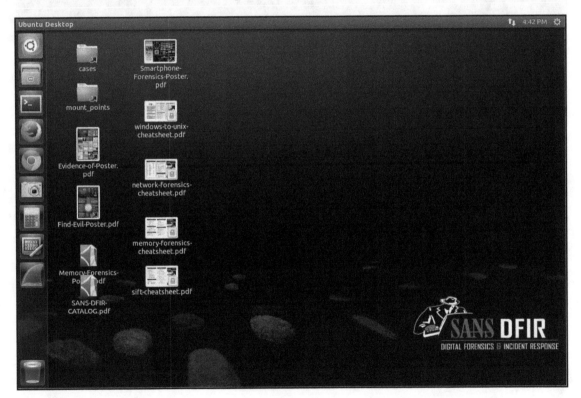

- **CAINE: Computer Aided Investigative Environment** (**CAINE**) is another forensic distribution that will be put to use further in this book. CAINE is a GNU / Linux platform that includes a number of tools that assist digital forensic examiners:

- **REMNUX**: REMNUX is a specialized tool that has aggregated a number of malware reverse engineering tools into an Ubuntu Linux based toolkit. There are a number of tools available on REMNUX such as tools specifically designed for analyzing Windows and Linux malware, examining suspicious documents, as well as the ability to intercept potential malicious network traffic in an isolated container:

- REMNUX can be downloaded as a virtual machine from `https://remnux.org` for a standalone virtual system. REMUX can also be added to either the SIFT workstation or CAINE utilizing the following command:

```
wget --quiet -O - https://remnux.org/get-remnux.sh | sudo
bash
```

- When incorporating different tools into a CSIRT digital forensics capability, it is important to keep in mind several factors. First, tools that have been developed by outsiders should absolutely be tested for efficacy. This can be done through the use of test data commonly available on the internet. Second, open source tools such as Linux distributions are sometimes not adequately maintained. Digital forensic analysts should ensure that tools such as SIFT, CAINE, and REMNUX are not past support or the tools will not receive updates. Finally, some tools that we will explore in this book are derived from network monitoring tools, but can also serve as tools in incident response. When using these tools, it is critical to document their use and the justification. If ever there were a question as to the entirety of the evidence obtained or analyzed with these tools, proper documentation can lessen the potential that their use would be seen as forensically unsound.

The National Institute of Standards and Technology have provided guidance on the proper testing of forensic tools through the Computer Forensics Tool Testing Program found at `http://www.cftt.nist.gov/`. In addition to specific guidance on testing, there are a number of reports on different forensic hardware and software products. Having this information available for the tools utilized, provides validation in the event that the tool use is ever challenged in a courtroom.

Jump kit

One facet to incident response that can present a challenge to CSIRT team members is the possibility that they may have to respond to incidents outside their own location. Off-site response is quite common in larger enterprises and is even the norm in CSIRTs that consult for other organizations. As a result, CSIRTs may often have to perform the entire response at another location without the support of a digital forensics laboratory. With this challenge in mind, CSIRTs should prepare several *Jump Kits*. These kits are preconfigured and contain the hardware and software necessary to perform the necessary tasks a CSIRT would be called on to perform during an incident. These kits should be able to sustain an incident investigation throughout the process, with the CSIRT identifying secure areas at the incident location in which to store and analyze evidence.

Jump kits should be portable and can be configured to fit within a secure hard sided case and be prepared to be deployed at any time. CSIRTs should ensure that, after each incident, the jump kit is restocked with any items that were utilized in the last incident, and that hardware and software is properly configured so that, during an incident, analysts can be confident in their availability.

At a minimum, the jump kit should contain:

- **Forensic laptop**: This laptop should contain enough RAM (32GB) to image a hard drive in a reasonable amount of time. The laptop should also contain a forensic software platform that was previously discussed. If possible, the laptop should also contain at least one of the Linux forensic OS such as CAINE or SIFT.
- **Networking cables**: Having several CAT5 cables of varying lengths is useful in the event that the CSIRT team has to access a network or patch into any network hardware such as a router or a switch.
- **Physical write blocker**: Each kit should have a physical write blocker that can be used to image any hard drives that the CSIRT personnel would encounter.
- **External USB hard drives**: The jump kit should contain several 1TB or 2TB USB hard drives. These will be used for imaging hard drives on potentially compromised systems.
- **External USB devices**: It is bad practice to put the evidence collected from log sources or the RAM capture of a potentially compromised system. The jump kit should contain several large capacity (64GB) USBs for offloading log files, RAM captures, or other information obtained from command-line outputs.
- **Bootable USB or CD/DVD**: While not utilized in every case, having several bootable Linux distributions can be useful in the event that the forensic laptop is currently performing another task.
- **Evidence bags or boxes**: It may become necessary to seize a piece of evidence and transport it offsite while an incident is ongoing. There should be the capability to secure evidence onsite and not have to search around for a proper container.
- **Anti-static bags**: In the event that hard drives are seized as evidence, they should be transported in anti-static bags.
- **Chain of custody forms**: As was previously discussed, chain of custody for each piece of evidence is critical. Having a dozen blank forms available saves the trouble of trying to find a system and printer to print out new copies.

- **Tool kit**: A small toolkit that contains screwdrivers, pliers, and a flashlight comes in handy when hard drives have to be removed, connections cut, or if the analyst has to access a dark corner of the data center.
- **Notepad and writing instrument**: Proper documentation is critical; handwritten notes in pen may seem old fashioned, but they are the best way to reconstruct events as the incident continues to develop. Several steno notebooks and pens as part of the kit ensure that CSIRT personnel do not have to hunt down these items while a critical event has just occurred. Jump kits should be inventoried at least monthly so that they are fully stocked and prepared for deployment. They should also be secured and accessible by CSIRT personnel only. Left out, these kits are often raided by other personnel in search of a screwdriver, network cable, or flashlight. For CSIRTs that support geographically dispersed organizations, having several kits at key locations such as major office headquarters, data centers, or other offsite locations, it may be pertinent to have several of these jump kits pre-staged for use. This saves the trouble of having to cart the kit through an airport.

Summary

Incident response spans a number of disciplines from legal to scientific. Those CSIRT members that have the responsibility for conducting digital forensic examinations should be very familiar with the legal and technical aspects of digital forensics. In addition, they should be familiar with the wide variety of tools and equipment necessary to acquire, examine, and present data discovered during an examination. The proper application of forensic techniques is critical to gain insight into the chain of events that led to the deployment of the CSIRT to investigate an incident. This chapter has delved into the various legal aspects of digital forensics such as the rules of evidence and laws pertaining to cyber crime. Next, the science of digital forensics was discussed, providing an understanding of how the techniques to be discuss have developed. To enhance this knowledge was how these techniques fit into a framework of digital investigations. This lead to the various tools available for digital forensic examiners. In the next chapter, the focus will be on jumping *on to the wire* with a discussion of network forensics.

3
Network Evidence Collection

The traditional focus of digital forensics has been to locate evidence on the host hard drive. Law enforcement officers interested in criminal activity such as fraud or child exploitation can find the vast majority of evidence required for prosecution on a single hard drive. In the realm of incident response though, it is critical that the focus goes far beyond a suspected compromised system. For example, there is a wealth of information to be obtained within the points along the flow of traffic from a compromised host to an external C2 server.

This chapter focuses on the preparation, identification, and collection of evidence that is commonly found among network devices and along the traffic routes within an internal network. This collection is critical during an incident where an external threat source is in the process of commanding internal systems or is in the process of pilfering data out of the network. Network-based evidence is also useful when examining host evidence as it provides a second source of event corroboration, which is extremely useful in determining the root cause of an incident.

Preparation

The ability to acquire network-based evidence is largely dependent on the preparations that are undertaken by an organization prior to an incident. Without some critical components of a proper infrastructure security program, key pieces of evidence will not be available for incident responders in a timely manner. The result is that evidence may be lost as the CSIRT members hunt down critical pieces of information. In terms of preparation, organizations can aid the CSIRT by having proper network documentation, up-to-date configurations of network devices, and a central log management solution in place.

Aside from the technical preparation for network evidence collection, CSIRT personnel need to be aware of any legal or regulatory issues in regards to collecting network evidence. CSIRT personnel need to be aware that capturing network traffic can be considered an invasion of privacy absent any other policy. Therefore, the legal representative of the CSIRT should ensure that all employees of the organization understand that their use of the information system can be monitored. This should be expressly stated in policies prior to any evidence collection that may take place.

Network diagram

To identify potential sources of evidence, incident responders need to have a solid understanding of what the internal network infrastructure looks like. One method that can be employed by organizations is to create and maintain an up- to- date network diagram. This diagram should be detailed enough so that incident responders can identify individual network components such as switches, routers, or wireless access points. This diagram should also contain internal IP addresses so that incident responders can immediately access those systems through remote methods. For instance, examine the following simple network diagram:

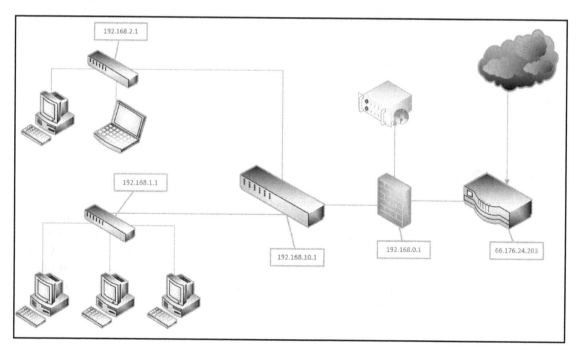

This diagram allows for a quick identification of potential evidence sources. In the preceding diagram, for example, suppose that the laptop connected to the switch at 192.168.2.1 is identified as communicating with a known malware C2 server. A CSIRT analyst could examine the network diagram and ascertain that the C2 traffic would have to traverse several network hardware components on its way out of the internal network. For example, there would be traffic traversing the switch at 192.168.10.1, through the firewall at 192.168.0.1 and finally the router out to the internet.

Configuration

Determining whether an attacker has made modifications to a network device such as a switch or a router can be made easier if the CSIRT has a standard configuration immediately available. Organizations should already have configurations for network devices stored for disaster recovery purposes, but they should have these available for CSIRT members in the event that there is an incident.

Logs and log management

The lifeblood of a good incident investigation is evidence from a wide range of sources. Even something like a malware infection on a host system requires corroboration from a variety of sources. One common challenge with incident response, especially in smaller networks, is how the organization handles log management. For a comprehensive investigation, incident response analysts need access to as much network data as possible. All too often, organizations do not dedicate the proper resources to enabling the comprehensive logs from network devices and other systems.

Prior to any incident, it is critical to clearly define the how and what an organization will log and as well as how it will maintain those logs. This should be established within a log management policy and associated procedure. The CSIRT personnel should be involved in any discussion as to what logs are necessary or not as they will often have insight into the value of one log source over another.

 The **National Institute of Standards and Technology (NIST)** has published a short guide to log management available at: http://nvlpubs. nist.gov/nistpubs/Legacy/SP/nistspecialpublication800-92.pdf.

Aside from the technical issues regarding log management, there are legal issues that must be addressed. The following are some issues that should be addressed by the CSIRT and its legal support prior to any incident:

- **Establish logging as a normal business practice**: Depending on the type of business and the jurisdiction, users may have a reasonable expectation of privacy absent any expressly stated monitoring policy. In addition, if logs are enabled strictly to determine a user's potential malicious activity, there may be legal issues. As a result, the logging policy should establish that logging of network activity is part of the normal business activity and that users do not have a reasonable expectation of privacy.

- **Logging as close to the event**: This is not so much an issue with automated logging as logs are often created almost as the event occurs. From an evidentiary standpoint, logs that are not created close to the event lose their value as evidence in a courtroom.

- **Knowledgable personnel**: The value of logs is often dependent on who created the entry and whether or not they were knowledgable about the event. In the case of logs from network devices, the logging software addresses this issue. As long as the software can be demonstrated to be functioning properly, there should be no issue.

- **Comprehensive logging**: Enterprise logging should be configured for as much of the enterprise as possible. In addition, logging should be consistent. A pattern of logging that is random will have less value in a court than a consistent pattern of logging across the entire enterprise.

- **Qualified custodian**: The logging policy should name a **data custodian**. This individual would speak to the logging and the types of software utilized to create the logs. They would also be responsible for testifying to the accuracy of the logs and the logging software used.

- **Document failures**: Prolonged failures or a history of failures in the logging of events may diminish their value in a courtroom. It is imperative that any logging failure should be documented and a reason is associated with such failure.

- **Log file discovery**: Organizations should be made aware that logs utilized within a courtroom proceeding are going to be made available to opposing legal counsel.

- **Logs from compromised systems**: Logs that originate from a known compromised system are suspect. In the event that these logs are to be introduced as evidence, the custodian or incident responder will often have to testify at length concerning the veracity of the data contained within the logs.

- **Original copies are preferred**: Log files can be copied from the log source to media. As a further step, any logs should be archived off the system as well. Incident responders should establish a chain of custody for each log file used throughout the incident and these logs are maintained as part of the case until an order from the court is obtained allowing their destruction.

Network device evidence

There are a number of log sources that can provide CSIRT personnel and incident responders with good information. A range of manufacturers provides each of these network devices. As a preparation task, CSIRT personnel should become familiar on how to access these devices and obtain the necessary evidence:

- **Switches**: These are spread throughout a network through a combination of core switches that handle traffic from a range of network segments and edge switches that handle the traffic for individual segments. As a result, traffic that originates on a host and travels out the internal network will traverse a number of switches. Switches have two key points of evidence that should be addressed by incident responders. First is the **content addressable memory (CAM)** table. This CAM table maps the physical ports on the switch to the **Network Interface Card (NIC)** on each device connected to the switch. Incident responders in tracing connections to specific network jacks can utilize this information. This can aid in the identification of possible rogue devices. The second way switches can aid in an incident investigation is through facilitating network traffic capture.
- **Routers**: Routers allow organizations to connect multiple LANs into either **Metropolitan Area Networks (MAN)** or **Wide Area Networks (WAN)**. As a result, they handle an extensive amount of traffic. The key piece of evidentiary information that routers contain is the routing table. This table holds the information for specific physical ports that map to the networks. Routers can also be configured to deny specific traffic between networks and maintain logs on allowed traffic and data flow.
- **Firewalls**: Firewalls have changed significantly since the days when they were considered just a different type of router. Next-generation firewalls contain a wide variety of features such as intrusion detection and prevention, web filtering, data loss prevention, and detailed logs about allowed and denied traffic. Firewalls oftentimes serve as the detection mechanism that alerts security personnel to potential incidents. Incident responders should have as much visibility into how their organization's firewalls function and what data can be obtained prior to an incident.

- **Network intrusion detection and prevention systems**: These systems were purposefully designed to provide security personnel and incident responders with information concerning potential malicious activity on the network infrastructure. These systems utilize a combination of network monitoring and rulesets to determine whether there is malicious activity. **Intrusion Detection Systems (IDSes)** are often configured to alert to specific malicious activity while **Intrusion Prevention Systems (IPSes)** can detect, but also block potential malicious activity. In either case, both types of platform's logs are an excellent place for incident responders to locate specific evidence on malicious activity.

- **Web proxy servers**: Organization often utilize web proxy servers to control how users interact with websites and other internet-based resources. As a result, these devices can give an enterprise-wide picture of web traffic that both originates and is destined for internal hosts. Web proxies also have the additional feature set of alerting to connections to known malware C2 servers or websites that serve up malware. A review of web proxy logs in conjunction with a possible compromised host may identify a source of malicious traffic or a C2 server exerting control over the host.

- **Domain controllers or authentication servers**: Serving the entire network domain, authentication servers are the primary location that incident responders can leverage for details on successful or unsuccessful logins, credentials manipulation, or other credentials use.

- **DHCP server**: Maintaining a list of assigned IP addresses to workstations or laptops within the organization requires an inordinate amount of upkeep. The use of **Dynamic Host Configuration Protocol (DHCP)** allows for the dynamic assignment of IP addresses to systems on the LAN. The DHCP servers often contain logs on the assignment of IP addresses mapped to the MAC address of the host's NIC. This becomes important if an incident responder has to track down a specific workstation or laptop that was connected to the network at a specific data and time.

- **Application servers**: A wide range of applications from email to web applications is housed on network servers. Each of these can provide logs specific to the type are application.

Network devices such as switches, routers, and firewalls also have their own internal logs that maintain data on access and changes. Incident responders should become familiar with the types of network devices on their organization's network and also be able to access these logs in the event of an incident.

Security information and event management system

A significant challenge that a great many organizations have is the nature of logging on network devices. With limited space, log files are often *rolled over*, where the new log files are written over older log files. The result is that in some cases, an organization may only have a few days or even a few hours of important logs. If a potential incident happened several weeks ago, the incident response personnel will be without critical pieces of evidence.

One tool that has been embraced by a number of enterprises is a **Security Information and Event Management (SIEM)** system. These appliances have the ability to aggregate log and event data from network sources and combine them into a single location. This allows the CSIRT and other security personnel to observe activity across the entire network without having to examine individual systems.

The following diagram illustrates how a SIEM integrates into the overall network:

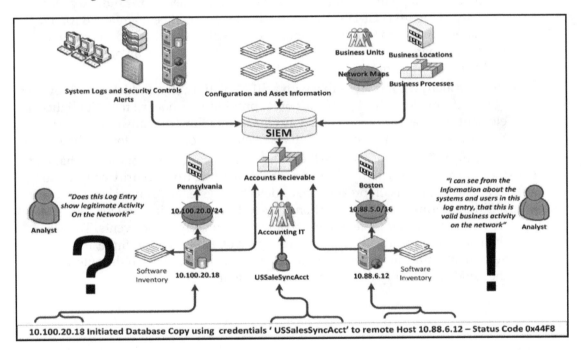

A variety of sources from security controls to SQL databases are configured to send logs to the SIEM. In this case, the SQL database located at `10.100.20.18` indicates that the user account **USSalesSyncAcct** was utilized to copy a database to the remote host located at `10.88.6.12`. The SIEM allows for quick examination of this type of activity. For example, if it is determined that the account **USSalesSyncAcct** had been compromised, CSIRT analysts can quickly query the SIEM for any usage of that account. From there, they would be able to see the log entry that indicated a copy of a database to the remote host. Without that SIEM, CSIRT analysts would have to search each individual system that might have been accessed, a process that may be prohibitive.

From the SIEM platform, security and network analysts have the ability to perform a number of different tasks related to incident response:

- **Log aggregation**:Typical enterprises have several thousand devices within the internal network, each with their own logs; the SIEM can be deployed to aggregate these logs in a central location.
- **Log retention**:Another key feature that SIEM platforms provide is a platform to retain logs. Compliance frameworks such as the **Payment Card Industry Data Security Standard (PCI-DSS)** stipulate that logs should be maintained for a period of 1 year with 90 days immediately available. SIEM platforms can aid with log management by providing a system that archives logs in an orderly fashion and allows for the immediate retrieval.
- **Routine analysis**: It is advisable with a SIEM platform to conduct period reviews of the information. SIEM platforms often provide a dashboard that highlights key elements such as the number of connections, data flow, and any critical alerts. SIEMs also allow for reporting so that stakeholders can keep informed of activity.
- **Alerting**: SIEM platforms have the ability to alert to specific conditions that may indicate malicious activity. This can include alerting from security controls such as anti-virus, intrusion prevention, or detection systems. Another key feature of SIEM platforms is event correlation. This technique examines the log files and determines whether there is a link or any commonality in the events. The SIEM then has the capability to alert on these types of events. For example, if a user account attempts multiple logins across a number of systems in the enterprise, the SIEM can identify that activity and alert to it.

- **Incident response**: As the SIEM becomes the single point for log aggregation and analysis, CSIRT analysts will often make use of the SIEM during an incident. CSIRT analysis will often make queries on the platform as well as download logs for offline analysis. Because of the centralization of log files, the time to conduct searches and event collection is significantly reduced. For example, a CSIRT analysis has indicated a user account has been compromised. Without a SIEM, the CSIRT analyst would have to check various systems for any activity pertaining to that user account. With a SIEM in place, the analyst simply conducts a search of that user account on the SIEM platform, which has aggregated user account activity, logs from systems all over the enterprise. The result is the analyst has a clear idea of the user account activity in a fraction of the time it would have taken to examine logs from various systems throughout the enterprise.

SIEM platforms do entail a good deal of time and money to purchase and implement. Adding to that cost is the constant upkeep, maintenance, and modification to rules that is necessary. From an incident response perspective though, a properly configured and maintained SIEM is vital to gathering network-based evidence in a timely manner. In addition, the features and capability of SIEM platforms can significantly reduce the time it takes to determine the root cause of an incident once it has been detected.

The following article has an excellent breakdown and use cases of SIEM platforms in enterprise environments: `https://gbhackers.com/security -information-and-event-management-siem-a-detailed-explanation /.`

Security onion

Full-featured SIEM platforms may be cost-prohibitive for some organizations. One option that is available is the open source platform security onion. The Security Onion ties a wide range of security tools, such as OSSEC, **Suricata**, and **Snort,** into a single platform. Security onion also has features such as dashboards and tools for deep analysis of log files.

For example, the following screenshot shows the level of detail available:

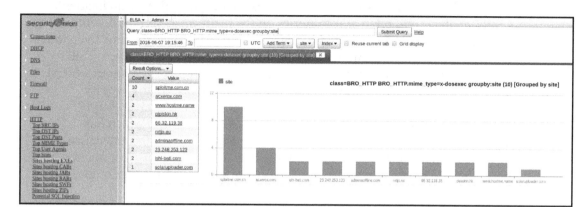

Although installing and deploying the Security Onion may require some resources in time, it is a powerful low-cost alternative providing a solution to organizations that cannot deploy a full-featured SIEM solution (the Security Onion platform and associated documentation is available at `https://securityonion.net/`).

Packet capture

Capturing network traffic is critical to having a full understanding of an incident. Being able to identify potential C2 traffic IP addresses may provide further information about the type of malware that might have infected a host. In other types of incidents, CSIRT members may be able to identify potential exfiltration methods that an external threat actor is utilizing.

One method is to set up what is referred to as a network tap. A network tap is a system in-line with the compromised host and the switch. For example, in the network diagram, if the host that is compromised is on the `192.168.1.0/24` subnet, the tap should be placed in between the host and the switch. This often involves placing a system in between the host and the switch.

Another option is to configure a **Switched Port Analyzer** (**SPAN**) port. In this configuration, the switch closest to the compromised host will have port mirroring enabled. This then sends the traffic from the entire segment the switch is on to the system that is on the mirrored port.

Finally, some network devices have built-in applications such as tcpdump that can be utilized to capture traffic for further analysis. This may be the quickest option as it does not require physical access to the network or the switch and can be set up remotely. The drawback to this method is that the storage on the switch may not support a large capture file and the added strain may increase the potential for some packets not being captured.

tcpdump

tcpdump is a command-line tool specifically designed for packet capture. tcpdump is often included with Linux distributions and is found on many network devices. For many of these devices, tcpdump has to be run as a root user or with root privileges as it will be monitoring the network traffic. The full page is available at `http://www.tcpdump.org/`.

To access the basic help menu, type the following into the Command Prompt:

```
caine@caine:~$ tcpdump -h
```

The command will produce the basic options available for tcpdump:

```
 File  Edit  View  Search  Terminal  Help
caine@caine:~$ tcpdump -h
tcpdump version 4.7.4
libpcap version 1.7.4
OpenSSL 1.0.2g  1 Mar 2016
Usage: tcpdump [-aAbdDefhHIJKlLnNOpqRStuUvxX#] [ -B size ] [ -c count ]
               [ -C file_size ] [ -E algo:secret ] [ -F file ] [ -G seconds ]
               [ -i interface ] [ -j tstamptype ] [ -M secret ] [ --number ]
               [ -Q in|out|inout ]
               [ -r file ] [ -s snaplen ] [ --time-stamp-precision precision ]
               [ --immediate-mode ] [ -T type ] [ --version ] [ -V file ]
               [ -w file ] [ -W filecount ] [ -y datalinktype ] [ -z command ]
               [ -Z user ] [ expression ]
```

The default setting of Tcpdump is to capture traffic on all available interfaces. Running the following command produces a list of all interfaces that tcpdump can capture traffic on:

```
caine@caine~$ tcpdump -D
```

The following screenshot shows that the `ens33` (Ethernet) and `lo` (loopback) interfaces are available for capturing traffic:

```
File  Edit  View  Search  Terminal  Help
caine@caine:~$ tcpdump -D
1.ens33 [Up, Running]
2.any (Pseudo-device that captures on all interfaces) [Up, Running]
3.lo [Up, Running, Loopback]
4.bluetooth0 (Bluetooth adapter number 0)
5.nflog (Linux netfilter log (NFLOG) interface)
6.nfqueue (Linux netfilter queue (NFQUEUE) interface)
7.usbmon1 (USB bus number 1)
8.usbmon2 (USB bus number 2)
```

To configure a basic capture on the Ethernet interface located at `ens33` with normal verbosity, type the following command:

```
caine@caine~$ sudotcpdump -i ens33 -v
```

The `-i` tells tcpdump which interface to perform the packet capture on. In this case, it is on the Ethernet interface `ens33`. The `-v` sets the verbosity of the packet capture. The following screenshot show what information is displayed by the command:

```
File  Edit  View  Search  Terminal  Help
     keeton.canonical.com.http > 172.16.137.138.50498: Flags [P.], cksum 0x3eea (
correct), seq 9930384:9931832, ack 1, win 64240, length 1448: HTTP
02:07:12.571664 IP (tos 0x0, ttl 128, id 18329, offset 0, flags [none], proto TC
P (6), length 1500)
     keeton.canonical.com.http > 172.16.137.138.50498: Flags [.], cksum 0x79ea (c
orrect), seq 9931832:9933292, ack 1, win 64240, length 1460: HTTP
02:07:12.571682 IP (tos 0x0, ttl 64, id 54879, offset 0, flags [DF], proto TCP (
6), length 40)
```

While this method works for determining whether traffic is traversing that interface, the individual packet information is useless to an analyst due to the speed with which the individual packets appear on the screen. For the packet capture to be any use, it is advisable to output the file so that later examination can be performed with a packet analysis tool such as Wireshark. Wireshark will be reviewed later on in this chapter and with greater detail during the analysis chapter. To configure tcpdump to output the packet capture to a file, the following command is used:

```
caine@caine~$ sudo tcpdump -i ens33 -vvv -w capture
```

The command tells tcpdump to capture network traffic and write the file out to `capture`. Unlike the previous capture, there is no traffic indicated on the screen. To stop the capture, type Ctrl+C, which produces the following information:

```
File  Edit  View  Search  Terminal  Help
caine@caine:~$ sudo tcpdump -i ens33 -vvv -w capture
tcpdump: listening on ens33, link-type EN10MB (Ethernet), capture size 262144 by
tes
^C3867 packets captured
3868 packets received by filter
0 packets dropped by kernel
```

The previous screenshot indicates that a total of `3868` packets were received and recorded in the capture file. Navigating to the root directory, the file can then be opened via Wireshark:

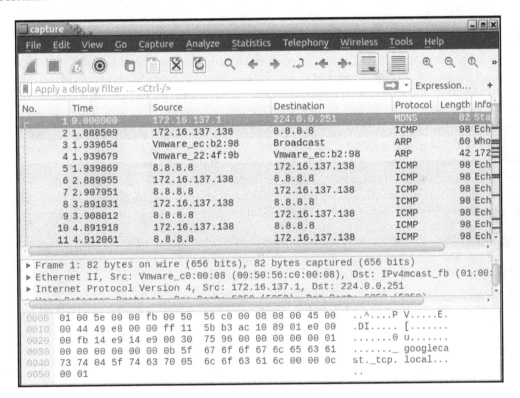

tcpdump can also be configured to focus the capture on specific source or destination IP addresses and ports. For example, if an incident response analyst needs to collect packets leaving a specific host at the IP address `192.168.10.54`, the following tcpdump command will produce the desired results:

```
caine@rootsudotcpdump -i ens33 src host 192.168.10.54
```

Packets going to a destination such as a known C2 server at the IP address can also be separated out from the background network traffic with the following command:

```
caine@rootsudotcpdump -i ens33 dst host 162.4.5.23
```

tcpdump is a powerful tool and has a great deal of options. Incident response analysts would be advised to examine and incorporate the various features into their toolkit.

WinPcap and RawCap

During an incident, it may become necessary to obtain a packet capture from a Windows system. In incidents such as a compromise of a web server or application server, the Windows system will not have a native application to conduct a packet capture. There are several tools available for packet capture on Windows systems. The first tool that can be utilized is WinPcap. This tool is generally recognized as the standard for packet capture on Windows systems and is available as a free download at `winpcap.org`. The drawback to this tool from a forensics perspective is that it has to be installed on the system. This can complicate a forensic analysis as any changes to the system have to be thoroughly documented. For this reason, it is a good preparatory step to ensure that high-risk systems such as web servers, file servers, and application servers have WinPcap installed.

Another option available to incident response analysts is the use of tools such as **RawCap**. RawCap has the same basic capability as WinPcap without the necessity to install on the local system. RawCap can be easily run from a USB device attached to the system and run. To perform a capture, first start the Windows Command Prompt as an administrator. Once in the Command Prompt, navigate to the folder containing the `RawCap.exe`. For a list of options, type the following:

```
D:\>RawCap.exe -help
```

The command will produce the following output:

```
D:\>RawCap.exe --help
NETRESEC RawCap version 0.1.5.0
http://www.netresec.com

Usage: RawCap.exe [OPTIONS] <interface_nr> <target_pcap_file>

OPTIONS:
 -f             Flush data to file after each packet (no buffer)
 -c <count>     Stop sniffing after receiving <count> packets
 -s <sec>       Stop sniffing after <sec> seconds

INTERFACES:
 0.     IP         : 169.254.205.201
        NIC Name   : Ethernet
        NIC Type   : Ethernet

 1.     IP         : 169.254.212.254
        NIC Name   : Local Area Connection* 3
        NIC Type   : Ethernet

 2.     IP         : 169.254.97.199
        NIC Name   : Local Area Connection* 2
        NIC Type   : Wireless80211

 3.     IP         : 192.168.23.1
        NIC Name   : VMware Network Adapter VMnet1
        NIC Type   : Ethernet

 4.     IP         : 192.168.106.1
        NIC Name   : VMware Network Adapter VMnet8
        NIC Type   : Ethernet

 5.     IP         : 192.168.0.24
        NIC Name   : Wi-Fi
        NIC Type   : Wireless80211
```

The output produces a list of interfaces. This is one of the advantages of RawCap in that even from a USB device, the incident response analyst can perform a packet capture on each of the interfaces. In this example, the capture will be performed on the wireless interface number 5.

To start the packet capture, RawCap requires the interface to capture and an output file to output the packet capture. To capture the traffic on the wireless interface and output to the file called RawCap.pcap, the following command is used:

```
D:\>RawCap.exe 5 RawCap.pcap
```

The command produces the following output:

```
D:\>RawCap.exe 5 RawCap.pcap
Sniffing IP : 192.168.0.24
File        : RawCap.pcap
Packets     : 619
```

Typing *Ctrl+C* will stop the capture. The capture file `RawCap.pcap` is saved to the same directory as the `RawCap.exe`. This file can then be opened with tools such as Wireshark for further analysis:

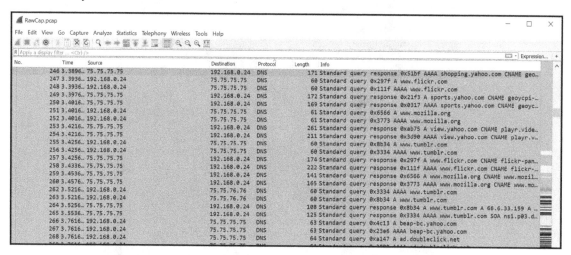

Wireshark

Wireshark is a Unix or Windows packet capture and analysis tool. Unlike tcpdump or tools such as RawCap, Wireshark is a GUI-based tool that has a number of features for not only packet capture, but also analysis. As a result, it may be difficult to deploy rapidly during an incident as the program has to be installed. Furthermore, the tool is only supported on the Windows and Mac operating systems. To install on a Linux system requires a bit more effort. The one distinct advantage that Wireshark has over the command-line options is that incident response analysts can perform a detailed inspection of the traffic as it is being captured.

Wireshark can be run on the system itself or run on a USB. Once installed, it has to be run as an administrator. The first step is to select an interface that Wireshark will capture on:

In the previous screenshot, the only interface that appears to be handling traffic is the **Wi-Fi:en0** interface. Double-clicking on the interface will start a packet capture. As was stated before, unlike tcpdump or RawCap, the actual capture is output to the screen for immediate analysis:

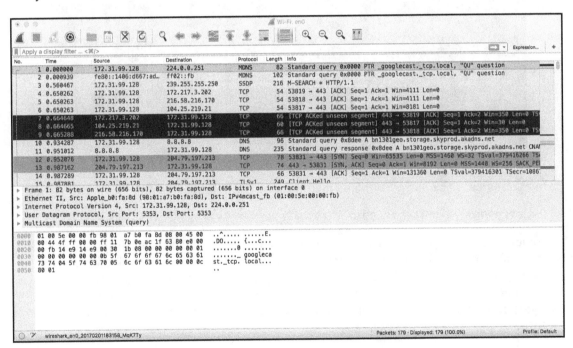

To stop the capture, hit the red box in the upper left-hand corner of the pane. The file can then be saved for further analysis.

Another tool that is included with Wireshark that is useful during evidence acquisition is **Mergecap**. Mergecap is a command-line tool that allows incident response analysts to combine multiple packet capture files from Wireshark, tcpdump, or RawCap. This is extremely useful in situations where incident response analysts obtain packet captures from several sources, but want to check for traffic to a specific host. To access the menu for Mergecap, type the following into the command prompt:

```
~$ mergecap -help
```

That command produces the following help information:

```
gerardjohansen@ubuntu:~$ mergecap -help
Mergecap (Wireshark) 2.0.2 (SVN Rev Unknown from unknown)
Merge two or more capture files into one.
See https://www.wireshark.org for more information.

Usage: mergecap [options] -w <outfile>|- <infile> [<infile> ...]

Output:
  -a                     concatenate rather than merge files.
                         default is to merge based on frame timestamps.
  -s <snaplen>           truncate packets to <snaplen> bytes of data.
  -w <outfile>|-         set the output filename to <outfile> or '-' for stdout.
  -F <capture type>      set the output file type; default is pcapng.
                         an empty "-F" option will list the file types.
  -I <IDB merge mode>    set the merge mode for Interface Description Blocks; defau
lt is 'all'.
                         an empty "-I" option will list the merge modes.

Miscellaneous:
  -h                     display this help and exit.
  -v                     verbose output.
```

To merge several packet capture files, the following command is used:

```
~$ mergecap -w switches.pcap switch1.pcap switch2.pcap switch3.pcap
```

By combining the output of three packet captures to one file, the incident response analyst has the ability to examine a wider range of activity across multiple network paths. If, for example, the analyst is searching for traffic coming from an unknown host to an external C2 server, they would be able to combine captures over the entire span of the network and then search for that particular IP rather than individually picking through each packet capture.

Evidence collection

In order to conduct a proper examination of log files and other network data such as packet captures, they often have to be moved from the log source and examined offline. As with any source of evidence, the log files or packet captures have to be handled with due care to ensure that they are not corrupted or modified during the transfer. One simple solution is to transfer the evidence immediately to a USB drive or similar removable medium. From there, a hash can be created for the evidence prior to any examination.

The acquisition of network evidence such as a packet capture or log file should be thoroughly documented. Incident response personnel may be acquiring log files and packet captures from a number of sources over the entire network. As a result, they should ensure that they can trace back every separate piece of evidence to its source as well as the date and time that the evidence was collected. This can be recorded in a network evidence log sheet and entries completed for each piece of evidence. For example, the following is a sheet with an entry:

File Name	Description	Location	Date	Time	Collected By	MD5 Hash
Switch1.pcap	Packet capture from Switch 1	192.168.2.1	2/7/17	1642	GTJ	6c1717e2c0da2bdc954a7b56d43f51b2

The log entry captures the necessary information:

- **File Name**: Each log file or packet capture should have its own unique name. Within the procedures in use by the CSIRT should be a naming convention for different types of evidence files.
- **Description**: A brief description of the file. There does not need to be too much detail unless it is a unique file and a detailed description is called for.
- **Location**: The location is important. In this case, the packet capture was obtained on the switch located at 192.168.2.1.
- **Date and time**: Record the date and time the file was transferred to the medium.

> **Note:** Prior to an incident, it is important to identify what type of time zone will be in use. From an evidentiary standpoint, the time zone does not really matter as long as it is consistent among the entire incident investigation.

- **Collected by**: Initials are sufficient for the log file.

- **MD5 hash**: A comprehensive overview of hashing will be covered in later chapters. For now, the hash is a one-way algorithm that is utilized to provide a digital fingerprint for the file. This hash will be recorded at the collection phase and after analysis to demonstrate that the file was not modified during the analysis phase. There are several ways to compute the hash. In this case, the MD5 hash can be computed using the installed hashing program MD5 sum on a Ubuntu install. MD5 sum has several different options that can be accessed via the command line. For the help menu, type the following:

```
~$ md5sum -help
```

That produces the following help menu:

```
gerardjohansen@ubuntu:~$ md5sum --help
Usage: md5sum [OPTION]... [FILE]...
Print or check MD5 (128-bit) checksums.

With no FILE, or when FILE is -, read standard input.

  -b, --binary         read in binary mode
  -c, --check          read MD5 sums from the FILEs and check them
      --tag            create a BSD-style checksum
  -t, --text           read in text mode (default)

The following five options are useful only when verifying checksums:
      --ignore-missing  don't fail or report status for missing files
      --quiet           don't print OK for each successfully verified file
      --status          don't output anything, status code shows success
      --strict          exit non-zero for improperly formatted checksum lines
  -w, --warn            warn about improperly formatted checksum lines

      --help     display this help and exit
      --version  output version information and exit

The sums are computed as described in RFC 1321.  When checking, the input
should be a former output of this program.  The default mode is to print a
line with checksum, a space, a character indicating input mode ('*' for binary,
' ' for text or where binary is insignificant), and name for each FILE.

GNU coreutils online help: <http://www.gnu.org/software/coreutils/>
Full documentation at: <http://www.gnu.org/software/coreutils/md5sum>
or available locally via: info '(coreutils) md5sum invocation'
```

The MD5 hash can be calculated for the packet capture from the switch by simply entering in the following command:

```
~$ md5sum Switch1.pcap
```

This produces the following output:

```
gerardjohansen@ubuntu:~$ md5sum Switch1.pcap
6c1717e2c0da2bdc954a7b56d43f51b2  Switch1.pcap
```

Log files and packet captures should be transferred to a storage device as soon as possible. Once the collection is complete, a chain of custody form should also be filled out for the external medium that contains the evidence files. From here, the files can be analyzed.

Summary

Evidence that is pertinent to incident responders is not just located on the hard drive of a compromised host. There is a wealth of information available from network devices spread throughout the environment. With proper preparation, a CSIRT may be able to leverage the evidence provided by these devices through solutions such as a SIEM. CSIRT personnel also have the ability to capture the network traffic for later analysis through a variety of methods and tools. Behind all of these techniques, though, are the legal and policy implications that CSIRT personnel and the organization at large needs to navigate. By preparing for the legal and technical challenges of network evidence collection, CSIRT members can leverage this evidence and move closer to the goal of determining the root cause of an incident and bringing the organization back up to operations.

This chapter discussed several sources of evidence available to incident response analysts. Logs from network devices, whether they report to a SIEM or through other methods can give insight into what transpired in the network. Packet captures provide details into the exact nature of network traffic. Finally, analysts have to be prepared to acquire these sources of evidence is a forensically sound manner. The next chapter will take the analyst off the network into acquiring the volatile data from host based systems.

4

Acquiring Host-Based Evidence

Host systems are far too often the target of malicious actions. They represent a possible initial target to gain a foothold in the network, pivot point, or the goal of threat actors. As a result, incident response analyst should be prepared to investigate these systems. Modern operating systems such as Microsoft Windows makes a number of changes during the execution of an application, changes to files, or the addition of user accounts. All of these changes leave traces of activity that can be evaluated by incident response analysts. Compounding the amount of data available to incident response analysis is the increasing storage and memory available in even the lowest-cost consumer systems. Commonly available systems are routinely manufactured with extensive memory and storage in terabytes; there is a great deal of data that could assist incident responders with determining a root cause analysis. As a result, incident response analysts should be prepared to acquire different types of evidence from systems for further analysis.

Preparation

In terms of preparation, incident response analysts should have the necessary tools at their disposal for acquiring host-based evidence. The techniques discussed within this chapter do not rely on any highly-specialized technology, but rather on tools that can be acquired for little or no cost. Outside of software, the only additional hardware that is required is external hard drives and common desktop computers.

When supporting an enterprise environment, it is a good idea that incident response personnel have a solid understanding of the types of systems commonly deployed. For example, in an enterprise that utilizes strictly Microsoft operating systems, the tools available should have the ability to support the wide range of versions of the Microsoft OS. In other circumstances, incident response personnel may support an enterprise where there is an 80/20 split of Microsoft and Linux systems; incident response personnel should be prepared with tools and techniques that support the acquisition of evidence.

Many of the tools and techniques that will be discussed in this chapter require administrator privileges. Incident responders should be provided with the necessary credentials to perform these tasks. It should be noted that analysts should use only existing accounts and that adding accounts to a possibly compromised system may make evidence inadmissible in a judicial proceeding. One technique is for incident response analysts to be given individual credentials that are enabled only during an incident. This allows the organization to separate out the legitimate use of credentials with possible malicious ones. This also allows the incident response team to recreate their actions. It is worth noting that highly technical adversaries will often monitor the network they are attacking during an active compromise to determine whether they are being detected. Therefore, these credentials should not indicate that they are tied to the incident response analysts or other personnel investigating a possible breach.

Evidence volatility

Not all evidence on a host system is the same. Volatility is used to describe how data on a host system is maintained after changes such as log-offs or power shutdowns. Data that will be lost if the system is powered down is referred to as volatile data. Volatile data can be data in the CPU, routing table, or ARP cache. One of the most critical pieces of volatile evidence is the memory currently running on the system. When investigating such incidents as malware infections, the memory in a live system is of critical importance. Malware leaves a number of key pieces of evidence within the memory of a system and, if lost, can leave the incident response analyst with little or no avenue to investigate.

Non-volatile data is the data that is stored on a hard drive and will usually persist after shut down. Non-volatile data includes **Master File Table** (**MFT**) entries, registry information, and the actual files on the hard drive. While malware creates evidence in memory, there are still items of evidentiary value in non-volatile memory.

Evidence acquisition

There are a variety of methods that are used to not only access a potential evidence source but the type of acquisition that can be undertaken. To define these methods better, it is important to have a clear understanding of the manner and type of acquisition that can be utilized:

- **Local**: Having access to the system under investigation is often a luxury for most enterprises at times. Even so, there are many times where incident response analysts or other personnel have direct physical access to the system.

- **Remote**: In a remote acquisition, incident response analysts leverage tools and network connections to acquire evidence. Remote acquisition is an obvious choice if the incident response analysts are dealing with geographical challenges. Remote acquisition can also be useful if incident response analysts cannot be onsite immediately.
- **Online acquisition**: An online acquisition of evidence occurs when the incident response analyst acquires the evidence from a system that is currently powered on and running. Some of the techniques demonstrated in this chapter have to be deployed on a live system (for example, running memory). Completely acquiring digital evidence from a live system may be a technique necessary in high - availability environments where a suspected system cannot be taken offline. These techniques allow incident response analysts to acquire and analyze evidence to determine whether a system is indeed compromised.
- **Offline acquisition**: The offline acquisition method is the one often used by law enforcement agencies to preserve digital evidence on the hard drive. This technique requires that the system be powered down and the hard drive removed. Once the drive is accessed, specialized tools are utilized to acquire the hard drive evidence. There are some drawbacks in focusing strictly on offline acquisition. First is the loss of any volatile memory. Second, it may be time-consuming to acquire a suspect system's hard drive, image it, and finally process the image for investigation. This may create a situation where incident responders do not have any idea of what has transpired for more than 24 hours.

Depending on the type of incident and any constraints in time or geography, incident response analysts should be prepared to perform any of these types of acquisitions. In terms of preparation, analysts should have the necessary tools and experience to conduct evidence acquisition in any of these methods.

To perform local acquisition, incident response analysts require an external hard drive or USB drive with sufficient space for the capture of at least the running memory of the system or systems that are being investigated along with other files if deemed necessary. In order to ensure the integrity of the evidence being collected, it is advisable to configure the USB drive into two partitions. The first partition should contain the necessary tools to perform the evidence acquisition and the second, a repository for the evidence. This also allows the incident response analyst to move evidence to a more permanent storage and subsequently wipe the evidence partition without having to reinstall all the tools.

Evidence collection procedures

There are a number of parallels between digital forensics and other forensic disciplines such as trace evidence. The key parallel is that organizations acquiring evidence need to have a procedure that is sound, reproducible, and well documented. The following are some guidelines for proper collection of digital evidence:

1. Photograph the system and the general scene. One the key pieces of equipment that can save time is a small digital camera. While it may seem overkill to photograph a system in place, in the event that actions taken by incident responders ever see the inside of a courtroom, having photos will allow for a proper reconstruction of the events. One word of caution though is make sure to utilize a separate digital camera. Utilizing a cell phone may expose the device to discovery in the event of a lawsuit or criminal proceeding. The best method is to snap all of the photos necessary and at a convenient time and place, and transfer them to permanent storage.

2. Determine whether the system is powered up. If the system is powered on, leave it on. If the system is powered off, do not power it on. A number of changes take place when turning a system on or off. In the event that the system is powered on, the volatile memory will be available for capture. If the system is turned off, preserving this state ensures any evidence in the non-volatile memory is preserved. In the event that incident response personnel feel that the system may be a danger to other systems, simply remove the network connection to isolate it.

3. Acquire the running memory. This is a critical piece of evidence that can produce a wealth of data concerning running processes, DLLs in use, and network connections. Due to this, procedures for acquiring memory are covered extensively in this chapter.

4. Acquire registry and log files. While these files are non-volatile in nature, having near-immediate access is beneficial, especially when investigating malware or other exploitation means.

5. Unplug the power from the back of the system. In the event that the system is a laptop, remove the battery as well. This preserves the state of the system.

6. Photograph the back or bottom of the system to capture the model and serial number. This procedure allows the incident response analyst to capture information necessary for the chain of custody.

7. Remove the cover to the system and photograph the hard drive to capture the model and serial number. Again, this aids in the reconstruction of the chain of custody.

8. Remove the hard drive from the system and package it in an anti-static bag. Secure the drive in a sealable envelope or box. Anti-static bags will protect the hard drive and the packaging should be such that any attempt to open it will be evident. This can be facilitated through purpose-designed evidence bags or simple mailing envelopes that allow for the sealing with tape. The seizing analyst should sign on any seals. Furthermore, indicate the incident number, evidence number, date, time, and seizing analyst somewhere on the exterior of the packaging.

9. Document all actions. Ensure that dates and times are recorded as well as which incident response analyst performed the action. Incident reporting is often the last stage of any response. As a result, hours or even days can pass before analysts are able to record their actions. As a result, pictures and notes taken during the initial seizure are invaluable to reconstruct the sequence of events.

Memory acquisition

Traditional digital forensics or what is often referred to now as **dead box forensics** has focused on the hard disk drive taken from a shut down system as the primary source of evidence. This approach works well when addressing criminal activity such as fraud or child exploitation where image files, word processing documents, and spreadsheets can be discovered in a forensically sound manner. The issue with this approach is that to properly acquire this evidence, the system has to be powered off, thereby destroying any potential evidence found within the volatile memory.

As opposed to traditional criminal activity, incident responders will find that a great deal of evidence of a security incident is contained within the memory of a potentially compromised system. This is especially true when examining systems that have been infected with malware or exploited utilizing a common platform such as metasploit. Trace evidence is often found within the memory of the compromised system. As a result, it is critical before powering down the system and removing the hard drive that the running memory is acquired for processing.

There are a number of free and commercial tools that can be leveraged by incident response analysts to acquire the running memory. Which tool is used will often be dependent on the type of techniques and tools that will be used during the analysis phase. Two popular frameworks for analysis of memory images are *Rekall* and *Volatility*. Both of these frameworks allow for detailed analysis of memory images.

Running memory can be acquired in two ways. First, memory can be acquired locally via a USB device or other writable medium that is directly connected to the suspect system. The other method to acquiring memory is through a remote connection. This can be facilitated through the use of specialized software that performs the acquisition over a network connection.

Local acquisition

If an incident response analyst has physical access to a potentially compromised system, they have the option of acquiring the memory and other evidence locally. This involves the use of tools run from a USB device or other similar removable medium that is connected to the potentially compromised system. From there, the tools are run and the evidence is collected. Local acquisition is often conducted in conjunction with seizing the hard drive and other evidence from the system. There are several tools that are available for local acquisition. For the purposes of this book, two such tools, Access Data's **FTK Imager** and **WinPmem** will be discussed.

When acquiring memory in this fashion, it is advisable to utilize an external drive with sufficient capacity for multiple files. Furthermore, incident response analysts should make use of a USB device with two partitions. The first of these partitions contains the tools necessary to perform the memory acquisition and the second partition will contain the evidence files. This way, incident response analysts can be sure that the evidence does not become co-mingled with their tools.

FTK Imager

Access Data's FTK Imager is a Windows software platform that performs a variety of imaging tasks including acquiring the running memory of a system. The software can be downloaded at `http://accessdata.com/product-download/digital-forensics/ftk-imager-version-3.4.3`. Once downloaded, install the executable in the **Tools** partition of the USB drive. Open the `FTK Imager` folder and run the executable as administrator. The following window will appear:

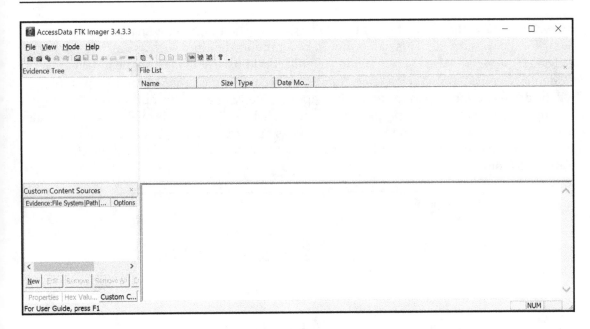

Click on **File** and then on **Capture Memory**. This opens up the following window:

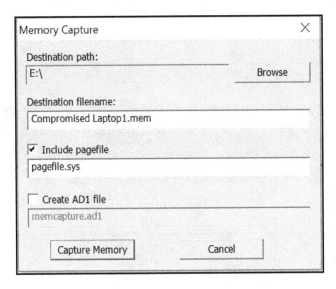

Browse to the **Evidence** partition of the USB drive attached to the system and provide a name for the capture file. This name should be a unique identifier such as `Laptop1` or `Evidence Item 1`. Also check Include pagefile checkbox. There may not be information of evidentiary value within the pagefile, but it may become important later on (the pagefile will be discussed later on in the analysis chapter). Finally, there is the option to create an `AD1` file that is Access Data's proprietary file format. This file is for the analysis of this image using the FTK analysis program. For the purposes of this book, the standard output is sufficient for the analysis that will be performed. Once the configurations are set, click on **Capture Memory:**

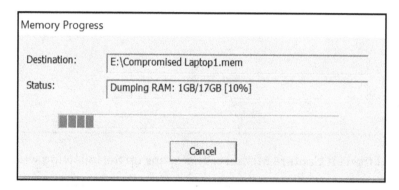

After running, FTK Imager will indicate whether the memory capture was successful or not:

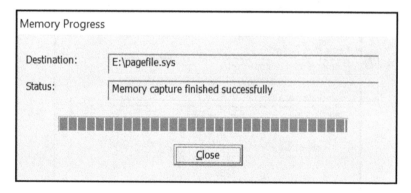

An examination of the evidence partition reveals the two files, as shown in the following screenshot:

Notice that the .mem file is approximately 17 GB. The RAM on this system that was utilized in the demonstration has 16 GB of RAM. This situation is common where the .mem file is not the exact size of the entire RAM space.

Winpmem

As was previously discussed, some memory acquisition tools work better with different memory analysis tools. In the case of the memory analysis tool Rekall, there are several memory acquisition tools provided by the same organization that created Rekall. The PMEM tools are available for capturing raw memory from Linux, macOS, and Windows systems. These tools are available at the Rekall website `http://releases.rekall-forensic.com/`.

In the following demonstration, the target system is the same that was utilized in the FTK Imager demonstration. As a result, the tool WinPmem, which is specifically designed to capture the memory of Windows systems, will be utilized.

Starting with version 2.0.1, the default output for the WinPmem tool is the **Advanced Forensic Framework 4 (AFF4)** file format. This format was created to allow for a number of separate data sources and workflows. This open source format is utilized for digital forensics evidence and other associated data.

 More information about the AFF4 file format is available at the following site:
`http://www.aff4.org/`.

To acquire the physical memory of the target system, open up a Windows Command Prompt as an administrator. Typing D:\winpmem-2.1.exe -h will produce the following help menu:

```
D:\>winpmem-2.1.exe -h

USAGE:

    winpmem-2.1.exe  [-l] [-u] [--write-mode] [--mode <MmMapIoSpace,
                     PhysicalMemory, PTERemapping>] [--driver <Path to
                     driver.>] [--format <map, elf, raw>] [-m] [-p
                     </path/to/pagefile>] ...   [-V] [-d] [-v] [-t] [-i
                     </path/to/file/or/device>] ...   [-e <string>] [-o
                     </path/to/file>] [-c <zlib, snappy, none>] [--]
                     [--version] [-h] </path/to/aff4/volume> ...
```

Next, configure Winpmem to acquire the memory of the system by typing the following:

```
D:\winpmem-2.1.exe --format raw -o e:\Laptop1
```

This command tells WinPmem to acquire the raw memory and output it to a folder created on the evidence partition of the USB drive in use. The command will produce the following:

```
D:\>winpmem-2.1.exe --format raw -o e:\Laptop1
Driver Unloaded.
CR3: 0x00001AA000
 7 memory ranges:
Start 0x00001000 - Length 0x0009C000
Start 0x00100000 - Length 0x00002000
Start 0x00103000 - Length 0xBE2FE000
Start 0xBE889000 - Length 0x1BD7E000
Start 0xDA770000 - Length 0x00775000
Start 0xDBAFF000 - Length 0x00001000
Start 0x100000000 - Length 0x31E800000
```

WinPmem then runs through the entire memory structure. During the processing, it will produce the following output:

```
Creating output AFF4 Directory structure.
Dumping Range 0 (Starts at 1000, length 9c000)
Dumping Range 1 (Starts at 100000, length 2000)
Dumping Range 2 (Starts at 103000, length be2fe000)
Dumping Range 3 (Starts at be889000, length 1bd7e000)
Dumping Range 4 (Starts at da770000, length 775000)
Dumping Range 5 (Starts at dbaff000, length 1000)
Dumping Range 6 (Starts at 100000000, length 31e800000)
 Reading 0x8000   0MiB / 16272MiB 0MiB/s
 Reading 0x4398000   67MiB / 16272MiB 255MiB/s
 Reading 0x89b0000   137MiB / 16272MiB 275MiB/s
 Reading 0xd288000   210MiB / 16272MiB 276MiB/s
 Reading 0x11858000   280MiB / 16272MiB 274MiB/s
 Reading 0x15f48000   351MiB / 16272MiB 283MiB/s
 Reading 0x1a998000   425MiB / 16272MiB 295MiB/s
 Reading 0x1f3f0000   499MiB / 16272MiB 296MiB/s
 Reading 0x23cb8000   572MiB / 16272MiB 289MiB/s
 Reading 0x283c8000   643MiB / 16272MiB 283MiB/s
 Reading 0x2cb68000   715MiB / 16272MiB 285MiB/s
 Reading 0x310d0000   784MiB / 16272MiB 276MiB/s
 Reading 0x346f8000   838MiB / 16272MiB 206MiB/s
 Reading 0x38c70000   908MiB / 16272MiB 276MiB/s
 Reading 0x3cbe8000   971MiB / 16272MiB 252MiB/s
 Reading 0x41240000   1042MiB / 16272MiB 280MiB/s
 Reading 0x45580000   1109MiB / 16272MiB 267MiB/s
```

At the conclusion, a review of the output file reveals that the entire physical memory is contained within a single file along with others as part of the AFF4 file container:

```
02/15/2017  10:02 AM           99,328 C%3a%2fWindows%2fSysNative%2fdrivers%2fWUDFPf.sys
02/15/2017  10:02 AM          216,064 C%3a%2fWindows%2fSysNative%2fdrivers%2fWUDFRd.sys
02/15/2017  10:02 AM          258,560 C%3a%2fWindows%2fSysNative%2fdrivers%2fxboxgip.sys
02/15/2017  10:02 AM           43,520 C%3a%2fWindows%2fSysNative%2fdrivers%2fxinputhid.sys
02/15/2017  10:02 AM        7,816,032 C%3a%2fWindows%2fSysNative%2fntoskrnl.exe
02/15/2017  10:02 AM               43 container.description
02/15/2017  10:02 AM          112,565 information.turtle
02/15/2017  10:01 AM   17,691,574,272 PhysicalMemory
02/15/2017  09:59 AM              433 PhysicalMemory%2finformation.yaml
             424 File(s) 17,794,139,025 bytes
               2 Dir(s)  439,895,343,104 bytes free
```

WinPmem is an easy tool to use, but one of the other great advantages is that there are versions for Linux and macOS systems as well as Microsoft OS. This allows incident response analysts to become familiar with one tool across all operating systems they might encounter in their organization.

Remote acquisition

The preferred method for the acquisition of memory is through direct contact with the suspect system. This allows for adaptability by incident response analysts in the event that a tool or technique does not work. This method is also faster at obtaining the necessary files, as it does not depend on a stable network connection. Although this is the preferred method, there may be geographical constraints, especially with larger organizations where the incident response analysts are a plane ride away from the location containing the evidence.

In the case of a remote acquisition, incident response analysts can leverage the same tools utilized in local acquisition. The one change is that incident response analysts are required to utilize a remote technology to access the suspect systems and perform the capture. As with any method that is utilized, incident response analysts should ensure that they document any use of remote technology. This will allow for proper identification of legitimate versus suspect connections later on.

Winpmem

Winpmem can be deployed on remote systems through such native applications as Remote Desktop or PsExec. Once installed on the remote system, the output of WinPmem can be piped to another system utilizing NetCat. For example, suppose that the incident response analyst is utilizing a system located at 192.168.0.56. If the analyst is able to access the compromised host via PSExec or RDS, they can establish a netcat connection back to their machine utilizing the following command:

```
C:/winpmem-2.1.exe - | nc 192.168.0.56 4455
```

The preceding command directs the system to perform the capture and send the output via Netcat to the incident response analyst workstation over port 4455. The drawback to this technique is that it requires access to the Command Prompt as well as the installation of both NetCat and WinPmem. This may not be the best option if the incident response analyst is dealing with a system that is already suspected of being compromised.

F-Response

Another option that is available to incident response analyst is the use of the tool F-Response. F-Response is a software platform that allows incident response analysts to perform remote acquisition of evidence over a network. One advantage to utilizing F-Response is that it does not require direct access via SSH or RDS to the remote system. Another key feature of F-Response is that the tool is designed to establish the connection while allowing the incident response analyst to utilize their preferred tools to perform the acquisition.

In the following example, F-Response is utilized to connect to a suspected compromised system over a network whereby the incident response analyst can utilize FTK Imager to acquire the memory of the suspect system. After installing F-Response Enterprise, navigate to the menu **Scan** and click on **Custom Scan**. From there, the incident response analyst can enter the suspect system's IP address. In this case, F-Response will be utilized to capture the memory from a system on the local network at the IP address 192.168.0.24:

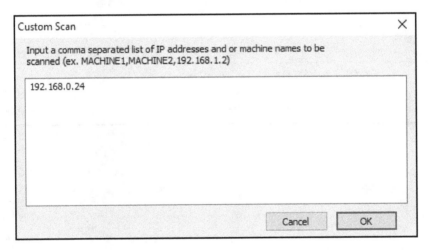

After inputting the target IP address, click **OK**. At this point, F-Response attempts to connect to the target system. If F-Response is able to connect to the target system, the system will appear in the upper pane as an icon. In this case, it appears with the Windows logo on the system. In the bottom pane, the target system indicates that it does not have F-Response installed:

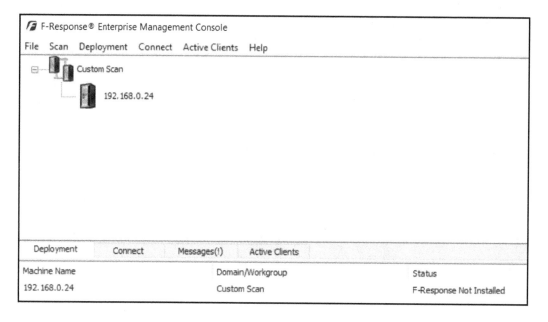

In order for F-Response to be able to acquire the necessary evidence, an agent has to be installed.by right-clicking on the system and choosing **Install/Start F-Response:**

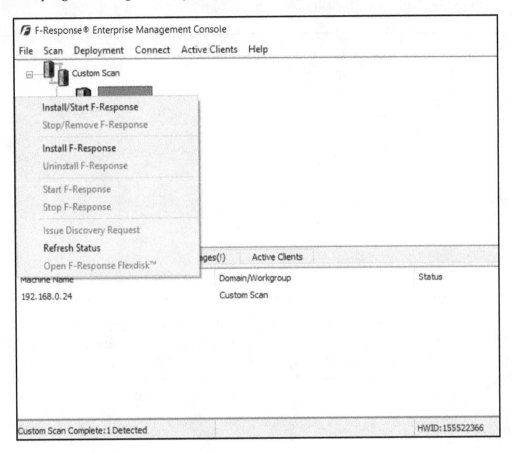

Once F-Response is installed on the remote system, there will be two indicators visible. First, a green F-Response icon will appear on the system icon in the top pane. In the bottom pane, a list of the system's available targets will appear:

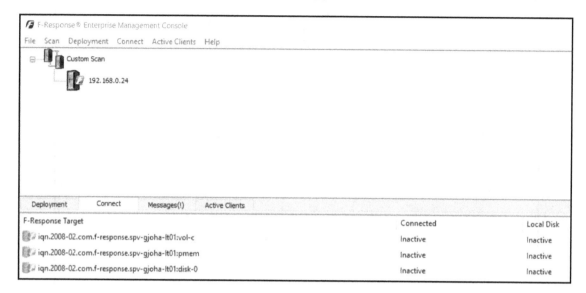

In the preceding screenshot, F-Response indicates that the target system has both a physical drive, indicated by the target ending in `disk-0`, and a logical drive, ending in `vol-c`. In addition to those drives, there is also the memory target that ends in `pmem`. In this case, the memory is the target. To acquire the memory, F-Response first has to be configured to mount the target. Right-click on the target and select **Login to F-Response Disk**:

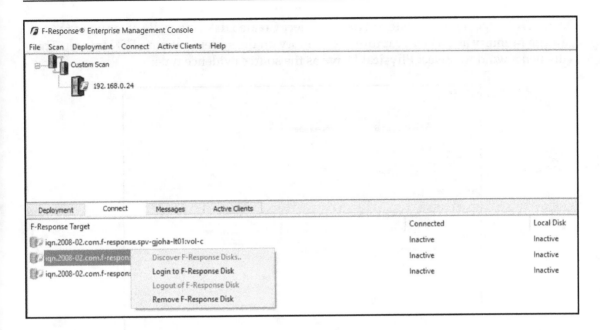

Once the F-Response has logged in, the bottom pane will indicate which disk is active:

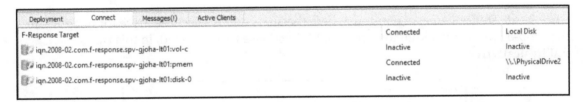

In this case, the memory target has been activated and now can be mounted as a physical drive as indicated by \\.\PhysicalDrive2 under local disk. From here, the memory can be acquired utilizing any number of tools. In this case, FTK Imager will be utilized to acquire the memory as a raw file.

Open FTK Imager and navigate to **File** and select **Create Disk Image**. Be careful not to try **Capture Memory** as this will capture the memory on the system running FTK Imager. This will open a window. Select **Physical Drive** as the source evidence type:

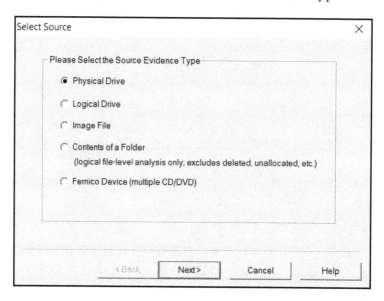

Click **Next**. This will open a window where the analyst will select the drive for imaging. In the drop-down menu, locate the drive that F-Response has indicated, in this case, **\\.\PhysicalDrive2:**

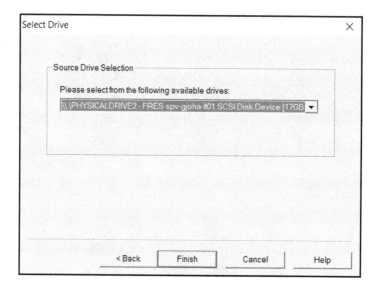

Click **Finish** and the **Create Image** window will appear:

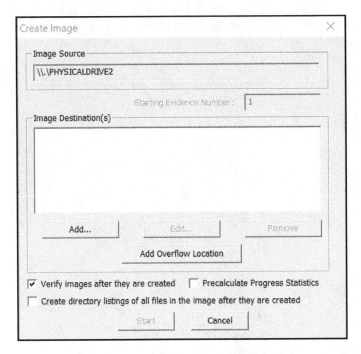

Click on the **Add** button and the **Select Image Type** window will appear. When capturing the memory, select the **Raw (dd)** or the **AFF** option and click **Next:**

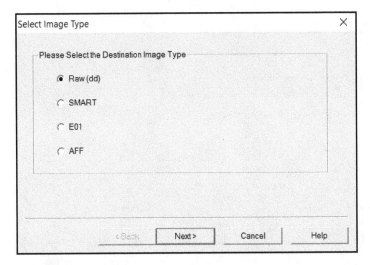

In the next window, complete the information concerning the case to include the **Case Number**, **Evidence Number**, a **Description**, and the **Examiner**. As an aside, including that this capture was performed via F-Response allows for proper documentation and if ever questioned, the incident response analyst would be prepared to answer questions concerning the acquisition:

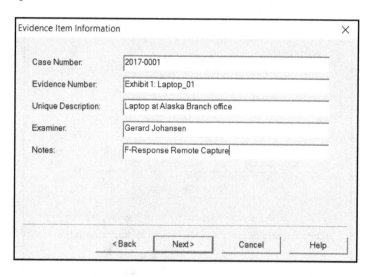

Click **Next**. In the next window, choose a destination folder. This should either be a section of the analyst system set aside for evidence or a USB hard drive. For memory images, set the **Image Fragment Size** to zero. This ensures that the entire memory image will be a single file:

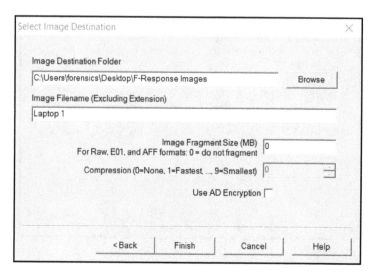

Click **Finish** and the **Create Image** window will appear. The **Image Destination** will be populated as well as the **Image Source**. Review this to ensure that each is appropriate. Once validated, click **Start:**

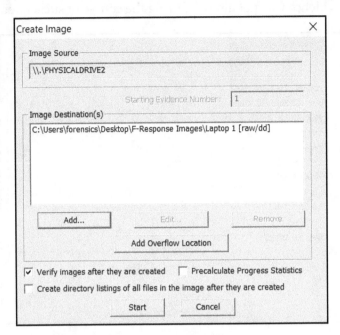

Click **Start** and the image file will process. This may take some time depending on the location of the remote system and the network connection that you have:

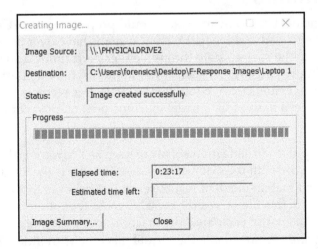

In addition to the preceding window, FTK Imager also provides the hash for the file created using **MD5** and **SHA1**. It is advised that incident response analysts take a screen capture of this for each separate piece of evidence. This allows incident response analysts to demonstrate that evidence was not altered during the course of subsequent analysis:

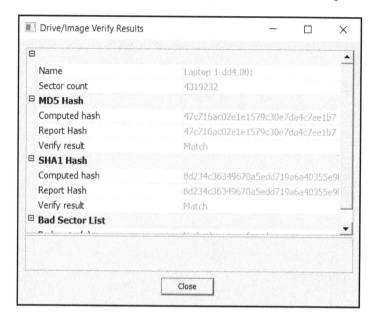

Virtual machines

Other systems that incident response analysts should prepare to acquire are virtual machines. The one distinct advantage that virtual systems have over physical systems is their ability to maintain the current state through either performing a snapshot of the system or through simply pausing. This allows incident response analysts to simply copy the entire file over to an evidence drive for later analysis. It is recommended that analysts ensure that they conduct a hash of the virtual machine pre and post copy to ensure the integrity of the evidence.

One key feature to popular virtualization software such as VMware is that the virtual machine file contains a file with the extension .vmem. This file is the virtual memory file for the system. In the event that an incident response analyst believes that a virtual system may have been compromised, this file serves the exact purpose that other memory images serve for physical devices. An analyst can pause the machine, copy the .vmem file from the folder to an evidence drive, and then re-enable the virtual machine with little disruption.

Non-volatile data

Although there is a great deal of data running in memory, it is still important to acquire the hard drive from a potentially compromised system. There is a great deal of evidence on these devices, even in the case of malware or other exploitation. Hard drive evidence becomes even more important when examining potential incidents such as internal malicious action or data loss. To ensure that this evidence is available and can be utilized in a court, incident responders should be well versed in the procedures previously discussed in this chapter.

In certain circumstances, incident responders may want to acquire two key pieces of data from suspected compromised systems before shutting down a running system. While not volatile in nature, the registry keys and log files can aid analysts during their investigation. Acquiring these files from an imaged hard drive is largely dependent on the time necessary to image and then process the entire hard disk drive. As a result, there are a few techniques that can be leveraged to acquire these key pieces of evidence.

In the event that analysts have access to the system, they can utilize the command line to access the log files by running the following command:

```
C:\wevtutil epl<Log Type> E:\<FileName>.evtx
```

This command can be repeated for security, application, and system logs.

FTK Imager also allows for the capture of registry key settings and other information that can aid in an investigation. Open FTK Imager and navigate to the **File** tab. Click on **Obtain Protected Files**. A dialog box will appear:

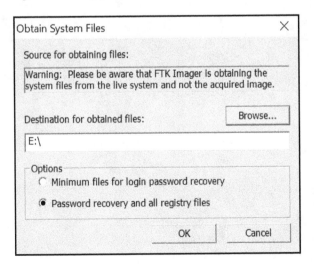

Click on **Browse** and navigate to the evidence file location. Next, click the radio button for **Password recovery and all registry files** and click **OK**. Once the tool completes, the registry and password data will be transferred to the evidence folder. From here, analysis can take place before the imaging process. This allows for a more rapid response to an incident.

Summary

Proper evidence handling starts the overall process that aims to determine the root cause of an incident and potentially identify the responsible party. In order for evidence to be of any use in an incident investigation, it has to be acquired in a sound manner. Incident responders should have a solid foundation in understanding the various types of acquisition, the tools and the techniques available, and apply those tools and techniques to the various situations that may arise. By applying solid techniques and properly documenting their actions, incident responders will be in a position to utilize the evidence to not only determine the root cause of an incident, but also be able to back up their actions in a courtroom if necessary. The next chapter will look at capturing the non-volatile data or that data contained on the disk drive.

5
Understanding Forensic Imaging

One critical task that incident response analysts will often have to perform is imaging of digital evidence. As was previously discussed in prior chapters, a great deal of evidence related to an incident can be found within log files, memory, and other areas that can be acquired relatively quickly. In some incidents, such as internal malicious activity such as fraud, industrial espionage, or data leakage, may require a more detailed search for evidence. This evidence includes the Master File Table entries, files, and specific user data that are contained on the hard drive of a suspect system. In the event that incident response analysts encounter such circumstances, they will be required to obtain an image of a suspect drive. As with any aspect of digital forensics, obtaining a usable and court- defensible image relies on the appropriate tools, techniques, and documentation. This chapter will explore the fundamental concepts of digital imaging and the preparation and use of tools to acquire a forensically sound image of a physical drive or other logical volume.

Overview of forensic imaging

Having a solid understanding of the facets of forensic imaging is important for incident response analysts. Having an understanding of the tools, techniques, and procedures ensures that evidence is handled properly and that the analyst has confidence in the evidence acquired. In addition, understanding the terminology allows the analysts to accurately prepare reports and testify as to their findings if the need arises.

One of the first concepts that should be understood is the difference between forensic imaging versus copying. Copying files from a suspect hard drive or other medium only provides analysts with the actual data associated with that file. Imaging, on the other hand, allows the analyst to capture the entire drive. This includes areas such as slack space, unallocated space, and possibly access deleted files. Imaging, also maintains the metadata on the volume to include the timestamps for files. This becomes critical in the event that a time line analysis is conducted to determine when specific files were accessed or deleted.

Oftentimes, the terms **cloning** and **imaging** are utilized in place of each other. When *cloning* a drive, a one-to-one copy of the drive is made. This means that the drive can then be inserted into a system and booted. *Cloning* a drive is often used to make a fully functional backup of a critical drive. While a cloned drive contains all the necessary files, it is cumbersome to work with, especially with forensic tools. As a result, an *image* file is taken. An image of a drive contains all the necessary files and in a configuration that will allow for detailed examination utilizing forensic tools.

The second concept that needs to be understood is the types of volumes that can be imaged. Volumes can be separated into either physical or logical. Physical volumes can be thought of as containing the entirety of a hard drive. This includes any partitions as well as the **master boot record**. When imaging a physical volume, the analyst captures all of this data. In contrast, a logical volume is a part of the overall hard drive. For example, in a hard drive that is divided into the master boot record and two partitions, a logical volume would be the D: drive. When imaging a logical volume, the analyst would only capture the data from that D: drive.

The following figure illustrates the data that is captured in imaging either a physical or logical volume:

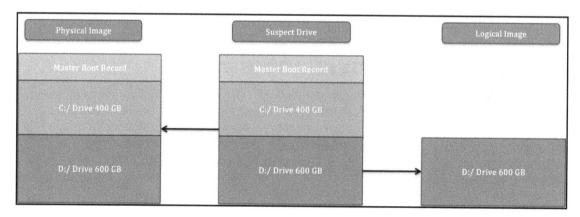

The type of incident that is being investigated largely dictates the type of imaging that is conducted. For example, if an analyst is able to identify a potential malicious file being executed from the D: drive and is intent on only capturing that data, it might be faster to image only that volume. In other cases, where activity such as employee misconduct is suspected, the analyst would need to trace as much activity as possible, and time is not as much as a factor, a full image of the physical volume is conducted.

In Chapter 3, *Network Evidence Collection,* there was an extensive discussion of the acquisition of evidence such as log files and running memory from a live or powered up system. In much the same way, incident response analysts have the capability to obtain a logical volume from a running system. This technique is referred to as **live imaging**. Live imaging may be the best option if the potentially compromised system cannot be taken offline, say in a high-availability production server, and the potential evidence is located within a logical volume.

Dead imaging is performed on a system that is powered down and the hard drive removed. In this type of imaging, the analyst is able to capture the entire disk including all volumes and the master book record. This may become necessary in incidents where analysts want to be sure to capture the entirety of the source evidence so that there is no location that is not examined.

A final aspect to forensic imaging that an analyst should have knowledge in is the type of image files that can be created and leveraged during an investigation. There are a number of image files, some very specialized, but for the purposes of this book, the focus will be on the two most common types of evidence files that analysts would most likely create and work with during an incident:

- **Raw image**: A *raw image* file contains only the data from the imaged volume. There is no additional data that is provided in this type of image, although some imaging tools such as FTK Imager include a separate file with imaging information. Raw image outputs include the extensions .raw, .img, or .dd.

- **EnCase evidence file**: The *EnCase evidence file* or E01 or EX01 file is a proprietary file format that was developed by **Guidance Software** as part of their EnCase forensic tools in 1998. This format was based on the **Expert Witness Format (EWF)** found in the ASR Data's Expert Witness Compression Format. The EnCase evidence file or E01 file contains metadata about the image. The metadata that is contained in both the header and footer captures and stores information about the drive type, operating system, and timestamps. Another key feature of the E01 file is the inclusion of a **Cyclical Redundancy Check (CRC)**. This CRC is a file integrity verification that takes place after every 64 KB of data is written to the image file. This CRC ensures the integrity of the preceding block of data over the entire image file. Finally, the E01 file contains the MD5 hash within the footer of the file. The following diagram illustrates what components of the E01 file are created during the imaging process:

File Header	64 KB Data	CRC	64 KB Data	CRC	64 KB Data	CRC	64 KB Data	CRC	MD5

The information presented is really an overview of some of the core concepts of imaging. As a result, there are a great many details concerning forensic imaging that could not be included within this book. Having a detailed understanding of forensic imaging will allow the incident response analyst to prepare an accurate report, but also be able to describe in detail how their actions produced the output that served as the foundation of their analysis.

Preparing a stage drive

Beyond having the necessary hardware and software to perform the forensic imaging, it is critical to pre-stage a location to hold the image or evidence file. For incident response teams, the best option to utilize as an evidence repository is an external USB or **FireWire** disk drive. This allows for a degree of portability, as incident responders may have to investigate an incident offsite or at a variety of locations without the benefit of a forensics laboratory.

There are two tasks that need to be performed on evidence drives prior to their use. The first is to ensure that the repository is free of any data. Incident response teams should have a policy and procedure that dictates that an evidence drive be wiped prior to each use. This includes drives that are *new in box*. This is due to the fact that a number of manufacturers ship drives with backup software or other data that needs to be removed prior to use. Wiping further ensures that previously utilized drives.

This is easily accomplished through a wiping program. There are a number of programs both free and commercial that can be utilized. For example, the program Eraser by Heidi Computers is a freeware wiping utility that can be utilized for both file and volume wiping (Eraser can be downloaded at `https://eraser.heidi.ie/`).

In the following example, a 2 TB external hard drive will be erased and prepared for use as an evidence drive. The following sequence should be repeated every time that a drive is going to be placed into a state that can be utilized for an incident investigation:

1. Start the application **Eraser**. In the GUI, click **Erase Schedule** and **New Task:**

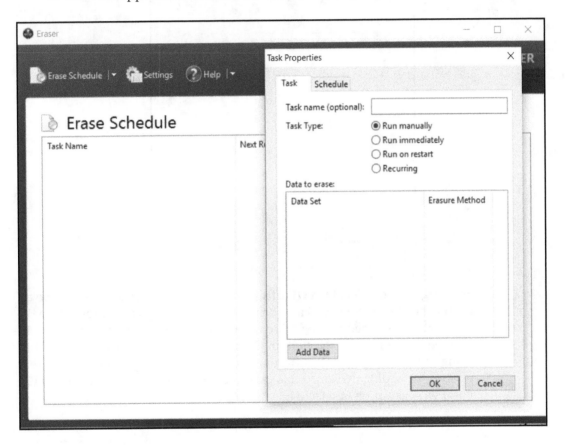

2. A task name can be assigned. This may be helpful in properly documenting the erasure of the evidence drive. Click the **Add Data** button. This will open another window:

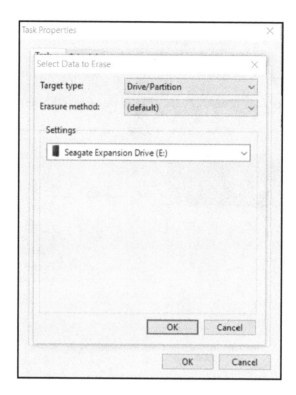

For **Target type,** select **Drive/Partition**. In the **Settings** area, there will be a drop-down list of partitions and drive letters. Pay very close attention to the drive letters assigned to the various drives and ensure that the external drive that requires wiping is selected. In this case, a new Seagate external HDD is being utilized. Finally, select the erasure method. There are several different options for wiping drives. In this case, the **US DoD 5220.22-M (8-306./E) (3 Pass)** wiping option is selected:

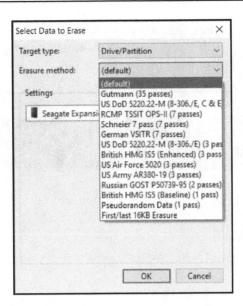

2. Click **OK** and the wiping task will be listed in the **Erase Schedule**.

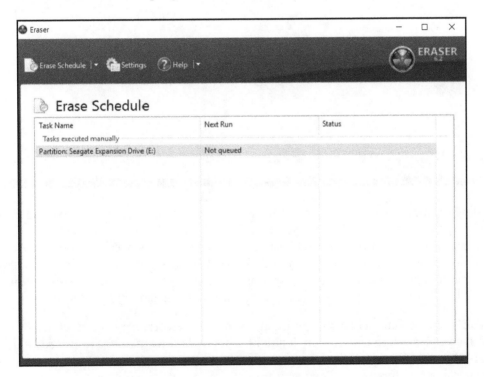

3. Right-click the **Partition: Seagate Expansion Drive(E:)** task and click **Run Now**. This will start the wiping process. As was stated before, ensure that the correct evidence drive is being wiped:

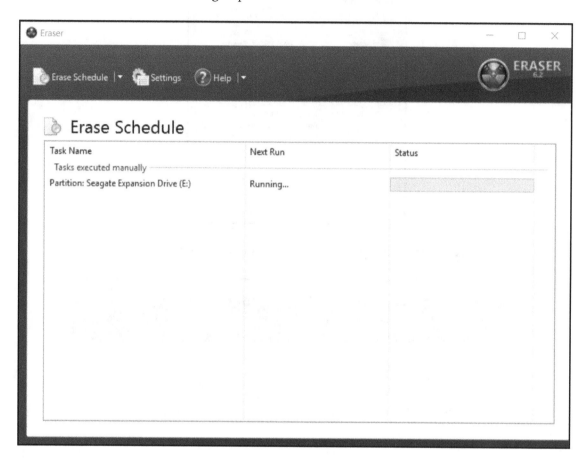

Depending on the size of the drive and the system that is performing the wipe, the process can last hours or even days. Once completed, the incident response analyst should capture any wiping information that verifies that the evidence drive has been properly wiped. This is important information to include in a written forensic analysis report as it demonstrates that the incident response analyst took appropriate measures to ensure that any evidence files were free from corruption or co-mingling with other files on the evidence drive.

It is recommended that incident response analysts have several drives available and that these drives be pre-wiped before any incident. This will allow incident response analysts to immediately utilize a wiped drive instead of having to wipe a drive onsite, which wastes time better spent on incident-related activity.

A second preparation step that can be undertaken is to encrypt the evidence drive. Software such as **VeraCrypt** or another disk encryption platform can be utilized to encrypt the partition of the evidence drive that contains the evidence files. Incident response analysts that are dealing with confidential information such as credit cards or medical records should encrypt the evidence drive regardless of whether it leaves the facility or not.

There are two methods that can be leveraged to encrypt the evidence drive. The first is to utilize the encryption software on the forensic workstation that is utilized in the imaging process. This approach is limited to imaging on drives that have been removed from the system and imaged on dedicated systems that have the encryption software installed. A second option is to include the encryption software on the evidence drive. In a previous chapter, an evidence drive was divided into two partitions. One partition was set aside for the evidence files. The second partition is utilized for tools such as those for dumping memory files or imaging. In this scenario, the encryption software can be loaded in the tools partition and the drive encrypted during the evidence imaging process. This limits the amount of changes to the system under investigation.

Imaging

Once a proper repository is configured for the image file, the incident response analyst is ready to perform the sequence to acquire the necessary evidence. In this chapter, three separate sequences are discussed. Two will be powered-off systems and one will examine the sequence for capturing a live image. The analyst should select the appropriate technique based upon the incident investigation. In any incident, no matter what technique is utilized, the incident response analyst should be prepared to properly document their actions for any subsequent forensic report.

Dead imaging

Dead imaging is conducted on media that is not powered on and in the case of hard drives, removed from the potentially compromised system. In terms of evidence preparation, this method is most comprehensive as it allows for the complete preservation and analysis of a physical volume. There are several methods and tools available, both commercial and freeware that allow for the proper imaging. In addition to software, often times incident response analysts will make use of a hardware write blocker. These devices ensure that no changes are made to the suspect media. As was discussed in Chapter 1, *Incident Response,* it is critical to be able to demonstrate to a court of law that no changes were made to the original evidence.

One advantage that imaging a hard drive or other digital media in this manner is that the process can be predefined and repeatable. Having a predefined process that is formalized as part of the incident response planning and procedures ensures that evidence is handled in...

1. This first step in the process is to physically inspect the evidence. There are two primary focal points that incident response analysts should inspect. The first is the chain of custody form. As the incident response analyst is taking custody of the evidence, they should have access to the form, ensure that all steps are properly documented, and finally make their own entry.

2. Second, the incident response analyst should inspect the evidence packaging to ensure that any seals have maintained integrity. One fast way to document this is to take a picture of the evidence in the original packaging:

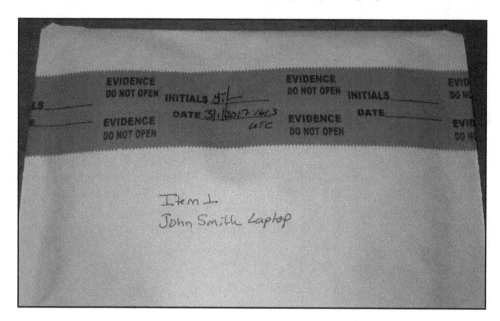

3. In the preceding image, the incident response analyst has captured the information concerning the piece of evidence as well as demonstrating that prior to the imaging, the integrity of the evidence has been maintained. After the seal is broken, the incident response analyst should take another photo of the contents of the packaging:

4. Once an image of the piece of evidence is taken, the incident response analyst should ensure that the piece of evidence matches the chain of custody form. Errors happen in an incident, and this is a way to ensure that mistakes in the chain of custody are corrected as early as possible. By confirming the chain of custody, any such mix-up can be rectified.

5. The next step is to configure the physical write blocker. In this case, a Tableau TK35u USB 3.0 Forensic IDE/SATA Bridge Kit is utilized as a physical write blocker. The suspect drive is attached via the included SATA drive adapter and a Firewire connection is made to the imaging laptop. When utilizing a physical write blocker, ensure that the device is able to indicate proper functioning:

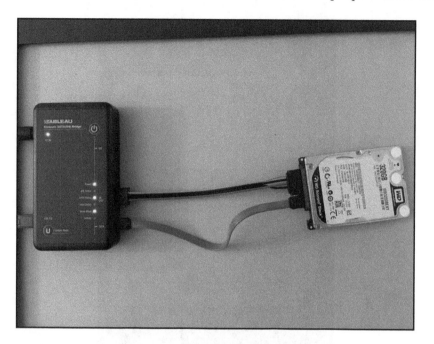

6. With the physical write blocker in place, the suspect drive is now ready for imaging. In this example, the freeware application FTK Imager will be used. FTK Imager requires administrator privileges to run. Open the executable and the following screen will appear:

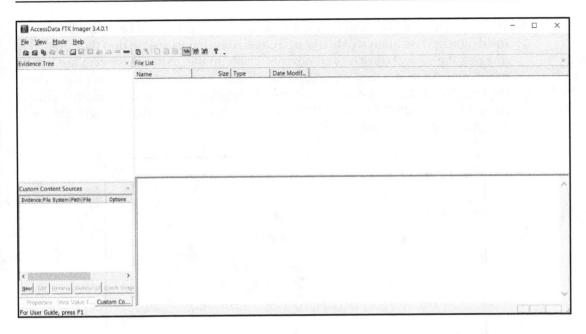

7. Click on **File** and **Create Disk Image**. This will open a window where the analyst needs to select the media source. In this case, the analyst will select **Physical Drive** so that the entire drive including the master boot record will be captured for further analysis. Select **Physical Drive** and click **Next:**

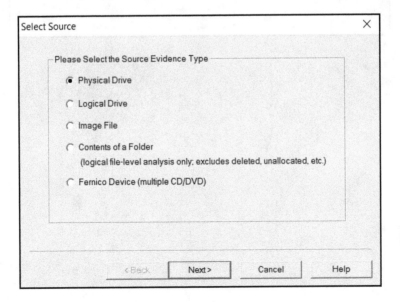

8. The next window allows the analyst to select which drive will be imaged. Incident response analysts should pay close attention to ensure that they are imaging the correct device as all devices visible to the operating system are listed. In this case, there are four separate drives listed. Two are drives contained within the imaging laptop. Another drive is the destination drive. In this case, the third drive, labeled \\.**PHYSICALDRIVE2**, is the correct suspect drive. Highlight the selection and click **Finish:**

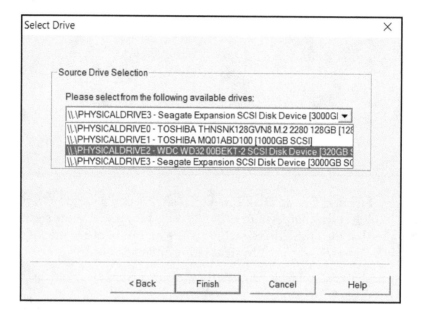

9. Once the suspect drive has been selected, set the destination drive. Click **Add:**

10. At this point, the analyst will choose the type of image file to create. There are four options available to the incident response analyst. In this case, the E01 file is selected. Click **Next:**

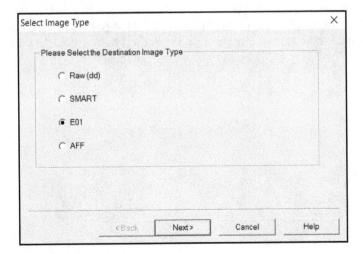

11. In the next window, the incident response analyst will enter the case information specific to the image. A discussion of reporting will be addressed in a later chapter. For now, the analyst should complete the fields with the greatest detail as possible as this information will be included in the forensic report. Once the fields have been completed, click **Next:**

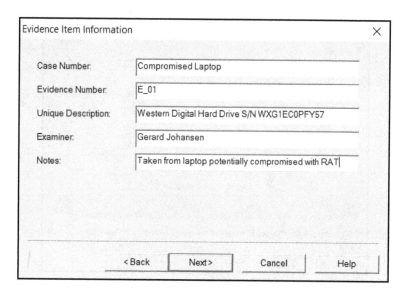

12. In the next window, verify that the image destination and filenames are correct. In addition, the incident response analyst will be able to set the image fragmentation size and compression. The fragmentation size may be set to 0 where the entire disk image will be contained within a single file. For now, the defaults will be utilized as mounting a disk image that is fragmented is not an issue. Once the entered information is verified as correct, click **Finish:**

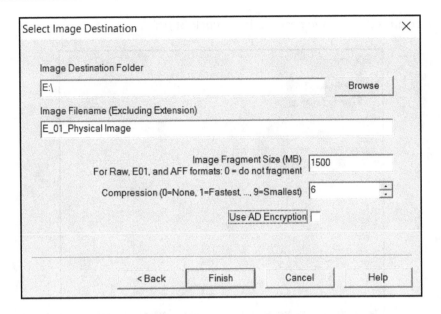

13. The **Create Image** window opens. This is the final stage where the analyst can cancel the image file creation. There are also two options that the analyst should enable, depending on the case. The first of these is for FTK Imager to verify the images after they are created. In this feature, FTK Imager will verify that there have been no changes made and that the image file is complete without errors. Second, FTK Imager can create a list of all files on the image. This may be handy for the analyst in the event that a specific file or files has evidentiary value. The analyst will be able to determine whether the file is on this system. This can save time if several drives have to be examined.

Once all settings have been verified, click **Start:**

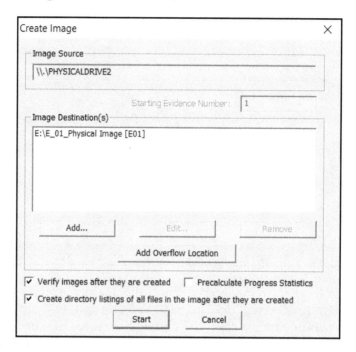

14. FTK Imager will then begin the process of imaging the drive. This can take several hours or even days depending on both the size of the drive being imaged and the type of imaging system. During the progress, the following window will appear:

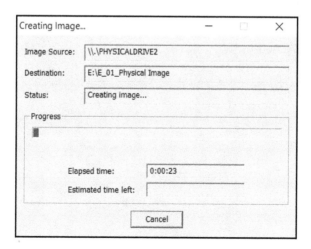

15. Once FTK Imager has completed the imaging process, a window will open. In this window, FTK Imager will provide the incident response analyst with detailed information. Of concern to the analysts should be that the hashes computed for both the drive and the image match. In this case, both the MD5 and SHA1 hashes match, indicating that the imaging process captured the drive properly and that there was no change to the evidence taken from the suspect drive. A good practice is to include this information as part of the forensic report:

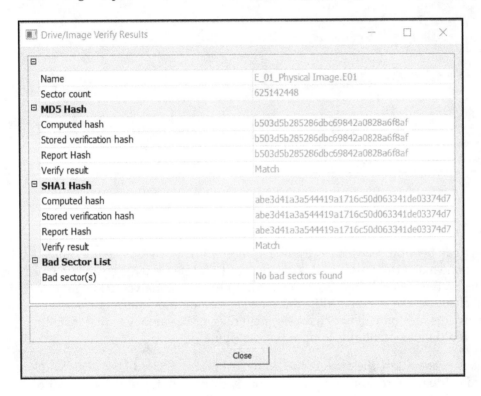

16. Navigate to the evidence drive. In the drive location, the entire image can be located. In this case, the image file has been broken up. In addition to the evidence files, a list of the files on the hard drive. Finally, FTK Imager provides a text file with detailed information concerning the imaging. This information should be captured and included with any subsequent forensic reporting:

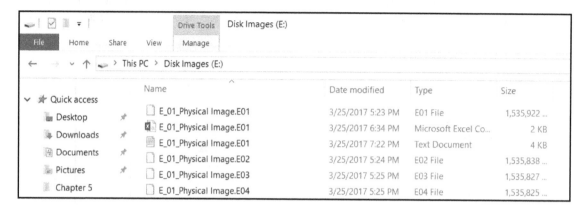

Live imaging

An image can be captured from a running system utilizing FTK Imager in much the same way. The one major difference in this case is that FTK Imager will be run from a USB device connected to the system. This allows the incident response analyst to image the drive without changing the system. While there will be certain files and registry settings updated, imaging in this fashion will not change system files in the same way that installing FTK Imager would on a potentially compromised system.

In terms of preparation, the analyst should have a preconfigured USB drive with separate tools and evidence partitions. As was previously discussed, the evidence partition should be wiped prior to any use. Also, the full-featured FTK Imager often has issues with DLL files not being in the correct place when attempting to run from a USB drive. To counter this, Access Data provides a light version called **FTK Imager Lite**. This can be downloaded at
`http://accessdata.com/product-download/digital-forensics/ftk-imager-lite-version-3.1.1.`

To image a drive, connect the USB to the target machine and simply start the FTK Imager Lite. Follow the same process that was outlined before. The imager will create the image in the same way. As opposed to the previous example where an entire disk is imaged, live imaging can focus directly on a partition of the drive. For example, in this case, the incident response analyst is only concerned with capturing the C: drive of the target system. When the **Source Drive Selection** is made, the analyst would select **C:\ - [NTFS]**:

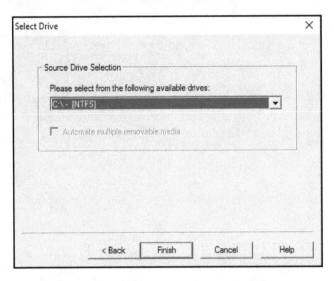

The remaining steps are the same for a live image as they were for a dead image in that the analyst will select the destination drive that has been previously configured for evidence files:

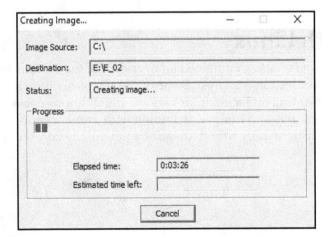

Finally, analysts will be given the same information that was provided in the dead imaging process:

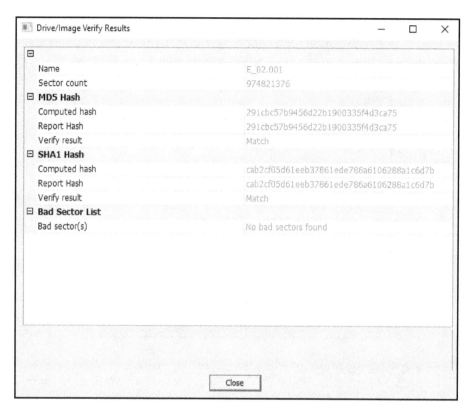

Imaging with Linux

Chapter 2, *Forensic Fundamentals*, contained an overview of the various forensic tools available to the incident response analyst. Some of these tools include Linux distributions that can be leveraged during an incident for various digital forensic tasks. The following example will demonstrate how a Linux distribution with forensics applications can be deployed to capture a forensically sound image of a potentially compromised computer.

The combination of a Linux distribution and a bootable USB device is an option for conducting forensic imaging of potentially compromised systems. Incident response analysts may find themselves in a situation where multiple systems need to be imaged and the analysts has only one write-blocker. A great deal of time will be wasted if the analyst must image each one of these systems in sequence. In this situation, the analyst can avoid that by creating a bootable USB drive for each system and imaging each one at the same time. All that is needed is an evidence drive and a bootable USB drive for each source of evidence. Utilizing this technique will allow the analyst to image each system at the same time, saving time that is better spent on other activities.

In this scenario, the Linux distribution CAINE will be utilized to image the hard drive from a potentially compromised system. The system is powered off and the bootable USB device containing the CAINE OS is installed. The suspected compromised system is powered on. Incident response analysts should be aware of how to change the boot order of a system to ensure that it boots to the USB device. Analysts should also be prepared to immediately power down the system if it attempts to boot into the native OS and not the USB device. Once the device boots up, insert the evidence drive into another available USB interface.

 Note: If the evidence drive does not have a bootable OS, it may cause issues as the boot sequence may try to find a valid OS on that drive. That is why it is necessary to wait until the Linux OS that is utilized boots up.

After inserting the evidence drive, open a Terminal and type the following:

```
caine@caine:~$fdisk -l
```

The `fdisk -l` command lists all of the partitions visible to the CAINE OS. The abridged output will look similar to this:

```
Disk /dev/sdb: 465.8 GiB, 500107862016 bytes, 976773168 sectors
Units: sectors of 1 * 512 = 512 bytes
Sector size (logical/physical): 512 bytes / 4096 bytes
I/O size (minimum/optimal): 4096 bytes / 4096 bytes
Disklabel type: dos
Disk identifier: 0x345601e6

Device     Boot    Start       End   Sectors   Size Id Type
/dev/sdb1  *        2048   1026047   1024000   500M  7 HPFS/NTFS/exFAT
/dev/sdb2        1026048 975847423 974821376 464.9G  7 HPFS/NTFS/exFAT
/dev/sdb3      975847424 976769023    921600   450M 27 Hidden NTFS WinRE

Disk /dev/sdc: 3.8 GiB, 4060086272 bytes, 7929856 sectors
Units: sectors of 1 * 512 = 512 bytes
Sector size (logical/physical): 512 bytes / 512 bytes
I/O size (minimum/optimal): 512 bytes / 512 bytes
Disklabel type: dos
Disk identifier: 0x000f1d04

Device     Boot Start       End Sectors  Size Id Type
/dev/sdc1  *     2048   7929855 7927808  3.8G  c W95 FAT32 (LBA)

Disk /dev/sdd: 3.7 TiB, 4000787029504 bytes, 7814037167 sectors
Units: sectors of 1 * 512 = 512 bytes
Sector size (logical/physical): 512 bytes / 4096 bytes
I/O size (minimum/optimal): 4096 bytes / 33553920 bytes
Disklabel type: gpt
Disk identifier: 30B0BF34-42D8-41E5-A90C-E5735893CFB6

Device         Start       End   Sectors  Size Type
/dev/sdd1         34    262177    262144  128M Microsoft reserved
/dev/sdd2     264192 7814035455 7813771264  3.7T Microsoft basic data
```

In the screenshot, there are three separate disks, each with their own partitions. The disk labeled /dev/sdc is the USB drive that contains the CAINE OS that the system has been booted from. The disk /dev/sdd is the evidence drive that the system will be imaged to. Finally, the target system is labeled as /dev/sdb. It is obviously important to identify the separate disks that appear to ensure that the right target drive is being imaged. In examining /dev/sdb closer, the analyst can see the three separate partitions that make up the entire physical volume. CAINE indicates the boot volume /dev/sdb1 in the entries with an asterisk. This information can be valuable as CAINE can be leveraged to either image the physical volume, such as this demonstration, or specific logical volumes.

After identifying the proper target drive of the system, it is critical that the imaging performed does not change any of the target system data. The CAINE OS has a built-in software write-blocker. On the desktop, find the application **Block On/Off**. This opens the software write-blocker that will be utilized. Examining the list of devices, the only one that is writable is the **sdd** that had been previously identified as the evidence drive. The other drives are set to **Read-Only**. This provides the incident response analysts with an assurance that the imaging will not alter the target drive (it is a good idea for analysts to screen capture such information for subsequent reporting):

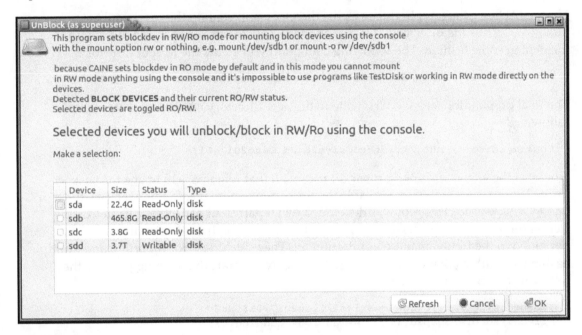

After verifying that the evidence drive is in place and the target system is set to read-only, the analyst will then configure the evidence drive so that it is properly mounted. First, a directory titled EvidenceDrive1 will be made mnt directory by entering the following command:

```
caine@caine:~$ sudo mkdir /mnt/EvidenceDrive1
```

Next, mount the disk sdd on that newly created mount directory by entering the following command:

```
caine@caine:~$sudomount /dev/sdd2 /mnt/EvidenceDrive1/
```

The evidence drive is now mounted on the mount point that was created. Next, change the directory into the evidence drive utilizing the following command:

```
caine@caine:~$sudomount /dev/sdd2 /mnt/EvidenceDrive1/
```

The next step is to make a directory that will contain the image file. First, change to the directory EvidenceDrive1 by entering the following:

```
caine@caine:~$ cd /mnt/EvidenceDrive1/
```

Next, make the directory. In this case, the directory will contain the case number Case2017-01 as the directory. It is a good idea to make this directory tie directly to the incident in some fashion. The following command will create the proper directory:

```
caine@caine :/ mnt /EvidenceDrive1$ mkdir Case2017-01
```

The final preparation step is to navigate to the new directory created by entering the following:

```
caine@caine :/ mnt /EvidenceDrive1$ cd Case2017-01/
```

Now that the analyst is in the proper directory, all that remains is to image the suspect drive. There are several tools available for performing an image. In this example, the tool Dc3dd will be used. This tool was developed by **Department of Defense Cyber Crime Center** forensic specialist Jesse Kornblum. This application has additional features that are not found in the Linux imaging application dd. These include error reporting and multiple hashing algorithms that can be leveraged on the fly. To start the imaging process, the following commands are entered:

```
caine@caine:/mnt/EvidenceDrive1/Case2017-01$ dc3dd
if=dev/sdbof=ideapad.imghash=md5 log=dc3ddlog.txt
```

The preceding command has the Dc3dd start imaging the disk at sdb to the evidence drive under the filename ideapad.img as well as hashing the output with MD5. Finally, the application will then create a log file dcddlog.txt that can be utilized for reporting purposes. The output produces the following:

```
caine@caine:/mnt/EvidenceDrive1/Case2017-01$ sudo dc3dd if=/dev/sdb of=ideapad.img hash=md5 log
=dc3ddlog.txt

dc3dd 7.2.641 started at 2017-04-02 19:18:35 +0100
compiled options:
command line: dc3dd if=/dev/sdb of=ideapad.img hash=md5 log=dc3ddlog.txt
device size: 976773168 sectors (probed),   500,107,862,016 bytes
sector size: 512 bytes (probed)
 6376849408 bytes ( 5.9 G ) copied (  1% ),   58 s, 105 M/s
```

Depending on the size of the drive, this process can take hours. During the processing, the analyst can keep track of the progress. Upon completion, the application will produce an output indicating how many sectors were utilized for input and how many sectors were used as output to the image file. Ideally, these should be that same. Finally, the MD5 hashing of the image file is calculated and utilized as part of the output:

```
dc3dd 7.2.641 started at 2017-04-02 19:18:35 +0100
compiled options:
command line: dc3dd if=/dev/sdb of=ideapad.img hash=md5 log=dc3ddlog.txt
device size: 976773168 sectors (probed),    500,107,862,016 bytes
sector size: 512 bytes (probed)
500107862016 bytes ( 466 G ) copied ( 100% ), 5854 s, 81 M/s

input results for device `/dev/sdb':
   976773168 sectors in
   0 bad sectors replaced by zeros
   d48a7ccafaead6fab7d284b4be300bd8 (md5)

output results for file `ideapad.img':
   976773168 sectors out

dc3dd completed at 2017-04-02 20:56:09 +0100
```

An examination of the evidence drive from a Windows system reveals the image and log file that were created with the application:

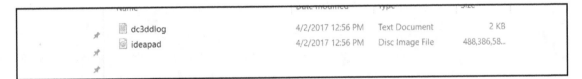

Name	Date modified	Type	Size
dc3ddlog	4/2/2017 12:56 PM	Text Document	2 KB
ideapad	4/2/2017 12:56 PM	Disc Image File	488,386,58...

An examination of the log file revealed the following information that should be incorporated into any subsequent reporting:

```
dc3dd 7.2.641 started at 2017-04-02 19:18:35 +0100
compiled options:
command line: dc3dd if=/dev/sdb of=ideapad.img hash=md5
log=dc3ddlog.txt
device size: 976773168 sectors (probed), 500,107,862,016 bytes
sector size: 512 bytes (probed)
500107862016 bytes ( 466 G ) copied ( 100% ), 5854.43 s, 81 M/s
input results for device `/dev/sdb':
 976773168 sectors in
 0 bad sectors replaced by zeros
 d48a7ccafaead6fab7d284b4be300bd8 (md5)
output results for file `ideapad.img':
 976773168 sectors out
dc3dd completed at 2017-04-02 20:56:09 +0100
```

Summary

Not every incident may dictate the need to obtain an image from a potentially compromised hard drive or other volume. Regardless, incident response analysts should be familiar with and able to perform this function when called upon. The evidence found on a hard drive may be critical to determine a sequence of events or to obtain actual files that can aid in determining the root cause. Finally, as with any process in a forensic discipline, imaging should be conducted in a systematic manner in which all steps are followed and properly documented. This will ensure that any evidence obtained will be sound and admissible in a courtroom. The next chapter will discuss examining network based evidence to what network activity is associated with an incident.

6
Network Evidence Analysis

Chapter 3, *Network Evidence Collection* explored how incident response analysts can acquire network-based evidence for later evaluation. That chapter focused on two primary sources of that evidence, network log files and network packet captures. This chapter will show which tools and techniques are available to examine the evidence acquired. Incorporating these techniques into an incident response investigation can provide incident response analysts with insight into the network activity of possible threats.

Analyzing packet captures

A great deal of Chapter 3, *Network Evidence Collection* covered the various methods to obtain packet captures from a range of sources and from a variety of locations. Packet captures contain a great deal of information that is potentially valuable to incident response analysts. Some of this information includes source and destination IP addresses, domains and ports, and the content of communications between hosts. In some instances, incident response analysts are able to reconstruct actual files, such as text documents and images in these packet captures.

This chapter makes references to several preconfigured packet captures which are examined. These packet captures are taken directly from the site malware-traffic-analysis.net by permission of the author. This site has a number of packet capture exercises, where incident response analysts can practice locating indicators of compromise.

Command-line tools

There are several command-line tools that can be utilized during the analysis of network packet captures. During more in-depth or lengthy incident response engagements, analysts may gather several packet captures files. It may be beneficial to combine these multiple packet captures into one single file to make analysis easier. The application **mergecap** does just that by combining several packet capture files. Mergecap is made as part of the CAINE OS and can be executed utilizing the following command:

```
caine@caine:~$ mergecap -w mergedpacketcapture.pcap packetcapture1.pcap
packetcapture2.pcap
```

Another command-line tool that is useful in analyzing packet captures is the tool **editcap.** Editcap allows analysts to manipulate the packet capture files into smaller segments for easier review. For example, an analyst may only want to look at captures that are broken up into 50,000 packet segments. This would be helpful if an analysts has a large packet capture and dividing makes searching easier. To do this, the analyst would type the following into the command line:

```
caine@caine:~$ editcap -F pcap -c evidence.pcap split.pcap
```

In the preceding command, `editcap` took the evidence file `evidence.pcap` and divided it out into 50,000 packet segments. Another technique that `editcap` can be leveraged for is to divide a larger packet capture into time segments. For example, if analysts want to divide a packet capture into 10-minute segments, they type in the following:

```
caine@caine:~$ editcap -F pcap-t+600 evidence.pcap split.pcap
```

Analysts may also find that, in some circumstances, they may want to isolate Domain Name Registration traffic. This is due in large to a variety of C2 traffic, data exfiltration, and the possible redirection to compromised websites, often leveraging vulnerabilities in the DNS system. The application DNS top parses packet capture files and ascertains the sources and count of DNS queries from internal hosts. For example, if an incident response analyst wants to determine whether any IP addresses were sending outbound DNS queries of the packet capture taken from
`http://www.malware-traffic-analysis.net/2017/02/21/index.html`. The command entered would be:

```
forensics@ubuntu:~/Documents/Packet Captures$ dnstop -l 3 2017-02-21-
Hancitor-malspam-traffic.pcap
```

The preceding command produces the following output:

```
Queries: 107 new, 107 total, EOF                    Sun Apr 23 17:21:20 2017

Sources          Count      %    cum%
-----------   ----------  ------  ------
10.2.21.201        107   100.0  100.0
```

The output indicates that only one host in the packet capture is the source of DNS queries, having made a total of 107. While this was a simple example, incident response analysts can utilize the preceding technique of combining multiple packet capture files and then utilizing DNSStop in order to gain a better sense of what DNS traffic is leaving the internal network and if that is something that warrants further investigation.

Wireshark

Wireshark is one of the most popular packet capture analysis tool available to incident response analysts. In addition to the ability to capture packets, there are a great many features that are available. As entire volumes and training courses are built around this platform, it is impossible to identify every feature. Therefore, this chapter will focus on some of the key features of Wireshark that are most applicable to an incident investigation.

There are a number of free resources about Wireshark and its capability. The Wireshark site wireshark.org contains a great deal of information. Furthermore, the site wiresharkuniversity.com contains exercises and training packet captures to hone skills around analysis.

Because Wireshark is a feature-rich tool, there are some settings that lend themselves more to network traffic analysis that are outside incident response activities. As a result, there are some changes to be made to better assist the incident response analyst with performing packet capture analysis in relation to an incident investigation:

- **Time**: The time setting in Wireshark allows for several options. These include the time of the packet since 1/1/1970 or since the start of the packet capture. One of these options which can be useful in an incident investigation is the date and time that the individual packets have been captured. This allows analysts to correlate the date and time of other suspicious or malicious activity with the date and time of specific traffic within the packet capture. To enable this, navigate to **View** and then to **Time Display Format**. From there, choose one of the time options such as **Date and Time of Day** or **Time of Day**. Another option to consider is utilizing the UTC time options as well. This is very useful if the internal network utilizes UTC rather than local time. Also, the time can be set all the way to nanoseconds.

- **Name resolution**: The name resolution setting allows analysts to toggle between seeing the IP address of source and destination hosts and hostname resolution. This is useful if an analyst is examining a packet capture and wants to determine if there are any suspicious hostnames found. For example, if the packet capture is opened, the following shows the IP addresses:

2920 95.230	74.125.141.100	172.16.4.193	TCP
2921 95.232	74.125.141.100	172.16.4.193	TLSv1.2
2922 95.232	172.16.4.193	74.125.141.100	TCP
2923 95.234	74.125.141.100	172.16.4.193	TCP
2924 95.234	74.125.141.100	172.16.4.193	TLSv1.2
2925 95.234	172.16.4.193	74.125.141.100	TCP
2926 95.234	172.16.4.193	74.125.141.100	TCP

- To determine the hostnames, navigate to **View** and then **Name Resolution**. Click on **Resolve Network Addresses**. Wireshark will then resolve the IP addresses to hostnames:

2920 95.230	www-google-analytics.1.go…	172.16.4.193	TCP
2921 95.232	www-google-analytics.1.go…	172.16.4.193	TLSv1.2
2922 95.232	172.16.4.193	www-google-analytics.1.google.com	TCP
2923 95.234	www-google-analytics.1.go…	172.16.4.193	TCP
2924 95.234	www-google-analytics.1.go…	172.16.4.193	TLSv1.2
2925 95.234	172.16.4.193	www-google-analytics.1.google.com	TCP
2926 95.234	172.16.4.193	www-google-analytics.1.google.com	TCP

- **Colorize packet list**: This feature allows analysts to toggle between a blank background of the packet list or to allow Wireshark to color-code the packets.

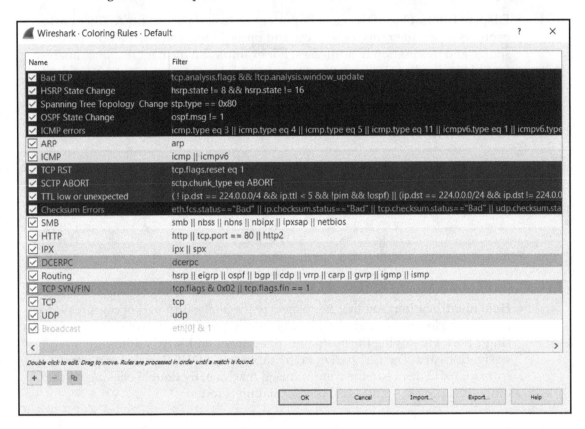

For the purposes of this chapter, an exploration of Wireshark will be done utilizing the packet capture: `http://www.malware-traffic-analysis.net/2017/01/28/index.html`. This packet capture is provided along with a scenario involving a user that downloads a crypto locker malware strain while conducting an online search. For the purposes of this chapter, several key elements of the packet capture will be identified. Prior to examining the packet capture, Wireshark was configured so that date and time are visible, as well as the hostnames identified.

The following are some of the features in Wireshark that provide key pieces of information from the packet capture:

- **Display filters**: One of the most important features is the ability to filter packet captures on a wide range of services and ports. Filters can also be utilized on the source and destination IP addresses. For example, an incident response analyst would like to filter traffic on the source IP address of 172.16.4.193. By right-clicking on the IP address in the packet capture window and navigating to **Apply as Filter** and then **Selected**, the analyst can select the IP address as a filter. This filter then appears in the filter bar.

No.	Time	Source	Destination	Protocol	Ler
2	2017-01-27 14:5...	172.16.4.193	224.0.0.252	LLMNR	
3	2017-01-27 14:5...	172.16.4.193	224.0.0.252	LLMNR	
4	2017-01-27 14:5...	172.16.4.193	224.0.0.252	LLMNR	
5	2017-01-27 14:5...	172.16.4.193	224.0.0.252	LLMNR	
6	2017-01-27 14:5...	172.16.4.193	172.16.4.255	NBNS	
7	2017-01-27 14:5...	172.16.4.193	172.16.4.255	NBNS	

ip.src == 172.16.4.193

- **Host identification**: Another key aspect to the analysis of packet captures is to identify the localhost, if applicable. Considering that this packet capture is from a single host, identifying the hostname, IP address, and MAC address is straightforward. The first packet in the capture is a DHCP packet originating from a CISCO device to the compromised machine. By double-clicking on the individual packet, a great deal of information is found:

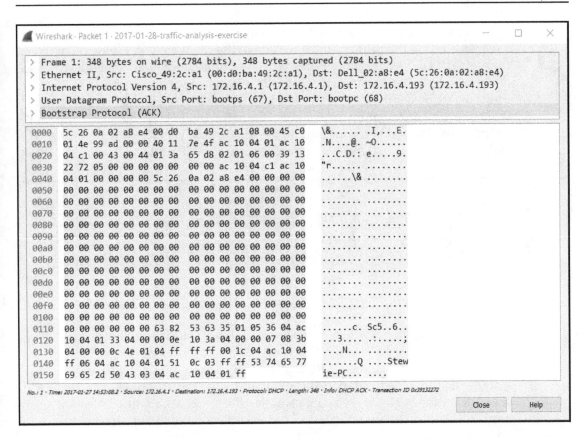

- In this packet, the analyst can identify the source of the traffic from the **Ethernet II** and **Internet Protocol Version 4** (**IPV4**) lines. In this case, the source of the traffic is the Cisco device located at `172.16.4.1` and the destination located at `172.16.4.193`. In the second window that contains the hexadecimal and ASCII characters, the analyst can determine the name of the compromised machine. In this case, Stewie-PC.

- In this case, there was a good deal of HTTP connections, due to the activity of the user. As a result, the primary transmission of the malware was quite possibly through an HTTP connection. Wireshark has a number of filters that allow analysts to limit the packet capture results with specific parameters. In the top green dialog box, enter `http`. Pay attention while entering in the filter as there will be several different filters available. Once the filter is typed in, click the right-facing arrow located at the far right of the dialog box. Wireshark will now limit the view of packets to those that are utilizing the HTTP protocol:

No.	Time	Source	Destination	Protocol
44	2017-01-27 14:53:14.4	172.16.4.193	a1293.d.akamai.net	HTTP
46	2017-01-27 14:53:14.4	a1293.d.akamai.net	172.16.4.193	HTTP
107	2017-01-27 14:53:53.4	172.16.4.193	dual.a-0001.a-msedge.net	HTTP
165	2017-01-27 14:53:53.6	dual.a-0001.a-msedge.net	172.16.4.193	HTTP
170	2017-01-27 14:53:53.7	172.16.4.193	dual.a-0001.a-msedge.net	HTTP
179	2017-01-27 14:53:53.8	dual.a-0001.a-msedge.net	172.16.4.193	HTTP
184	2017-01-27 14:53:53.8	172.16.4.193	dual.a-0001.a-msedge.net	HTTP
185	2017-01-27 14:53:53.9	172.16.4.193	dual.a-0001.a-msedge.net	HTTP
193	2017-01-27 14:53:53.9	dual.a-0001.a-msedge.net	172.16.4.193	HTTP

- Parsing through the packet capture source and destination hostnames, one host name appears to be suspicious. This host, `p27dokhpz2n7nvgr.1jw21x.top` does not look like a standard URL that an analyst would find in a packet capture. Another feature of Wireshark is the ability to follow the TCP or HTTP stream of communication between the source and destination hosts. Right-click on the host name `p27dokhpz2n7nvgr.1jw21x.top` and the following appears:

Click on **HTTP Stream** and a second window appears. This window contains the HTTP packets in a format that can be read. The incident response analyst can review this output to determine what types of files may have been sent or received.

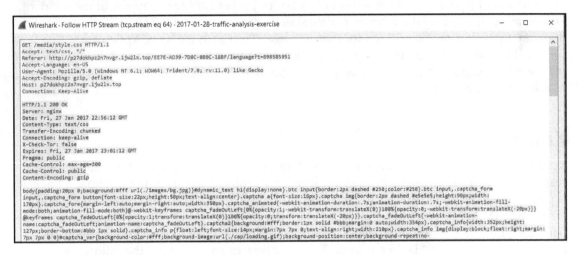

- In addition to examining the actual communications stream, Wireshark allows analysts to export specific objects from the packet capture. Click on **File** and then **Export Objects** and then HTTP and a window will appear listing all of the HTTP connections. The list can be sorted on any of the fields at the top of the window. In this case, select the **Hostname** and scroll down until the suspected URL is located:

Analysts can then parse through the results for any items of evidentiary value. For example, the last entry, packet 6002, is a PNG file titled **bitcoin.png**. Highlight the line and click **Save**. The file can then be downloaded for review.

Wireshark is a powerful tool for conducting detailed analysis of packet captures. The ability to drill down to indiviudal packets and disect them allows analysts to gain a very detailed sense of what is contained within the traffic running to and from external hosts, as well as to and from internal hosts. This visibility can afford the analyst possible insight into how an infected host communicates with an external host, or even identify other hosts that may have become compromised.

Xplico and CapAnalysis

As powerful a tool as Wireshark is, there may come a time when conducting a detailed examination of a packet capture, especially a larger packet capture, may not fit the incident. Furthermore, if an analyst wishes to isolate specific traffic such as HTTP or DNS traffic, there are tools that can be utilized for that purpose. Two such tools are Xplico and CapAnalysis. Both of these tools can be run on Linux operating systems and provide a platform for incident response analysts to gain an overall sense of what traffic is contained within a packet capture.

Xplico

Xplico is an open source **Network Forensic Analyst Tool (NFAT)** that allows an incident response analyst to extract specific application and protocol data contained within a packet capture. Xplico is able to extract information contained within common protocols such as HTTP, SIP, IMAP, IMAP, SMTP, and TCP. Finally, Xplico is able to utilize the DNS packages contained within the packet capture as a reverse DNS lookup, giving detailed information on captured DNS requests. To get Xplico up and running, the following procedure can be utilized:

1. Xplico is already installed on several well-known forensic platforms, such as DEFT and the CERT-Toolkit. Xplico is also installable on most Linux platforms. To install on Ubuntu-based platforms such as Paladin or CAINE, type the following into the Command Prompt:

```
sudo bash -c 'echo "deb http://repo.xplico.org/ $(lsb_release -s -
c) main" >>
/etc/apt/sources.list'
```

This will add the Xplico site to the Ubuntu sources list.

2. Next, the keys for Xplico need to be downloaded. Type the following into the command prompt:

```
sudo apt-key adv --keyserver keyserver.ubuntu.com --recv-keys 791C25CE
```

3. Next, ensure that all of the necessary packages are up to date by typing the following into the command prompt:

```
sudo apt-get update
```

4. Next, install Xplico utilizing the following command:

```
sudo apt-get install xplico
```

5. After installing, it may be necessary to start two services, the first is the Apache Web Server and the second, the actual Xplico service. Type the following two commands into the command prompt:

```
service apache2 start
service xplico start
```

6. Finally, navigate to the URL `http://localhost:9876`. The default username and password is **xplico** and **xplico** (administrator privileges can be accessed by utilizing the username **admin** and the password **xplico**). After authenticating, Xplico will open the interface to begin an analysis.

To begin an analysis of an existing packet capture:

1. Click on **New Case** located on the left side of the screen. This will open the following window:

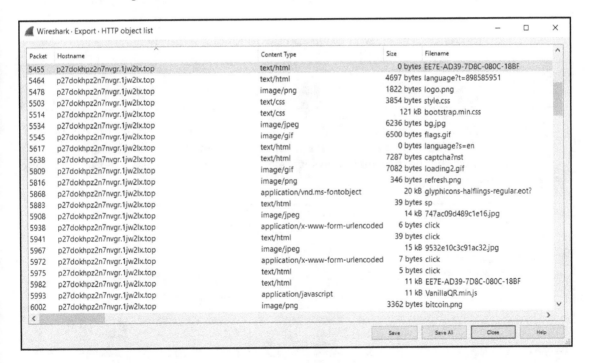

2. Xplico has the ability to perform both a live acquisition of a packet capture or analyze an existing packet capture. In this case, the existing packet capture analyzed previously in this chapter will be examined. Leave **Uploading PCAP capture file/s** checked. Next, create a **Case name**. It is a good standard operating procedure to utilize the case number of the incident across all platforms, so in this instance, the case name will be set to **IR 2017-001 Suspected Ransomeware**. After entering the case name, click **Create**. The following window will appear:

3. Double-click on the filename. This will open a new window. Click on **New Session**. This will open another new window in this case, the name **Packet Capture 2017-01-28** will be used. Click **Create** and the following window will open:

4. Double-click on the session name and the following window will open:

5. Navigate to the upper right-hand corner where the packet capture file can be uploaded. Select the appropriate packet capture and click **Upload**. Depending on the size of the file, this may take several minutes. Once complete, the session data fields will be filled in:

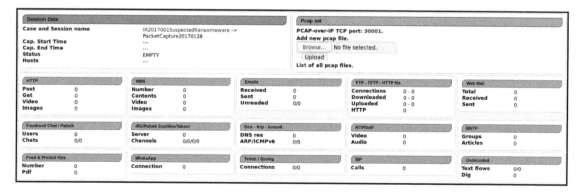

6. Below the session data, Xplico provides an overview of the various applications and protocol traffic were was contained within the packet capture:

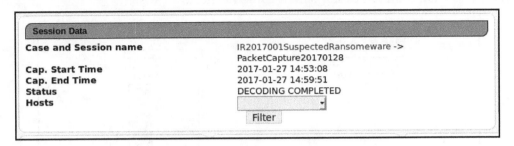

Session Data	
Case and Session name	IR2017001SuspectedRansomeware -> PacketCapture20170128
Cap. Start Time	2017-01-27 14:53:08
Cap. End Time	2017-01-27 14:59:51
Status	DECODING COMPLETED
Hosts	
	Filter

7. Analysts can then drill down to specific elements of the packet capture. For example, to examine the HTTP traffic, navigate to the left side of the screen and click on **Web** and then **site**. This produces a list of every separate URL that was contained within the packet capture:

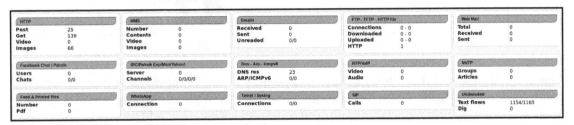

HTTP		MMS		Emails		FTP - TFTP - HTTP file		Web Mail	
Post	25	Number	0	Received	0	Connections	0 - 0	Total	0
Get	139	Contents	0	Sent	0	Downloaded	0 - 0	Received	0
Video	0	Video	0	Unreaded	0/0	Uploaded	0 - 0	Sent	0
Images	66	Images	0			HTTP	1		

Facebook Chat / Paltalk		IRC/Paltalk Exp/Msn/Yahoo!		Dns - Arp - Icmpv6		RTP/VoIP		NNTP	
Users	0	Server	0	DNS res	23	Video	0	Groups	0
Chats	0/0	Channels	0/0/0/0	ARP/ICMPv6	0/0	Audio	0	Articles	0

Feed & Printed files		WhatsApp		Telnet / Syslog		SIP		Undecoded	
Number	0	Connection	0	Connections	0/0	Calls	0	Text flows	1154/1165
Pdf	0							Dig	0

8. A quick review of the results shows the suspicious URL that was located utilizing Wireshark. Under the **Web** tab is a feature that reconstructs the images transferred in the packet capture. Clicking **Images** provides a gallery view that can be quickly analyzed. In this case, an icon for **bitcoin** is visible:

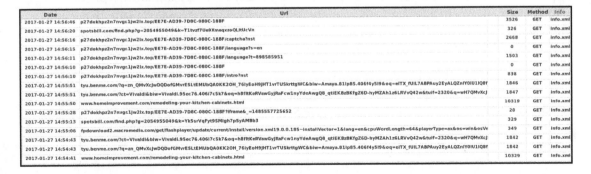

Date	Url	Size	Method	Info
2017-01-27 14:56:46	p27dokhpz2n7nvgr.1jw2lx.top/EE7E-AD39-7D8C-080C-18BF	3526	GET	Info.xml
2017-01-27 14:56:20	spotsbill.com/find.php?g=2054955049&k=T1tvzf7Ue9XmaqxzoQLltUcVn	326	GET	Info.xml
2017-01-27 14:56:16	p27dokhpz2n7nvgr.1jw2lx.top/EE7E-AD39-7D8C-080C-18BF/captcha?nst	2668	GET	Info.xml
2017-01-27 14:56:15	p27dokhpz2n7nvgr.1jw2lx.top/EE7E-AD39-7D8C-080C-18BF/language?s=en	0	GET	Info.xml
2017-01-27 14:56:11	p27dokhpz2n7nvgr.1jw2lx.top/EE7E-AD39-7D8C-080C-18BF/language?t=898585951	1503	GET	Info.xml
2017-01-27 14:56:10	p27dokhpz2n7nvgr.1jw2lx.top/EE7E-AD39-7D8C-080C-18BF	0	GET	Info.xml
2017-01-27 14:56:10	p27dokhpz2n7nvgr.1jw2lx.top/EE7E-AD39-7D8C-080C-18BF/intro?nst	838	GET	Info.xml
2017-01-27 14:55:51	tyu.benme.com/?q=zn_QMvXcJwDQDofGMvrESLtEMUbQA0KK2OH_76iyEoH9JHT1vrTUSkrttgWC&biw=Amaya.81lp85.406f4y5l9&oq=eiTX_fUIL7ABPAuy2EyALQZnlY0lU1IQ8f	1846	GET	Info.xml
2017-01-27 14:55:51	tyu.benme.com/?ct=Vivaldi&biw=Vivaldi.95ec76.406i7c5k7&oq=h8fltKeRVawGyjRaFcw1nyYdeAwgQ8_qtiEKBzBKfgZ6D-hyMZAh1z6LRVvQ42w&tuif=2320&q=wH7QMvXcJ	1847	GET	Info.xml
2017-01-27 14:55:50	www.homeimprovement.com/remodeling-your-kitchen-cabinets.html	10319	GET	Info.xml
2017-01-27 14:55:28	p27dokhpz2n7nvgr.1jw2lx.top/EE7E-AD39-7D8C-080C-18BF?iframe&_=1485557725652	20	GET	Info.xml
2017-01-27 14:55:13	spotsbill.com/find.php?g=2054955049&k=Yk5srVqFyt9SMlgh7pSyAMBb3	329	GET	Info.xml
2017-01-27 14:55:06	fpdownload2.macromedia.com/get/flashplayer/update/current/install/version.xml19.0.0.185~installVector=1&lang=en&cpuWordLength=64&playerType=ax&os=win&osVe	349	GET	Info.xml
2017-01-27 14:54:43	tyu.benme.com/?ct=Vivaldi&biw=Vivaldi.95ec76.406i7c5k7&oq=h8fltKeRVawGyjRaFcw1nyYdeAwgQ8_qtiEKBzBKfgZ6D-hyMZAh1z6LRVvQ42w&tuif=2320&q=wH7QMvXcJ	1842	GET	Info.xml
2017-01-27 14:54:43	tyu.benme.com/?q=zn_QMvXcJwDQDofGMvrESLtEMUbQA0KK2OH_76iyEoH9JHT1vrTUSkrttgWC&biw=Amaya.81lp85.406f4y5l9&oq=eiTX_fUIL7ABPAuy2EyALQZnlY0lU1IQ8f	1842	GET	Info.xml
2017-01-27 14:54:41	www.homeimprovement.com/remodeling-your-kitchen-cabinets.html	10329	GET	Info.xml

Another key feature is the ability of analysts to perform a quick review of DNS information that is contained within the packet capture. This allows the analyst to gain a sense of what external hosts were communicating with the internal host:

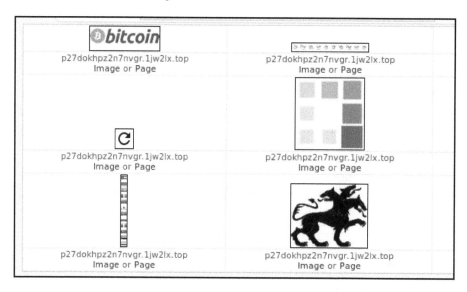

Xplico is a simple tool that allows incident response analysts to quickly identify potential evidence contained within a packet capture. For example, in the packet capture that was analyzed, a few simple steps have produced a suspect URL and IP address that can be investigated further.

CapAnalysis

CapAnalysis is a freeware toolset that performs a variety of tasks, similar to Xplico. CapAnalysis allows incident response analysts to review large packet capture files and parse out TCP, UDP, and ESP streams. Analysts also have the ability to filter out IP addresses, ports, protocols, as well as tie data flows to specific geographical areas.

CapAnalysis can be downloaded from the site `http://www.capanalysis.net/ca/#download`. The download package contains an installer. Simply click on the **Install** button and the package will install.

Date	Host	CName	IP	Info
2017-01-27 14:55:27	p27dokhpz2n7nvgr.1jw2lx.top		198.105.121.50	Info.xml
2017-01-27 14:55:27	api.blockcypher.com	bc-prod-web-lb-430045627.us-east-1.elb.amazonaws.com	107.23.24.131	Info.xml
2017-01-27 14:55:12	spotsbill.com		5.188.223.104	Info.xml
2017-01-27 14:55:06	fpdownload2.macromedia.com	fpdownload2.wip4.adobe.com	66.152.103.73	Info.xml
2017-01-27 14:54:43	tyu.benme.com		194.87.234.129	Info.xml
2017-01-27 14:54:43	www.google-analytics.com	www-google-analytics.l.google.com	74.125.141.100	Info.xml
2017-01-27 14:54:42	retrotip.visionurbana.com.ve		139.59.160.143	Info.xml
2017-01-27 14:54:41	www.homeimprovement.com		104.28.18.74	Info.xml
2017-01-27 14:54:29	da6ab9a9cf82c8f939081a82c7d90031.clo.footprintdns.com	cy4prdapp01-canary.cloudapp.net	13.78.149.173	Info.xml
2017-01-27 14:54:28	40bbdaf00bf29a6114a5019e397a2a15.clo.footprintdns.com	bm1prdapp01-canary.cloudapp.net	104.211.160.15	Info.xml
2017-01-27 14:54:27	3a0849bc3c36a673eb2ddd2fcf0494a.clo.footprintdns.com	sg1prdapp02-canary.cloudapp.net	111.221.104.81	Info.xml
2017-01-27 14:54:12	report.footprintdns.com	dnsprobeselector.cloudapp.net	138.91.83.37	Info.xml
2017-01-27 14:54:10	e623e8223493b6793a476840214720b1.clo.footprintdns.com	r53.canarytest.net	54.174.33.196	Info.xml
2017-01-27 14:54:10	1e46ba9c0151d4d34a7939daabd778ad.clo.footprintdns.com	ec2-52-79-148-45.ap-northeast-2.compute.amazonaws.com	52.79.148.45	Info.xml
2017-01-27 14:54:09	6b8960d1b061131b015f93f32d0a56f4.clo.footprintdns.com	cy4prdapp01-canary.cloudapp.net	13.78.149.173	Info.xml
2017-01-27 14:54:09	2.bing.com	dual.a-0001.a-msedge.net	204.79.197.200	Info.xml

Once installed, navigate to `http://localhost:9877`. From here, analysts can configure a password for access. After configuring a password, CapAnalysis opens into the following home page:

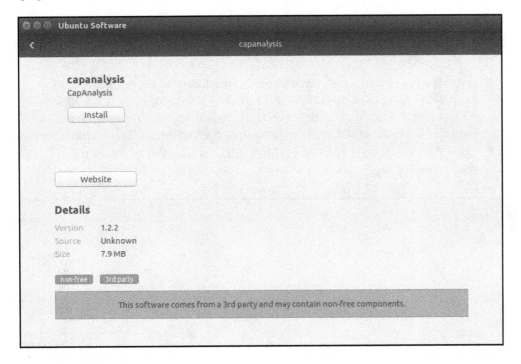

1. Click on **New** to begin the process of analyzing a packet capture. This opens the following:

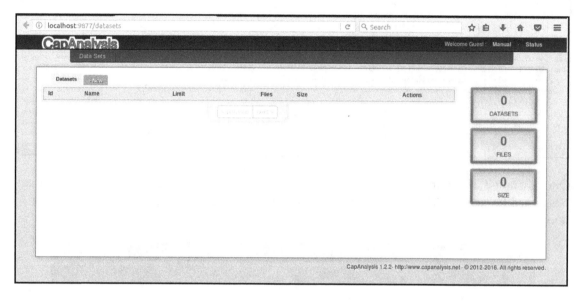

2. Enter the case number as name to the **Name** field. Again, as with previous examples, the case name **2017 001 Suspected Ransomeware** (CapAnalysis only allows alpha-numeric characters, so hyphens should be removed from the case name) will be utilized. Once the name has been entered, click **Submit**.

3. Once the new dataset has been added, click on the tab **Data Sets** which will open the following page:

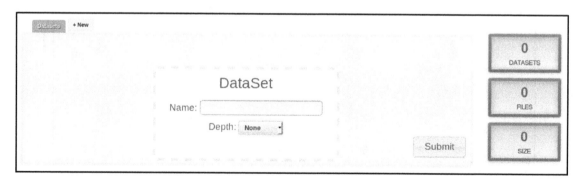

4. Click on **Files** to add the packet capture to the dataset. The next window allows the analyst to either import a packet capture from a URL, conduct a packet capture, or analyze an existing packet capture. Drag and drop the existing packet capture to the appropriate location or click the button **Click Here** to navigate to the appropriate folder. Once they are loaded, the following will appear:

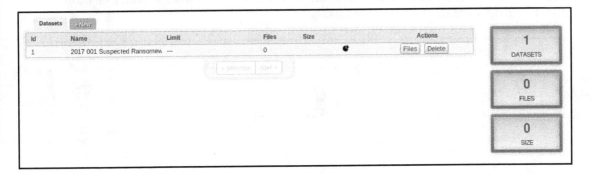

5. Click the tab **DATASETS** and the datasets window will show the file that was uploaded:

6. Double-click on the name **2017 001 Suspected Ransomeware** and the following window appears:

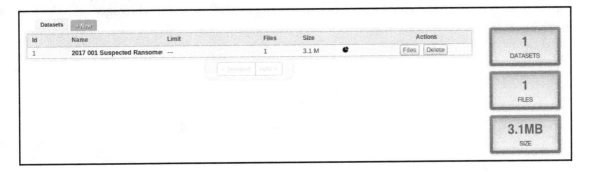

The tabs at the top of the window allow the analyst to drill down to specific information. There are several features that make CapAnalysis a good tool for analyzing packet captures. The **Overview** tab allows analysts to gain a sense of the protocols, data flows, and geographical regions data is flowing back and forth from. For example, analyzing the packet capture from the beginning of this chapter, the analyst would see that a good deal of HTTP traffic is flowing back and forth from the Russian Federation, as well as a number of other countries outside the United States.

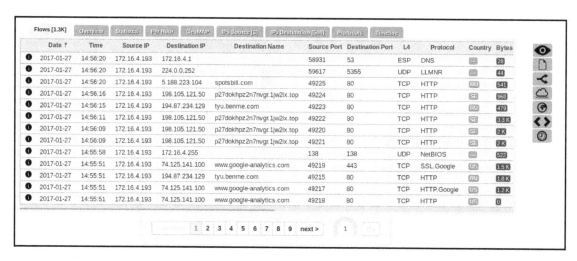

If the organization based in the United States does not have a significant presence outside that geographical region, the analyst could use this as an indication that the packet capture contains evidence related to a potential compromise. Moving forward, the analyst may want to look at data that relates only to the Russian Federation. To do this, navigate to the right side and click on the globe icon. This allows the analyst to select which geographical areas to focus on:

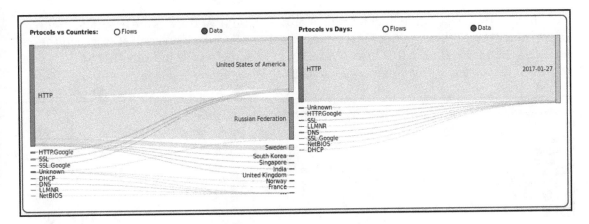

From here, select only the **Russian Federation** and then click **Apply**. This option then limits the data visible to only data that is moving back and forth between the host and IP addresses associated with the Russian Federation:

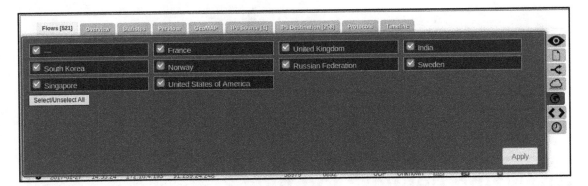

From here, the analyst can then determine if any of these IP addresses are associated with known botnet controllers or other malicious sites. For example, if an analyst searched the site `virustotal.com` for the IP address `91.239.24.50`, the results indicate that the IP address is associated with a number of malicous files:

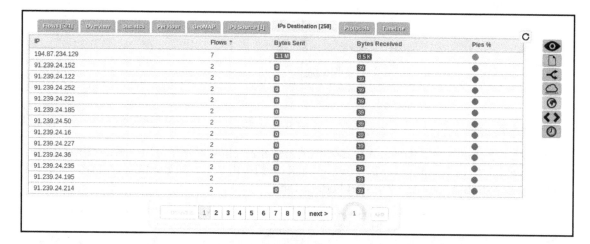

Tools such as Xplico and CapAnalysis allow the incident response analyst to gain insight into the wealth of data contained within a packet capture in a more user-friendly way. The way that the data is presented in these solutions further allows the analyst to triage potential incidents by quickly reviewing the data and determining whether there is in fact a potential incident that requires more detailed investigation.

Analyzing network log files

Chapter 3, *Network Evidence Collection,* contained a good deal of information concerning the acquisition of network-based evidence and the types of log files that are of importance to incident response analysts. Aside from the previously covered packet capture, there was a good deal focused on the acquisition of log files from a variety of sources. These log files can provide some insight into the potential indicators of compromise that can aid in an incident investigation. The main challenge though for analysts is sifting through all of the non-relevant logs to find those that have some evidentiary value.

Log file analysis can be performed in a variety of ways. The specific method that is used may often depend on the type of incident, the tools available, and the amount of log data that has to be analysed. The following are some of the methods that can be utilized:

- **Manual log review**: In a manual log review, raw log files are dumped into a tool such as a text editor. From there, the analyst will review the logs line by line. This is a low-cost solution, but it is really only useful with a limited amount of data. For example, an analyst would not be able to perform this type of analysis on a large enterprise firewall connection log. Rather, it may be useful to determine which users logged into a seldom used web application on a particular day.
- **Filtered log review**: Log review tools allow analysts to filter out log files along specific parameters. This can include showing a list of any known malicious activity. The one drawback is that logs may not immediately indicate known malicious activity, but rather are innocuous at the onset.
- **Log file searching**: Another key feature in most log analysis tools is the ability to search log files for specific expressions. Tools for searching can search for both regex and Boolean expressions and allow the analyst to limit logs to a specific time period, source IP address, or other specific condition. This allows analysts to quickly isolate specific log files. Depending on the search terms, this may return a good deal of information that has to then be reviewed manually.
- **Log file correlation**: Separate log activity can be correlated with other logs based upon either preconfigured rules or algorithms. Log correlation is often made part of log management tools or SIEM platforms with rulesets that have been created. This method is very powerful, as it automates the process, but it does require a good deal of upfront labor to configure and tune to the specific environment.
- **Log file data mining**: The next step up from correlation is the ability to mine log files and extract meaning from these. This gives greater context and insight into the specific activity. Currently, there are several tools, such as **ElasticSearch** and **Logstash**, which have been integrated into a platform for more useful information.

The amount of logs that are produced in a network over a month or so can be staggering. This amount only increases with the addition of new sources. Sorting through these manually is near impossible. In terms of log review, it is better to have a solution that provides some measure of automation, even in small networks. These tools give analysts the ability to sort through the proverbial stack of hay for that critical needle.

DNS blacklists

One technique that performs a combination of filtering and manual log review is utilizing scripting languages such as Python. These scripts can parse through firewall logs or other inputs to highlight specific areas of focus for the analyst. One such script is DNS Blacklists which is available at https://bitbucket.org/ethanr/dns-blacklists/. This script takes a text file created by the log source or analyst and compares it to lists of IP addresses and domains that have been blacklisted.

The folder containing the script contains two other folders that are compared against each other. One folder contains the text files of IP and domain blacklists. These blacklists can be obtained from open sources or threat intelligence providers. The script runs the suspicious log files or IP addresses against the blacklists to determine whether there are any matches.

For example, the IP addresses identified in the packet capture that resolve to the Russian Federation geographical area have been placed into a text file. Next, the analyst obtains the most up-to-date blacklists available. These are placed into the bad_lists folder. Once the data is placed into the appropriate folders, the following is entered into the command line:

```
forensics@ubuntu:~/Documents/dns_blacklists$ python dns_blacklists.py
bad_lists/ Suspect_IPS/
```

This command runs the script with the blacklists contained in the bad_lists folder against the log files or IP addresses in the Suspect_IPS folder. The command produces the following output:

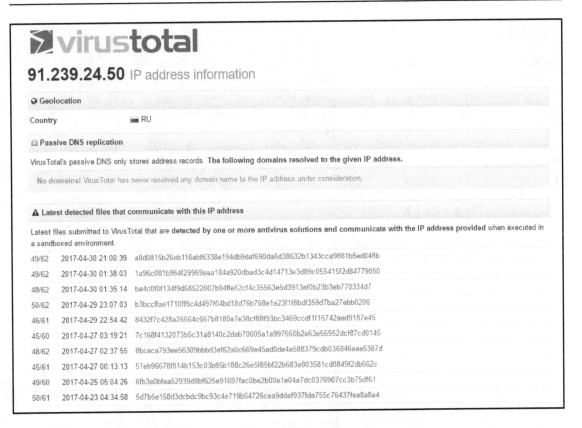

The output indicates that the IP address `198.105.121.50` has been located in one of the blacklists. From here, some research on that IP address may indicate whether there is any other malicious activity associated with it. This technique is useful if an analyst needs to triage log files or a large list of IP addresses. Positive results from running this script can be further used to drill down to specific log file entries for further examination.

SIEM

In Chapter 3, *Network Evidence Collection*, there was also discussion of the use of **Security Information and Event Management (SIEM)** platforms. These platforms not only serve as an aggregation point for log files from network devices, they also allow analysts to perform queries on the logs that have been aggregated. For example, there were IP addresses associated with potential malicious activity discovered during the analysis of the packet capture file. This file was limited to a single host on the internal network. One question that analysts would like to answer is how many other hosts could possibly be infected? If the SIEM aggregates connection log files from devices such as the exterior facing firewall and web proxy, the analyst would be able to determine if any other internal hosts connected to those suspect IP addresses.

There are a wide variety of SIEM platforms available, from freeware solutions to enterprise security management platforms. Most of these platforms allow analysts to conduct filtered, searching, and correlation log reviews. Many of the more robust commercial platforms provide rulesets for detecting specific types of attacks and updates to these rulesets as new attacks become known. Analysts could also query the SIEM for connection logs for the host IP address to any other systems. This would normally be the behavior seen in an incident where malware has infected a machine and an attacker is attempting to compromise other machines.

In organizations where incident response personnel are separate from those that have responsibility for the maintenance of the SIEM, it is a good idea to review the communications structure so that incident response analysts have access to these platforms. The wealth of information and data that is available can be leveraged to determine what activity on the internal network is connected to a possible incident, as well as evidence that can be utilized to determine the root cause.

ELK Stack

Alongside SIEM technology, incident response analysts can also leverage a bundle of applications for log analysis. This bundle, referred to as the ELK Stack, combines three tools together that allows for the analysis of large sets of data. The ELK Stack is comprised of three components. The first of these is **Elasticsearch**. Elasticsearch is a log searching tool that allows for near real-time searching of log data. This is accomplished through full text searching, powered by **Lucene**. This allows analysts to perform queries against log files for such elements as user IDs, IP addresses, or log entry numbers. Another key feature of Elasticsearch is the ability for the platform to expand the solution as the enterprise grows larger and with more data sources. This is useful for organizations that may want to test this capability and then add data sources and log files incrementally.

The next component in the ELK Stack is Logstash. Logstash is the mechanism that handles the intake of log files from the sources across the network, process log entries, and finally, allows for their output through a visualization platform. Logstash can be configured and deployed easily. The integration of Logstash with Elasticsearch provides the incident response analyst the ability to conduct fast queries against a large amount of log data.

The final component of the ELK Stack is **Kibana**. Kibana serves as the visual interface or dashboard of the ELK Stack. This platform allows analysts to gain insight into the data through the use of dashboards. Kibana also allows analysts to drill down into specific key data points for detailed analysis. Incident response analysts can customize the dashboards so that the most critical information, such as intrusion detection logs or connection logs, are immediately available for review.

For example, the Kibana dashboard utilizes a number of pie charts to display log activity. Utilizing these allows for an overview of what information is available to an analyst.

```
forensics@ubuntu:~/Documents/dns_blacklists$ python dns_blacklists.py bad_lists/ Suspect_
IPS/
Note: DNS resolution and reverse resolution is currently not supported.
Parsing blacklist files...
- - - - - - - - - - - - - - - - - - - - - - - - - - - - - - - - - - - - - - - - - - - - - - - - - - - - - -
IP_Blacklist.txt
all.php.txt
zeus_badips.txt
dom-bl-base.txt
hosts.txt
Mandiant_APT1_Report_Appendix_D.txt
zeus_baddomains.txt

Parsing check files...
- - - - - - - - - - - - - - - - - - - - - - - - - - - - - - - - - - - - - - - - - - - - - - - - - - - - - -
IR2017_001


============================================================================
The following hostnames were found in the blacklists:
============================================================================


============================================================================
The following IPs were found in the blacklists:
============================================================================
198.105.121.50
```

In addition, there is the ability to drill down into greater detail for specific events:

These can also be further expanded, giving analysts depth into the specific event:

```
▼  May 2nd 2017, 09:20:14.553    @version: 1 @timestamp: May 2nd 2017, 09:20:14.553 host: 127.0.0.1 port: 38,946 tags: bro, external_des
                                 tination, internal_source message: 1493716750.786102 CUOTxP26KHkqdEjAzi 192.168.0.35 59093 239.255.255.250
                                 1900 udp - 3.002940 692 0 S0 T F 0 D 4 804 0 0 (empty) - - forensics-virtual-machine-eth1 type: bro_conn
                                 syslog-facility: user syslog-file_name: /nsm/bro/logs/current/conn.log syslog-host: forensics-virtual-mac
                                 hine syslog-host from: forensics-virtual-machine syslog-priority: notice syslog-sourceip: 127.0.0.1
```

The ELK Stack is an open source platform and it can be configured by installing the separate components. This may be time consuming and does not allow for a proper evaluation of the stack. As a result, there are a few virtual machines or scripts that run that allow for evaluation of the toolset. For example, **Phil Hagen** of SANS has configured a virtual machine that is used in the SANS training classes. The VM and associated configuration files are available at: `https://github.com/philhagen/sof-elk`.

Another option available is to place the ELK Stack on top of a **Security Onion** installation. `Chapter 3`, *Network Evidence Collection* contained an overview of the Security Onion log management platform. The engineers have created an evaluation installation of the ELK Stack for review. The stack is installed through a script run on an existing Security Onion installation. The files and associated instructions can be found here: `http://blog.securityonion.net/2017/03/towards-elk-on-security-onion.html`.

The number of features of the ELK Stack and their use are too many to include as they can take up a whole volume themselves. Incident response analysts who are involved in parsing and examining log files would be best served by evaluating, and possibly deploying, the ELK Stack in their environment if there is currently no solution in place that allows for the aggregation and deep mining of log files for incident investigations.

Summary

Security incidents not only produce trace evidence on host systems, but also leave traces throughout the devices and traffic flows within a network. The ability to analyze this trace evidence will allow incident response analysts to have a better understanding of what type of incident they are investigating, as well as potential actions that can be taken. Tools such as Wireshark and CapAnalysis afford analysts the ability to rip apart network traffic and individual packets to discover a wealth of information. Log analysis, either conducted manually or using tools such as the ELK Stack, can also provide analysts with a way to determine what log entries indicate compromise. This trace evidence, taken in conjunction with evidence obtained from potentially compromised websites, goes a long way in allowing analysts to reconstruct the events of an incident.

7
Analyzing System Memory

For the longest time, law enforcement and other organizations performing digital forensic tasks associated with incident investigations often relied on methodologies that focused on evidence contained within the hard drive. Procedures dictated that the system be powered down and the hard drive removed for imaging. While this methodology and associated procedures were effective at ensuring the integrity of the evidence, this overlooked the wealth of information that was contained within the **Random Access Memory (RAM)**, or memory for short, of the targeted system. As a result, incident response analysts began to focus a great deal of attention on ensuring that appropriate methods were employed that maintained the integrity of this evidence, as well as giving them a platform in which to obtain information of evidentiary value.

This chapter will focus on the types of evidence that can be located within the memory of a system, the tools and techniques available to incident response analysts, and finally, how to analyze this information to obtain a clear understanding of how the system was compromised. In addition, these techniques can also be integrated into the analysis of other evidence, such as network log files and files located on the targeted system.

Memory evidence overview

When discussing analyzing the memory of a system, there are two terms that are used interchangeably. The first is RAM. RAM is the portion of the computer internal systems where the operating system places data utilized by applications and the system hardware while that application or hardware is in use. What makes RAM different from storage is the volatile nature of the data. Often, if the system is shut off, the data will be lost.

There is a good deal of data contained within RAM at the time a system is running that is valuable in an incident investigation. These include the following:

- Running processes
- Loaded **Dynamic Link Libraries(DLL)**
- Open Registry Keys
- Network connections

Memory analysis

As the necessity for analyzing the memory of systems has increased, there are several tools that analysts have at their disposal. This chapter will focus on three such tools; all of them are either open source or freeware and can be deployed easily. These tools allow analysts to gain critical insight into the activity of exploits and malware that have impacted a system.

 Throughout this chapter, a memory capture will be utilized. This memory capture is from a Windows system that has been infected by the Stuxnet virus. The memory image can be downloaded from the following site: jonrajewski.com/data/Malware/stuxnet.vmem.zip.

Memory analysis methodology

When examining system memory, it is advisable for analysts to follow a methodology. This ensures that all potential evidence is uncovered and can be utilized in an incident investigation. There are a variety of methodologies that can be leveraged. Which specific methodology that is used can often be dependent on the type of incident. For example, a methodology that is geared towards identifying **indicators of compromise** around a malware infection may yield a great deal of information, but may not be the best approach if the analysts has evidence from other network sources of a suspect IP address.

SANS six-part methodology

The SANS institution makes use of a six-part methodology for the analysis of memory images. This process is designed to start from an overall view of what is running to identifying and accessing the malicious software. The SANS methodology follows the following steps:

1. **Identify rogue processes:** Malware often hides its behavior behind processes that on the surface may seem legitimate. Uncovering these involves identifying what processes are running, the location in the operating system they are running from, and verifying that only legitimate processes are in use. Sometimes processes are hidden in plain sight where adversaries change a single letter in a process name. Other times, they will attempt to execute a process from an illegitimate source.

2. **Analyze process DLLs and handles:** Once a process or multiple processes have been identified as rogue, the next step is to examine the DLL files associated with the process as well as other factors such as account information.

3. **Review network artifacts:** Malware, especially multi-stage malware, requires connection to the internet. Even systems that are fully compromised often beacon out to C2 servers. Active and listening network connections are contained within the memory of these systems. Identifying external host IP addresses may give some insight into what type of compromise has taken place.

4. **Look for evidence of code injection:** Techniques such as process hollowing and unmapped sections of the memory are often used by advanced malware coders. Memory analysis tools assist analysts with finding the evidence of these techniques.

5. **Check for signs of a rootkit:** Achieving persistence is a goal with many external threat actors. If they are able to achieve the initial compromise of the system, it is critical that they maintain that.

6. **Dump suspicious process and drivers:** After locating any suspicious processes or executables, analysts need to be able to acquire them for later analysis with additional tools.

Network connections methodology

In many incidents, the first indication that a system is compromised is attempted or completed connections to external hosts. Detection mechanisms such as firewalls or web proxies may indicate that a system or systems are attempting to communicate with suspect external hosts. From this starting position, it may be possible to identify potential malware on a system:

1. **Suspicious network connections:** Conducting a review of network connections on hosts that have been associated with external connections will often provide the process that is attempting to communicate.

2. **Process name:** Examining the process from the network connections allows analysts to perform similar actions found within the SANS methodology. It is advisable for the analyst to also determine if the identified process is one that often requires a network connection.

3. **Parent process ID:** Further insight into the parent process is useful in determining if the process is legitimate and has a legitimate need to communication via a network connection.

4. **Associated entities:** Finally, examining the associated DLLs and other artifacts brings us to the stage where they can be acquired and analyzed.

Tools

There are several tools available to analysts for the review of memory images. For the purposes of this chapter, three tools will be examined. The first of these, **MandiantRedline**, is a GUI-based memory analysis tool that examines memory images for signs of rogue processes and scores them based upon several factors. The remaining tools, Volatility and Rekall, are command-line tools that allow analysts to drill into the details of the memory image and identify potential malicious code.

Redline

One powerful tool that analysts should include in their toolkits is Mandiant Redline. This Microsoft Windows application provides a feature rich platform for analyzing memory images. These features include the ability to create a memory collector, although the tool will work with memory captures that have been performed via tools previously discussed. There is also the ability to utilize previously discovered **Indicators of Compromise** (**IOCs**) to aid in the examination. The tool can be downloaded at fireeye.com/MandiantRedline/FireEyeRedline.

The download package includes a Microsoft Self Installer:

1. Once installed, double-click on the icon and the following screen will appear. There are a number of options broken out into two categories: **CollectData** and **AnalyzeData**. In this case, the existing memory capture previously indicated will be analyzed.

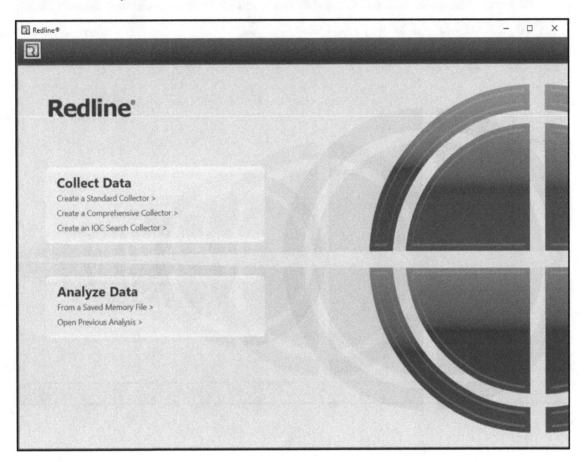

2. Click on **From a Saved Memory File** under the **Analyze Data** category. This will open a second window. Under **Location of Saved Memory Image**, navigate to the location of the memory file, and select it. Once completed, click **Next**.

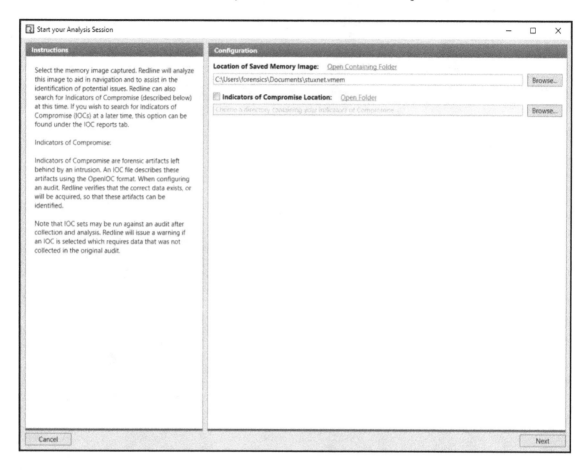

3. Once the memory file is loaded, the next screen will require a name for the session file that will be created by Redline. In this case, the filename IR 2017-001 Suspected Ransomeware will be utilized. Furthermore, select a folder that will contain all the data from this analysis session. It is a good practice to have separate folders for each session to ensure that each analysis is segregated. In the event that several systems are examined, this reduces the risk of comingling evidence. Once those parameters are set, click **OK**.

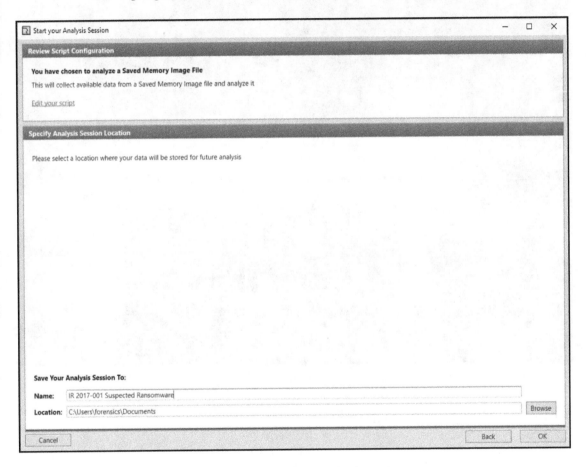

4. Redline will then begin the process of putting the data into a format for analysis. Depending on the size of the image, this may take several minutes.

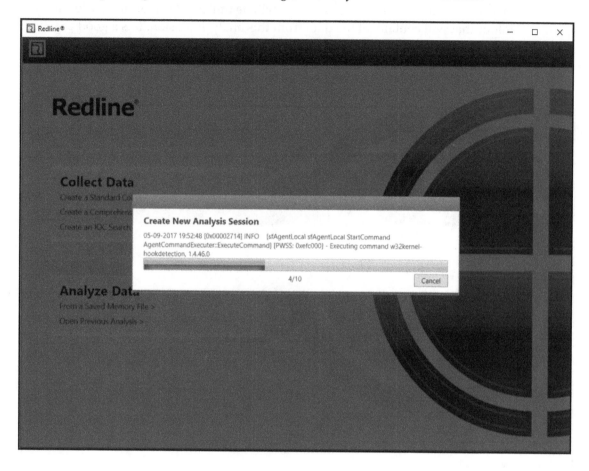

5. After creating the analysis session, the following window will appear. For memory images that do not contain any other information, click on the section titled **I am Reviewing a Full Live Response or Memory Image.**

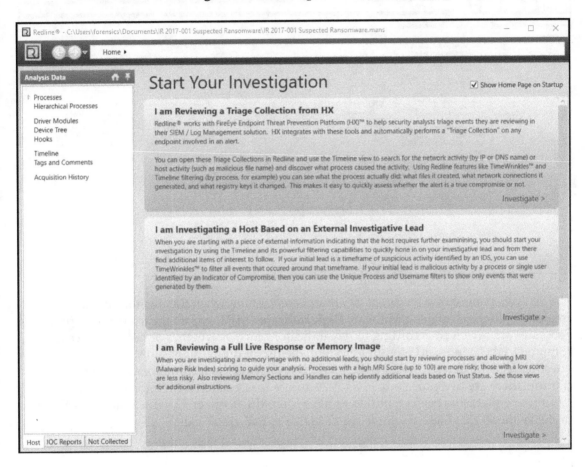

6. The next window will appear that details the results from the analysis:

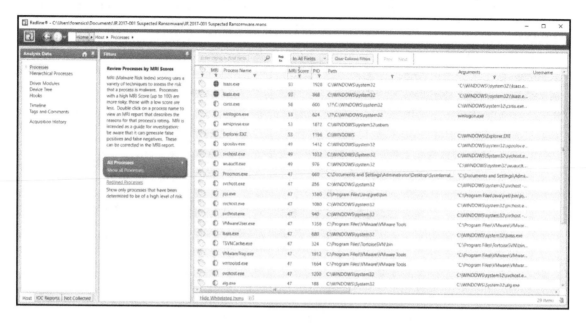

The analysis pane shows the processes that were running when the memory image was created. Redline calculates a **Malware Risk Indicator(MRI)** score for each running process. Processes are reviewed according to risk indicators such as whether or not the process is common to the Windows Operating System, the use of digital signatures, or if the process in question appears to have been injected. When reviewing the results from this memory capture, there are two processes, PIDs 1928 and 868, associated with the executable lsass.exe that have been identified as having an MRI score of 93, which indicates a very high likelihood that these two processes are tied to malicious code.

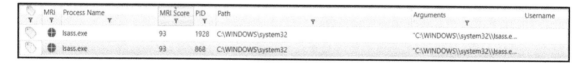

To gain more detail on one of the suspect processors, click anywhere on the bar containing the process. From there, the following window will open:

In the lower portion of the window, there are several tabs that provide analysts with details concerning the process under analysis. In this case, click the tab titled **MRI Report**. This will open a window with several sections. The first of these sections will be details concerning the process:

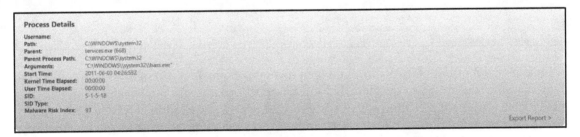

In this case, the analyst can see that the process is being executed via the `System32` folder under the **services.exe** process. Redline also allows the analyst to export the data in the form of a Microsoft Word document for inclusion in any reporting. Further down the window, Redline also provides insight into the MRI score.

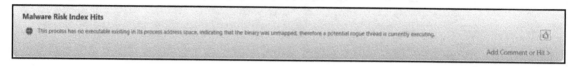

Finally, the MRI tab allows analysts to examine the **Named Memory Sections** of the suspect process. This includes not only process counts, but the associated DLL files associated with the suspect process.

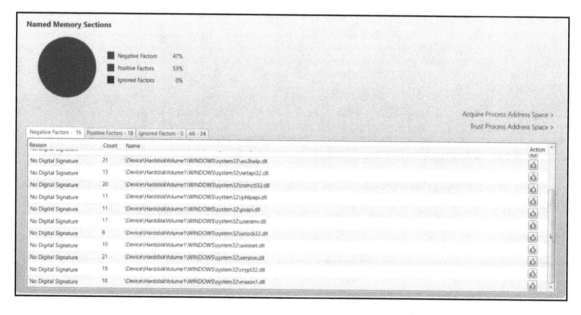

Redline provides an easier platform in which to analyze a memory image. As was demonstrated, the ability to graphically locate suspect processes is very useful, especially in incidents where there are a number of systems that need to be examined. While Redline does provide a good deal of information, it often takes the integration of Rekall or Volatility to get to the final stage of examining a potential malicious file.

Volatility

Volatility is an open source advanced memory forensics framework. The primary tool within the framework is the Volatility Python script that utilizes a large number of plugins to perform the analysis of memory images. As a result, Volatility is able to be run on any operating system that supports Python. In addition, Volatility can be utilized against memory image files from most of the commonly distributed operating systems including Windows for Windows XP to Windows Server 2016, macOS, and finally common Linux distributions.

There are a number of plugins available for Volatility with more being developed. For the purposes of examining system memory, several plugins will be examined to ensure that the analyst has sufficient information to conduct a proper analysis. It is recommended though that prior to using Volatility that the analyst ensures that software is up to date and that any new plugins are explored to determine their applicability to the current incident investigation.

Installing Volatility

There are several ways that Volatility can be installed. One simple method is to download the entire Volatility package via the Linux application Git and run the `vol.py` script against the image file. To install Volatility on a Linux platform, first download the package via Git utilizing the following command:

```
forensics@ubuntu:~$ git clone
https://github.com/volatilityfoundation/volatility.git
```

Once the download finishes, extract the package and navigate to the folder containing the Python script `setup.py`. Then execute the script via the following command:

```
forensics@ubuntu:~/volatility-master$sudo python setup.py install
```

Once the install completes, open another Command Prompt and enter the following:

```
forensics@ubuntu:~$ volatility
```

If the following appears, than the installation was successful:

```
Volatility Foundation Volatility Framework 2.6
ERROR :volatility.debug: You must specify something to do (try -h)
```

One of the advantages to installing Volatility rather than running the script from the Volatility folder is the ability to open a Terminal within the folder containing the image file and running Volatility directly from there. This saves a bit of typing and makes organizing evidence a bit more efficient. After installing Volatility, the following convention is utilized in analyzing a memory image:

```
forensics@ubuntu:~/Documents$ volatility -f <File Name> --profile=<Image
Profile><Plugin>
```

In the preceding convention, the -f points Volatility to the file that is being analyzed. The second part of the command is the image profile. This is required so that Volatility can locate the necessary data based upon the operating system (obtaining the profile is covered in the following section). Finally, the plugin name is entered. There are several other options available, such as pointing Volatility to a process ID or to output the results to a text file.

Identifying the image

One of the key preliminary steps that must be completed prior to conducting a detailed examination of the system memory is to determine the exact OS of the system under investigation. Even if the analyst is certain of the OS, it is still a good practice to run the memory images against Volatility's imageinfo plugin. The output of this plugin identifies the potential profile of the memory image that becomes critical to utilizing the other plugins available.

To determine the profile of the memory image, type the following into the command line:

forensics@ubuntu:~/Documents$ volatility -f stuxnet.vmemimageinfo

This produces the following output:

```
forensics@ubuntu:~/Documents$ volatility -f stuxnet.vmem imageinfo
Volatility Foundation Volatility Framework 2.6
INFO    : volatility.debug    : Determining profile based on KDBG search...
          Suggested Profile(s) : WinXPSP2x86, WinXPSP3x86 (Instantiated with Win
XPSP2x86)
                     AS Layer1 : IA32PagedMemoryPae (Kernel AS)
                     AS Layer2 : FileAddressSpace (/home/forensics/Documents/stu
xnet.vmem)
                      PAE type : PAE
                           DTB : 0x319000L
                          KDBG : 0x80545ae0L
          Number of Processors : 1
     Image Type (Service Pack) : 3
                KPCR for CPU 0 : 0xffdff000L
             KUSER_SHARED_DATA : 0xffdf0000L
          Image date and time  : 2011-06-03 04:31:36 UTC+0000
    Image local date and time_ : 2011-06-03 00:31:36 -0400
```

From this output, the analyst is provided with a good deal of information. This includes the most likely profile of the memory image, the number of processors, and the date and time that the memory image was created.

Volatility requires that for each plugin, the profile indicated in the `imageinfo` output is within the command. This allows Volatility to properly parse out the necessary information from the memory image.

pslist

The `pslist` command lists the current processes running in memory. This plugin outputs the offset, process name, process ID (PID), the number of threads and handles, and the date and time the process started and exited. Because the pslist plugin walks the doubly-linked list indicated by `PsActiveProcessHead`, it does not have the ability to detect hidden or unlinked process. To execute the plugin, enter the following into the Command Prompt:

```
forensics@ubuntu:~/Documents$ volatility -f stuxnet.vmem --
profile=WinXPSP2x86 pslist
```

The command produces the following output:

```
forensics@ubuntu:~/Documents$ volatility -f stuxnet.vmem --profile=WinXPSP2x86 pslist
Volatility Foundation Volatility Framework 2.6
Offset(V)   Name            PID   PPID   Thds   Hnds   Sess   Wow64 Start                      Exit

----------  --------------- ----- ------ ------ ------ ------ ----- -------------------------- ----------
0x823c8830 System             4      0     59    403  ------      0
0x820df020 smss.exe         376      4      3     19  ------      0 2010-10-29 17:08:53 UTC+0000
0x821a2da0 csrss.exe        600    376     11    395       0      0 2010-10-29 17:08:54 UTC+0000
0x81da5650 winlogon.exe     624    376     19    570       0      0 2010-10-29 17:08:54 UTC+0000
0x82073020 services.exe     668    624     21    431       0      0 2010-10-29 17:08:54 UTC+0000
0x81e70020 lsass.exe        680    624     19    342       0      0 2010-10-29 17:08:54 UTC+0000
0x823315d8 vmacthlp.exe     844    668      1     25       0      0 2010-10-29 17:08:55 UTC+0000
0x81db8da0 svchost.exe      856    668     17    193       0      0 2010-10-29 17:08:55 UTC+0000
0x81e61da0 svchost.exe      940    668     13    312       0      0 2010-10-29 17:08:55 UTC+0000
0x822843e8 svchost.exe     1032    668     61   1169       0      0 2010-10-29 17:08:55 UTC+0000
0x81e18b28 svchost.exe     1080    668      5     80       0      0 2010-10-29 17:08:55 UTC+0000
0x81ff7020 svchost.exe     1200    668     14    197       0      0 2010-10-29 17:08:55 UTC+0000
0x81fee8b0 spoolsv.exe     1412    668     10    118       0      0 2010-10-29 17:08:56 UTC+0000
0x81e0eda0 jqs.exe         1580    668      5    148       0      0 2010-10-29 17:09:05 UTC+0000
0x81fe52d0 vmtoolsd.exe    1664    668      5    284       0      0 2010-10-29 17:09:05 UTC+0000
```

Comparing the results to those that were located in the Redline example, the two processes that were identified can be located in the following screenshot. Although these processes are here, there is little to indicate that they are suspect. This is the advantage with combining Redline with Volatility or Rekall as the analyst is able to focus immediately on suspect processes.

```
0x81c498c8 lsass.exe          868   668    2    23    0    0 2011-06-03 04:26:55 UTC+0000
0x81c47c00 lsass.exe          1928  668    4    65    0    0 2011-06-03 04:26:55 UTC+0000
```

psscan

`psscan` is a useful plugin that allows the analyst to examine processes that have been terminated. As was previously discussed, `pslist` only shows the active processes. `psscan` can provide data as to the possibility of a rootkit through the examination of those processes that have been unlinked or hidden. The following command will execute the plugin:

```
forensics@ubuntu:~/Documents$ volatility -f stuxnet.vmem --
profile=WinXPSP2x86 psscan
```

```
forensics@ubuntu:~/Documents$ volatility -f stuxnet.vmem --profile=WinXPSP2x86 psscan
Volatility Foundation Volatility Framework 2.6
Offset(P)            Name            PID    PPID PDB         Time created                  Time exited
------------------   ------------    ----   ---- ----------  ----------------------------  ----------------------------
0x0000000001e0cda0   cmd.exe         968    1664 0x0a9403a0  2011-06-03 04:31:35 UTC+0000  2011-06-03 04:31:36 UTC+0000
0x0000000001e47c00   lsass.exe       1928   668  0x0a9403c0  2011-06-03 04:26:55 UTC+0000
0x0000000001e498c8   lsass.exe       868    668  0x0a940360  2011-06-03 04:26:55 UTC+0000
0x0000000001e543a0   Procmon.exe     660    1196 0x0a940260  2011-06-03 04:25:56 UTC+0000
0x0000000001fa5650   winlogon.exe    624    376  0x0a940060  2010-10-29 17:08:54 UTC+0000
0x0000000001fb8da0   svchost.exe     856    668  0x0a9400e0  2010-10-29 17:08:55 UTC+0000
0x000000000200eda0   jqs.exe         1580   668  0x0a9401e0  2010-10-29 17:09:05 UTC+0000
0x0000000002018b28   svchost.exe     1080   668  0x0a940140  2010-10-29 17:08:55 UTC+0000
0x0000000002061da0   svchost.exe     940    668  0x0a940100  2010-10-29 17:08:55 UTC+0000
0x000000000206b660   VMwareUser.exe  1356   1196 0x0a9402e0  2010-10-29 17:11:50 UTC+0000
0x0000000002070020   lsass.exe       680    624  0x0a9400a0  2010-10-29 17:08:54 UTC+0000
0x0000000002086978   TSVNCache.exe   324    1196 0x0a940180  2010-10-29 17:11:49 UTC+0000
0x0000000002114938   ipconfig.exe    304    968  0x0a940380  2011-06-03 04:31:35 UTC+0000  2011-06-03 04:31:36 UTC+0000
0x00000000021a5390   wmiprvse.exe    1872   856  0x0a9401c0  2011-06-03 04:25:58 UTC+0000
0x00000000021c5da0   VMwareTray.exe  1912   1196 0x0a9402c0  2010-10-29 17:11:50 UTC+0000
0x00000000021e52d0   vmtoolsd.exe    1664   668  0x0a940200  2010-10-29 17:09:05 UTC+0000
```

A review of the results indicates that neither of the suspicious processes have terminated. It is helpful though to have this output handy in the event that subsequent analysis reveals an associated process to either of the suspect processes.

pstree

Often when examining system memory, it is necessary to have an understanding of what parent processes child processes are executed under. One indicator of a system being compromised is the identification of a process executed outside the normal parent process. The `pstree` plugin provides examiners a tree-like structure that identifies the parent process that is executing a potential suspect process. The Stuxnet image is run with this plugin, utilizing the following command:

```
forensics@ubuntu:~/Documents$ volatility -f stuxnet.vmem --
profile=WinXPSP2x86 pstree
```

This produces the following output:

```
forensics@ubuntu:~/Documents$ volatility -f stuxnet.vmem --profile=WinXPSP2x86 pstree
Volatility Foundation Volatility Framework 2.6
Name                               Pid    PPid   Thds   Hnds Time
-------------------------------------------------------------------------------------
0x823c8830:System                     4      0     59    403 1970-01-01 00:00:00 UTC+0000
. 0x820df020:smss.exe               376      4      3     19 2010-10-29 17:08:53 UTC+0000
.. 0x821a2da0:csrss.exe             600    376     11    395 2010-10-29 17:08:54 UTC+0000
.. 0x81da5650:winlogon.exe          624    376     19    570 2010-10-29 17:08:54 UTC+0000
... 0x82073020:services.exe         668    624     21    431 2010-10-29 17:08:54 UTC+0000
.... 0x81fe52d0:vmtoolsd.exe       1664    668      5    284 2010-10-29 17:09:05 UTC+0000
..... 0x81c0cda0:cmd.exe            968   1664      0 ------ 2011-06-03 04:31:35 UTC+0000
...... 0x81f14938:ipconfig.exe      304    968      0 ------ 2011-06-03 04:31:35 UTC+0000
.... 0x822843e8:svchost.exe        1032    668     61   1169 2010-10-29 17:08:55 UTC+0000
..... 0x822b9a10:wuauclt.exe        976   1032      3    133 2010-10-29 17:12:03 UTC+0000
..... 0x820ecc10:wscntfy.exe       2040   1032      1     28 2010-10-29 17:11:49 UTC+0000
.... 0x81e61da0:svchost.exe         940    668     13    312 2010-10-29 17:08:55 UTC+0000
.... 0x81db8da0:svchost.exe         856    668     17    193 2010-10-29 17:08:55 UTC+0000
..... 0x81fa5390:wmiprvse.exe      1872    856      5    134 2011-06-03 04:25:58 UTC+0000
.... 0x821a0568:VMUpgradeHelper    1816    668      3     96 2010-10-29 17:09:08 UTC+0000
.... 0x81fee8b0:spoolsv.exe        1412    668     10    118 2010-10-29 17:08:56 UTC+0000
.... 0x81ff7020:svchost.exe        1200    668     14    197 2010-10-29 17:08:55 UTC+0000
.... 0x81c47c00:lsass.exe          1928    668      4     65 2011-06-03 04:26:55 UTC+0000
.... 0x81e18b28:svchost.exe        1080    668      5     80 2010-10-29 17:08:55 UTC+0000
.... 0x8205ada0:alg.exe            188    668      6    107 2010-10-29 17:09:09 UTC+0000
.... 0x823315d8:vmacthlp.exe        844    668      1     25 2010-10-29 17:08:55 UTC+0000
.... 0x81e0eda0:jqs.exe           1580    668      5    148 2010-10-29 17:08:55 UTC+0000
.... 0x81c498c8:lsass.exe          868    668      2     23 2011-06-03 04:26:55 UTC+0000
.... 0x82279998:imapi.exe          756    668      4    116 2010-10-29 17:11:54 UTC+0000
... 0x81e70020:lsass.exe           680    624     19    342 2010-10-29 17:11:49 UTC+0000
0x820ec7e8:explorer.exe           1196   1728     16    582 2010-10-29 17:11:49 UTC+0000
. 0x81c543a0:Procmon.exe            660   1196     13    189 2011-06-03 04:25:56 UTC+0000
. 0x81e86978:TSVNCache.exe          324   1196      7     54 2010-10-29 17:11:49 UTC+0000
. 0x81e6b660:VMwareUser.exe        1356   1196      9    251 2010-10-29 17:11:50 UTC+0000
. 0x8210d478:jusched.exe           1712   1196      1     26 2010-10-29 17:11:50 UTC+0000
. 0x81fc5da0:VMwareTray.exe        1912   1196      1     50 2010-10-29 17:11:50 UTC+0000
```

From an examination of these results, the analyst is able to determine that the process ID (PID) 1928 has been identified as having the parent process ID (PPID) 668, which corresponds to **services.exe**. An indicator of compromise that analysts should be looking for is the execution of a process outside a normal parent process. Having a solid understanding of what processes execute under what parent will go a long way to identifying suspect processes with this method.

DLLlist

Analysts can also check the loaded DLL files associated with a process. This allows the analyst to determine if a suspect process has accessed these files when it was executed. For example, if an analyst would like to examine the DLL files associated with one of the suspect processes, PID 868, the following command is run:

```
forensics@ubuntu:~/Documents$ volatility -f stuxnet.vmem --
profile=WinXPSP2x86 -p 868 dlllist
```

```
forensics@ubuntu:~/Documents$ volatility -f stuxnet.vmem --profile=WinXPSP2x86 -p 868 dlllist
Volatility Foundation Volatility Framework 2.6
*************************************************************************
lsass.exe pid:     868
Command line : "C:\WINDOWS\\system32\\lsass.exe"
Service Pack 3

Base          Size        LoadCount LoadTime                         Path
----------   ---------   ---------- ----------------------------    ----
0x01000000    0x6000      0xffff                                     C:\WINDOWS\system32\lsass.exe
0x7c900000    0xaf000     0xffff                                     C:\WINDOWS\system32\ntdll.dll
0x7c800000    0xf6000     0xffff                                     C:\WINDOWS\system32\kernel32.dll
0x77dd0000    0x9b000     0xffff                                     C:\WINDOWS\system32\ADVAPI32.dll
0x77e70000    0x92000     0xffff                                     C:\WINDOWS\system32\RPCRT4.dll
0x77fe0000    0x11000     0xffff                                     C:\WINDOWS\system32\Secur32.dll
0x7e410000    0x91000     0xffff                                     C:\WINDOWS\system32\USER32.dll
0x77f10000    0x49000     0xffff                                     C:\WINDOWS\system32\GDI32.dll
```

The output indicates that there are several DLL files. Later on in this chapter, these DLL files will be acquired for further examination.

Handles

The handles plugin allows analysts to view what type of handles are open in an existing process. This includes a wide variety of information including registry keys and files associated with that process. To identify the open handles for the PID 868 that was previously identified, the following command is used:

```
forensics@ubuntu:~/Documents$ volatility -f stuxnet.vmem --
profile=WinXPSP2x86 -p 868 handles
```

That preceding command produces the output found in the following screenshot. As the output indicates, the suspect process has several open handle processes, threads, and a registry key.

```
forensics@ubuntu:~/Documents$ volatility -f stuxnet.vmem --profile=WinXPSP2x86 -p 868 handles
Volatility Foundation Volatility Framework 2.6
Offset(V)     Pid     Handle     Access  Type              Details
----------    -----   --------   ------- ------------      --------
0x8225b710    868       0xc      0x100020 File             \Device\HarddiskVolume1\WINDOWS\system32
0x81eddc18    868       0x7a4    0x1f03ff Thread           TID 592 PID 940
0x82083a60    868       0x7ac    0x1f0003 IoCompletion
0x81c427a8    868       0x7b0    0x1f0003 IoCompletion
0x82083a60    868       0x7b4    0x1f0003 IoCompletion
0x822bbda8    868       0x7b8    0x1f03ff Thread           TID 1884 PID 868
0x81f9eae8    868       0x7bc    0x1f0003 Event
0x81c36ef8    868       0x7c0    0x1f0003 Event
0x81c8ee00    868       0x7c4    0x1f0003 Event
0x81f6cff0    868       0x7c8    0x1f0003 Event
0x81e61da0    868       0x7cc    0x1f0fff Process          svchost.exe(940)
0x822bbda8    868       0x7d0    0x1f03ff Thread           TID 1884 PID 868
0x81d9c670    868       0x7d4    0xf016e WindowStation     Service-0x0-3e7$
0x822563f0    868       0x7d8    0xf00cf Desktop           Default
0x81d9c670    868       0x7dc    0xf016e WindowStation     Service-0x0-3e7$
0x821a4678    868       0x7e0   0x21f0003 Event
0xe2a6e830    868       0x7e4   0x20f003f Key              MACHINE
0x81c68458    868       0x7e8    0x1f0003 Semaphore
0xe2b19ae0    868       0x7ec   0x21f0001 Port
0xe1613978    868       0x7f0    0xf000f Directory         Windows
0x81fb0a88    868       0x7f4    0x100003 Semaphore
0xe16008f8    868       0x7f8    0x3 Directory            KnownDlls
0xe10096e0    868       0x7fc    0xf0003 KeyedEvent        CritSecOutOfMemoryEvent
```

svcscan

The `svcscan` plugin allows the analyst to list out the services running. This plugin gives more detail to the running processes in the event that the analyst requires additional details such as the display name, binary path, or service type. The following command will list the processes:

```
forensics@ubuntu:~/Documents$ volatility -f stuxnet.vmem --
profile=WinXPSP2x86 svcscan
```

The abridged output is shown in the following screenshot. As can be seen, the output provides a great deal more information concerning the active processes than the `pslist` plugin:

```
Offset: 0x38afa0
Order: 259
Start: SERVICE_AUTO_START
Process ID: 1032
Service Name: winmgmt
Display Name: Windows Management Instrumentation
Service Type: SERVICE_WIN32_SHARE_PROCESS
Service State: SERVICE_RUNNING
Binary Path: C:\WINDOWS\System32\svchost.exe -k netsvcs

Offset: 0x38b030
Order: 260
Start: SERVICE_DEMAND_START
Process ID: -
Service Name: WmdmPmSN
Display Name: Portable Media Serial Number Service
Service Type: SERVICE_WIN32_SHARE_PROCESS
Service State: SERVICE_STOPPED
Binary Path: -

Offset: 0x38b0c0
Order: 261
Start: SERVICE_DEMAND_START
Process ID: -
Service Name: Wmi
Display Name: Windows Management Instrumentation Driver Extensions
Service Type: SERVICE_WIN32_SHARE_PROCESS
Service State: SERVICE_STOPPED
Binary Path: -
```

netscan and sockets

As was discussed previously, incident response analysts may have identified a potentially compromised host through an alert or review for a network-based system such as a firewall or proxy server. In the event that this is the case, the analyst may be able to include or exclude a system as potentially compromised by gaining insight into the current network connections.

The plugin netscan scans the memory image for network artifacts. The plugin will find TCP and UDP endpoints and listeners as well as provide the local and foreign IP address. netscan will only work with 32- and 64-bit Windows Vista, Windows 7, and Windows 2008 Server. One key feature that is of help to incident response analysts with the netscan plugin is that for the network connections, the process owner is indicated in the output. This is useful in determining if a connection is utilizing Internet Explorer or another process such as Remote Desktop Services or SMB.

For the older Windows XP and Windows 2003 Server, the `sockscan` plugin can be utilized. This plugin produces less information than netscan, but does provide the connections found within the memory image. For example, to run the plugin against the Stuxnet memory images, utilize the following command:

```
forensics@ubuntu:~/Documents$ volatility -f stuxnet.vmem --
profile=WinXPSP2x86 sockscan
```

The command produces the following output:

```
forensics@ubuntu:~/Documents$ volatility -f stuxnet.vmem --profile=WinXPSP2x86 sockscan
Volatility Foundation Volatility Framework 2.6
Offset(P)      PID    Port  Proto Protocol        Address          Create Time
---------- -------- ------ ------ --------------- ---------------- ----------
0x01e20898    1200   1900     17 UDP             127.0.0.1        2011-06-03 04:25:47 UTC+0000
0x01e79778    1080   1142     17 UDP             0.0.0.0          2010-10-31 16:36:16 UTC+0000
0x01eb3d70    1080   1141     17 UDP             0.0.0.0          2010-10-31 16:36:16 UTC+0000
0x01eb9e98    1580   5152      6 TCP             127.0.0.1        2010-10-29 17:09:05 UTC+0000
0x01fa4d18     680      0    255 Reserved        0.0.0.0          2010-10-29 17:09:05 UTC+0000
0x01fa54b0       4    445     17 UDP             0.0.0.0          2010-10-29 17:08:53 UTC+0000
0x01fc2008     680    500     17 UDP             0.0.0.0          2010-10-29 17:09:05 UTC+0000
0x021dbe98    1032    123     17 UDP             127.0.0.1        2011-06-03 04:25:47 UTC+0000
0x02260008     680   4500     17 UDP             0.0.0.0          2010-10-29 17:09:05 UTC+0000
0x02261c08       4    445      6 TCP             0.0.0.0          2010-10-29 17:08:53 UTC+0000
0x023a5008     188   1025      6 TCP             127.0.0.1        2010-10-29 17:09:09 UTC+0000
0x02494aa8     940    135      6 TCP             0.0.0.0          2010-10-29 17:08:55 UTC+0000
```

From here, the analyst can see what connections are open, the process they are tied to, and what time the connection was created. This is useful information taken in conjunction with data from network-based sources such as packet captures or firewall logs.

LDR modules

A common practice with malware coders is attempting to hide the activities of the malware. One technique is to attempt to hide the DLL files associated with the malicious code. This can be accomplished by unlinking the suspect DLL from the **ProcessEnvironmentBlock** (**PEB**). While this may provide some obfuscation on the surface, there is still trace evidence of the DLLs existence, contained within the **VirtualAddressDescriptor** (**VAD**). The VAD is a mechanism that identifies a DLL file's base address and full path. The `ldrmodules` plugin compares the list of processes and determines if they are in the PEB. The following command runs the `ldrmodules` against the image file:

```
forensics@ubuntu:~/Documents$ volatility -f stuxnet.vmem --
profile=WinXPSP2x86 -p 868 ldrmodules
```

The command produces the output found in the following screenshot:

```
forensics@ubuntu:~/Documents$ volatility -f stuxnet.vmem --profile=WinXPSP2x86 -p 868 ldrmodules
Volatility Foundation Volatility Framework 2.6
Pid      Process              Base         InLoad InInit InMem MappedPath
-------- -------------------- ------------ ------ ------ ----- ----------
     868 lsass.exe            0x00080000 False  False  False
     868 lsass.exe            0x7c900000 True   True   True  \WINDOWS\system32\ntdll.dll
     868 lsass.exe            0x77e70000 True   True   True  \WINDOWS\system32\rpcrt4.dll
     868 lsass.exe            0x7c800000 True   True   True  \WINDOWS\system32\kernel32.dll
     868 lsass.exe            0x77fe0000 True   True   True  \WINDOWS\system32\secur32.dll
     868 lsass.exe            0x7e410000 True   True   True  \WINDOWS\system32\user32.dll
     868 lsass.exe            0x01000000 True   False  True
     868 lsass.exe            0x77f10000 True   True   True  \WINDOWS\system32\gdi32.dll
     868 lsass.exe            0x77dd0000 True   True   True  \WINDOWS\system32\advapi32.dll
```

From this output, the **lsass.exe** process does have an issue with the associated processes where there is no DLL file, but the file does not appear in the PEB under the **InInit** column for both the first and seventh entry. This is further evidence that the process is suspect and requires further investigation.

psxview

Another good plugin that aids in discovering hidden processes is the `psxview` plugin. This plugin compares the active processes indicated within `psActiveProcessHead` with any other possible sources within the memory image. To run the plugin, type the following command:

```
forensics@ubuntu:~/Documents$ volatility -f stuxnet.vmem --
profile=WinXPSP2x86 psxview
```

The command produces the following output:

```
forensics@ubuntu:~/Documents$ volatility -f stuxnet.vmem --profile=WinXPSP2x86 psxview
Volatility Foundation Volatility Framework 2.6
Offset(P)  Name                  PID pslist psscan thrdproc pspcid csrss session deskthrd ExitTime
---------- --------------------- --- ------ ------ -------- ------ ----- ------- -------- --------
0x01e47c00 lsass.exe            1928 True   True   True     True   True  True    True
0x021a5390 wmiprvse.exe         1872 True   True   True     True   True  True    True
0x021c5da0 VMwareTray.exe       1912 True   True   True     True   True  True    True
0x02479998 imapi.exe             756 True   True   True     True   True  True    True
0x02273020 services.exe          668 True   True   True     True   True  True    True
0x02018b28 svchost.exe          1080 True   True   True     True   True  True    True
0x021ee8b0 spoolsv.exe          1412 True   True   True     True   True  True    True
0x02061da0 svchost.exe           940 True   True   True     True   True  True    True
0x024b9a10 wuauclt.exe           976 True   True   True     True   True  True    True
0x0200eda0 jqs.exe              1580 True   True   True     True   True  True    True
0x021f7020 svchost.exe          1200 True   True   True     True   True  True    True
0x01e543a0 Procmon.exe           660 True   True   True     True   True  True    True
0x022ecc10 wscntfy.exe          2040 True   True   True     True   True  True    True
0x02070020 lsass.exe             680 True   True   True     True   True  True    True
0x01e498c8 lsass.exe             868 True   True   True     True   True  True    True
0x01fa5650 winlogon.exe          624 True   True   True     True   True  True    True
0x0230d478 jusched.exe          1712 True   True   True     True   True  True    True
0x025315d8 vmacthlp.exe          844 True   True   True     True   True  True    True
0x0206b660 VMwareUser.exe       1356 True   True   True     True   True  True    True
0x021e52d0 vmtoolsd.exe         1664 True   True   True     True   True  True    True
0x01fb8da0 svchost.exe           856 True   True   True     True   True  True    True
0x024843e8 svchost.exe          1032 True   True   True     True   True  True    True
0x0225ada0 alg.exe               188 True   True   True     True   True  True    True
0x023a0568 VMUpgradeHelper      1816 True   True   True     True   True  True    True
0x022ec7e8 explorer.exe         1196 True   True   True     True   True  True    True
0x02086978 TSVNCache.exe         324 True   True   True     True   True  True    True
0x025c8830 System                  4 True   True   True     True   False False   False    2011-06-03 04:31:36 UTC+0000
0x02114938 ipconfig.exe          304 True   True   False    True   False False   False
0x023a2da0 csrss.exe             600 True   True   True     True   False False   True
0x022df020 smss.exe              376 True   True   True     True   False False   False
0x01e0cda0 cmd.exe               968 True   True   False    True   False False   False    2011-06-03 04:31:36 UTC+0000
```

A **False** within the column indicates that the process is not found in that area. This allows the analyst to review that list and determine if there is a legitimate reason that the process may not be there, or if it is indicative of an attempt to hide the process.

Dlldump

In the event that an analyst is able to identify a suspect process within the memory image, the plugin **dlldump** can be utilized to dump the contents of those DLL files to the local system. This allows the analysts to examine the contents of the DLL files as well as compare them to legitimate files to determine if they are malicious. For example, the process **lsass.exe** with the PID of 868 was identified as potentially malicious in several sections of this chapter. To acquire the DLL files and have them accessible to the local system, type the following:

```
forensics@ubuntu:~/Documents$ sudo volatility -f stuxnet.vmem --
profile=WinXPSP2x86 -p 868 dlldump --dump-dir /home/
```

The command produces the following output:

```
forensics@ubuntu:~/Documents$ sudo volatility -f stuxnet.vmem --profile=WinXPSP2x86 -p 868 dlldump --dump-dir /home/
[sudo] password for forensics:
Volatility Foundation Volatility Framework 2.6
Process(V) Name                 Module Base Module Name           Result
---------- -------------------- ----------- --------------------- ------
0x81c498c8 lsass.exe            0x001000000 lsass.exe             OK: module.868.1e498c8.1000000.dll
0x81c498c8 lsass.exe            0x07c900000 ntdll.dll             OK: module.868.1e498c8.7c900000.dll
0x81c498c8 lsass.exe            0x077e70000 RPCRT4.dll            OK: module.868.1e498c8.77e70000.dll
0x81c498c8 lsass.exe            0x077f10000 GDI32.dll             OK: module.868.1e498c8.77f10000.dll
0x81c498c8 lsass.exe            0x077dd0000 ADVAPI32.dll          OK: module.868.1e498c8.77dd0000.dll
0x81c498c8 lsass.exe            0x07c800000 kernel32.dll          OK: module.868.1e498c8.7c800000.dll
0x81c498c8 lsass.exe            0x07e410000 USER32.dll            OK: module.868.1e498c8.7e410000.dll
0x81c498c8 lsass.exe            0x077fe0000 Secur32.dll           OK: module.868.1e498c8.77fe0000.dll
```

In this case, elevated privileges may be necessary to write the files onto the local system, hence the use of **sudo** in the command. The **--dump-dir /home/** command points to the directory that Volatility should place the DLL files. An examination of that location reveals the following:

```
forensics@ubuntu:/home$ ls
forensics                            module.868.1e498c8.77fe0000.dll
module.868.1e498c8.1000000.dll       module.868.1e498c8.7c800000.dll
module.868.1e498c8.77dd0000.dll      module.868.1e498c8.7c900000.dll
module.868.1e498c8.77e70000.dll      module.868.1e498c8.7e410000.dll
module.868.1e498c8.77f10000.dll
```

From here, the analyst can analyze the DLL files utilizing a PE examination tool. For example, the DLL **module.868.1e498c8.7c800000.dll** that was part of the dump was examined utilizing the tool **PeStudio 8.60**. PeStudio is designed to identify artifacts within the files, such as DLL and other PE files, indicative of malicious software and is freely available at https://www.winitor.com/index.html. When the DLL file is examined, there are several indications that the file is malicious:

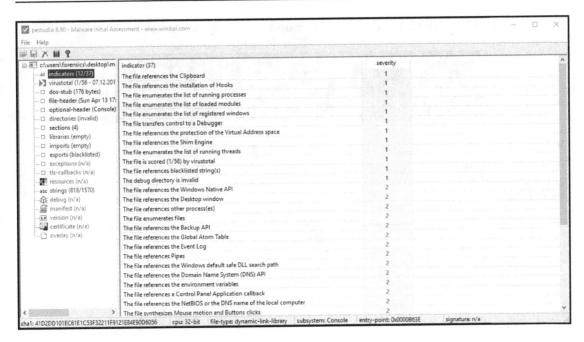

From this cursory examination, it is evident that there are a number of different elements indicating that this DLL is malicious. In a future chapter, there will be a detailed treatment of some of the methods available for reviewing malicious software.

memdump

During the course of the analysis it may become necessary to dump the memory resident pages associated with a process. In this case, the memdump plugin is run against the memory image, with the output directed to the home folder, utilizing the following command:

```
forensics@ubuntu:~/Documents$ sudo volatility -f stuxnet.vmem --
profile=WinXPSP2x86 -p 868 memdump--dump-dir /home/
```

Volatility will indicate the progress of the dump:

```
forensics@ubuntu:~/Documents$ sudo volatility -f stuxnet.vmem --profile=WinXPSP2x86 -p 868 memdump  --dump-dir /home/
Volatility Foundation Volatility Framework 2.6
************************************************************
Writing lsass.exe [   868] to 868.dmp
```

Once the plugin is finished, the dump file is found within the home folder:

```
forensics@ubuntu:/home$ ls
868.dmp                        module.868.1e498c8.77f10000.dll
forensics                      module.868.1e498c8.77fe0000.dll
module.868.1e498c8.1000000.dll module.868.1e498c8.7c800000.dll
module.868.1e498c8.77dd0000.dll module.868.1e498c8.7c900000.dll
module.868.1e498c8.77e70000.dll module.868.1e498c8.7e410000.dll
```

Once the dump is complete, the file can then be viewed utilizing a hex editor such as **HexEditorNeo** (available at `https://www.hhdsoftware.com/free-hex-editor`). This allows for the detailed examination of the file, as well as performing string searches for such elements as IP addresses.

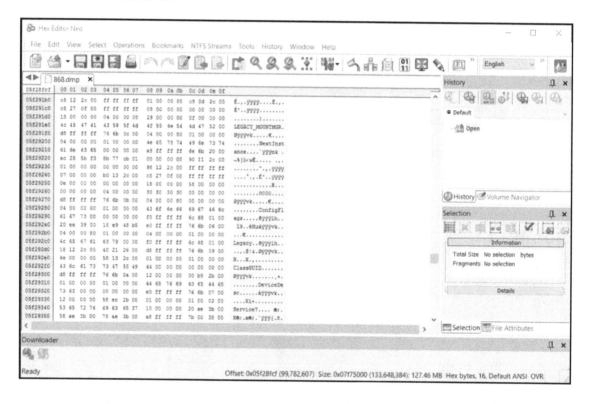

procdump

A review of the results from a variety of sources has indicated that the process 868 and the associated executable `lsass.exe` are suspected of containing malware. While the data thus far is very useful, it is often necessary to obtain confirmation from external sources that the executable in question is malicious. This can include something as simple as checking the hash of the executable against third-party sources all the way to forwarding the executable to a malware reverse engineering team.

To acquire the executable from the memory image, utilize the `procdump` plugin. The following command will dump the executable to the `home` folder:

```
forensics@ubuntu:~/Documents$ sudo volatility -f stuxnet.vmem --
profile=WinXPSP2x86 -p 868 procdump--dump-dir /home/
```

 Great care should be taken in regards to utilizing plugins such as dlldump or procdump. If the file is indeed malicious, it has the potential to infect the system utilized to acquire it. It is highly recommended that this procedure be conducted on a virtualization platform or other isolation technique to ensure that the executable does not infect the analysis system.

Once dumped, the executable can then be evaluated. In this case, the `lsass.exe` file was uploaded to the virustotal.com site to see if there was an indication that it was malicious:

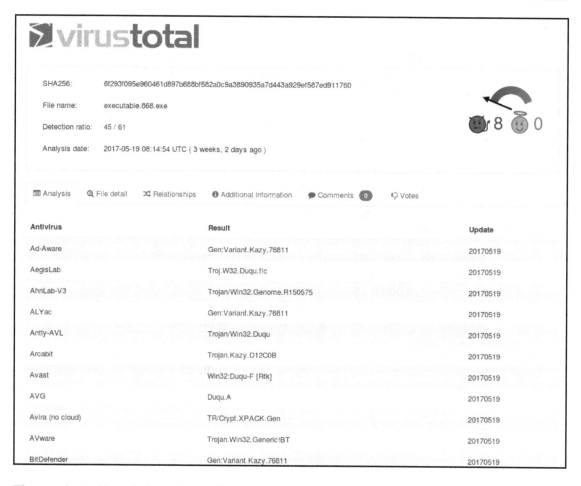

The results indicated that 45 out of 61 anti-virus provider sites view this as malicious code. This is a strong indicator that the executable is malicious software.

Rekall

Another platform that is similar to Volatility is Rekall. Rekall was developed by Google and purports to be the most complete memory analysis framework. The software is available for Linux, macOS, and Windows platforms. Instructions on how to download and set up Rekall can be found at https://github.com/google/rekall/releases. The one major advantage that Rekall has over Volatility is that Google has also released the memory acquisition tool Pmem. This tool is designed to work with the Rekall framework giving a single point for the acquisition and analysis toolset.

Rekall has some deep similarities with Volatility. For example, there are a number of plugins that are similarly named and that perform very similar functions(the site `http://www.rekall-forensic.com/docs/Manual/Plugins/` has a complete list of these plugins). To configure an analysis utilizing Rekall, first install on the appropriate operating system, in this case, Rekall will be run on a Windows 10 system. Navigate to the folder where the `Rekall.exe` program is located. From there, load the image that is to be analyzed utilizing the following command:

```
C:\Program Files\Rekall>rekal.exe -f \Images\stuxnet.vmem
```

Unlike Volatility, this command essentially loads the image file so that the analyst does not keep having to point Rekall to its location. Once the command is run, the following output appears:

```
C:\Program Files\Rekall>rekal.exe -f \Images\stuxnet.vmem

-------------------------------------------------------------
The Rekall Digital Forensic/Incident Response framework 1.6.0 (Gotthard).

"We can remember it for you wholesale!"

This program is free software; you can redistribute it and/or modify it under
the terms of the GNU General Public License.

See http://www.rekall-forensic.com/docs/Manual/tutorial.html to get started.
-------------------------------------------------------------
[1] stuxnet.vmem 18:14:11>
```

The output includes a new prompt from which the plugins and other analysis tasks are run. To run a plugin, the analyst needs only to type the plugin into the prompt and hit Enter.

imageinfo

The `imageinfo` plugin performs a similar operation to the Volatility plugin, as well as providing the same information.

```
[1] stuxnet.vmem 18:15:22> imageinfo
-------------------------> imageinfo()
        key             value
-------------------     -----
Kernel DTB              0x319000
NT Build                2600.xpsp.080413-2111
NT Build Ex             -
Signed Drivers          -
Time (UTC)              2011-06-03 04:31:36Z
Time (Local)            2011-06-03 00:31:36-0400
Sec Since Boot          56949.578125
NtSystemRoot            C:\WINDOWS
Out 18:15:24> Plugin: imageinfo (ImageInfo)
```

pslist

The pslist plugin also performs the same type of analysis as Volatility. This includes the process name, process ID, and parent process ID.

```
[1] stuxnet.vmem 18:36:42> pslist
                         > pslist()
_EPROCESS            name        pid   ppid  thread_count handle_count session_id wow64     process_create_time       process_exit_time
------------------------------- ----- ----- ------------ ------------ ---------- ------- -----------------------  -----------------------
0x823c8830 System              4     0            59          403          - False  -
0x8205ada0 alg.exe            188   668             6          107          0 False  2010-10-29 17:09:09Z     -
0x81f14938 ipconfig.exe       304   968             0            -          0 False  2011-06-03 04:31:35Z     2011-06-03 04:31:36Z
0x81e86978 TSVNCache.exe      324  1196             7           54          0 False  2010-10-29 17:11:49Z     -
0x820df020 smss.exe           376     4             3           19          - False  2010-10-29 17:08:53Z     -
0x821a2da0 csrss.exe          600   376            11          395          0 False  2010-10-29 17:08:54Z     -
0x81da5650 winlogon.exe       624   376            19          570          0 False  2010-10-29 17:08:54Z     -
0x81c543a0 Procmon.exe        660  1196            13          189          0 False  2011-06-03 04:25:56Z     -
0x82073020 services.exe       668   624            21          431          0 False  2010-10-29 17:08:54Z     -
0x81e70020 lsass.exe          680   624            19          342          0 False  2010-10-29 17:08:54Z     -
0x82279998 imapi.exe          756   668             4          116          0 False  2010-10-29 17:11:54Z     -
0x823315d8 vmacthlp.exe       844   668             1           25          0 False  2010-10-29 17:08:55Z     -
0x81db8da0 svchost.exe        856   668            17          193          0 False  2010-10-29 17:08:55Z     -
0x81c498c8 lsass.exe          868   668             2           23          0 False  2011-06-03 04:26:55Z     -
0x81e61da0 svchost.exe        940   668            13          312          0 False  2010-10-29 17:08:55Z     -
0x81c0cda0 cmd.exe            968  1664             0            -          0 False  2011-06-03 04:31:35Z     2011-06-03 04:31:36Z
0x822b9a10 wuauclt.exe        976  1032             3          133          0 False  2010-10-29 17:12:03Z     -
0x822843e8 svchost.exe       1032   668            61         1169          0 False  2010-10-29 17:08:55Z     -
0x81e18b28 svchost.exe       1080   668             5           80          0 False  2010-10-29 17:08:55Z     -
0x820ec7e8 explorer.exe      1196  1728            16          582          0 False  2010-10-29 17:11:49Z     -
0x81ff7020 svchost.exe       1200   668            14          197          0 False  2010-10-29 17:08:55Z     -
0x81e6b660 VMwareUser.exe    1356  1196             9          251          0 False  2010-10-29 17:11:50Z     -
0x81fee8b0 spoolsv.exe       1412   668            10          118          0 False  2010-10-29 17:08:56Z     -
0x81e0eda0 jqs.exe           1580   668             5          148          0 False  2010-10-29 17:09:05Z     -
0x81fe52d0 vmtoolsd.exe      1664   668             5          284          0 False  2010-10-29 17:09:05Z     -
0x8210d478 jusched.exe       1712  1196             1           26          0 False  2010-10-29 17:11:50Z     -
0x821a0568 VMUpgradeHelper   1816   668             3           96          0 False  2010-10-29 17:09:08Z     -
0x81fa5390 wmiprvse.exe      1872   856             5          134          0 False  2011-06-03 04:25:58Z     -
0x81fc5da0 VMwareTray.exe    1912  1196             1           50          0 False  2010-10-29 17:11:50Z     -
0x81c47c00 lsass.exe         1928   668             4           65          0 False  2011-06-03 04:26:55Z     -
0x820ecc10 wscntfy.exe       2040  1032             1           28          0 False  2010-10-29 17:11:49Z     -
    18:36:43> Plugin: pslist (WinPsList)
```

Event logs

`evtlogs` is a plugin available for the Windows XP and Windows 2003 server operating systems. This plugin is able to extract and parse out the event logs that are currently in memory. Event logs in memory sometimes have evidentiary value, as they may indicate specific actions taken by the system during or after a compromise.

```
[1] stuxnet.vmem 18:35:13> evtlogs
                         > evtlogs()
TimeWritten Filename Computer Sid Source Event Id Event Type Message
2010-08-22 17:34:29Z AppEvent.Evt JAN-DF663B3DBF1 S-82-1442861056 LoadPerf 1000     Info      'RSVP';'QoS RSVP'
2010-08-22 17:34:42Z AppEvent.Evt JAN-DF663B3DBF1 S-80-1660971008 LoadPerf 1000     Info      'PSched';'PSched'
2010-08-22 17:34:44Z AppEvent.Evt JAN-DF663B3DBF1 S-82-1828744960 LoadPerf 1000     Info      'RemoteAccess';'Routing and Remote Access'
2010-08-22 17:34:56Z AppEvent.Evt JAN-DF663B3DBF1 S-84-1912630528 LoadPerf 1000     Info      'TermService';'Terminal Services'
2010-08-22 17:34:57Z AppEvent.Evt JAN-DF663B3DBF1 S-77-1140872192 LoadPerf 1000     Info      'MSDTC';'MSDTC'
2010-08-22 17:34:57Z AppEvent.Evt JAN-DF663B3DBF1 S-0-1811939328 MSDTC    4104     Info
2010-08-22 17:34:57Z AppEvent.Evt JAN-DF663B3DBF1 S-48-805306368 MSDTC    2444     Info      '0';'0';'0';'0';'0';'0'
2010-08-22 17:35:05Z AppEvent.Evt JAN-DF663B3DBF1 S-87-1761624320 LoadPerf 1000     Info      'WmiApRpl';'WmiApRpl'
2010-08-22 17:35:05Z AppEvent.Evt JAN-DF663B3DBF1 S-87-1761624320 LoadPerf 1001     Info      'WmiApRpl';'WmiApRpl'
2010-08-22 17:35:05Z AppEvent.Evt JAN-DF663B3DBF1 S-87-1761624320 LoadPerf 1000     Info      'WmiApRpl';'WmiApRpl'
2010-08-22 17:35:08Z AppEvent.Evt JAN-DF663B3DBF1 S-1-5-18 WinMgmt 63       Warning   'HiPerfCooker_v1';'Root\\WMI'
2010-08-22 17:35:09Z AppEvent.Evt JAN-DF663B3DBF1 S-1-5-18 WinMgmt 63       Warning   'CmdTriggerConsumer';'Root\\cimv2'
2010-08-22 17:35:09Z AppEvent.Evt JAN-DF663B3DBF1 S-1-5-18 WinMgmt 63       Warning   'CmdTriggerConsumer';'Root\\cimv2'
2010-08-22 17:35:09Z AppEvent.Evt JAN-DF663B3DBF1 S-1-5-18 WinMgmt 5603     Warning   'Rsop Planning Mode Provider';'root\\RSOP'
2010-08-22 17:35:09Z AppEvent.Evt JAN-DF663B3DBF1 S-1-5-18 WinMgmt 5603     Warning   'Rsop Planning Mode Provider';'root\\RSOP'
2010-08-22 17:35:10Z AppEvent.Evt JAN-DF663B3DBF1 S-67-1845523456 LoadPerf 1000     Info      'ContentIndex';'ContentIndex'
2010-08-22 17:35:10Z AppEvent.Evt JAN-DF663B3DBF1 S-67-1845523456 LoadPerf 1000     Info      'ContentFilter';'ContentFilter'
2010-08-22 17:35:10Z AppEvent.Evt JAN-DF663B3DBF1 S-73-1090539520 LoadPerf 1000     Info      'ISAPISearch';'ISAPISearch'
2010-08-22 17:36:01Z AppEvent.Evt JAN-DF663B3DBF1 S-1-5-18 WinMgmt 5603     Warning   'Rsop Planning Mode Provider';'root\\RSOP'
2010-08-22 17:36:01Z AppEvent.Evt JAN-DF663B3DBF1 S-1-5-18 WinMgmt 5603     Warning   'Rsop Planning Mode Provider';'root\\RSOP'
2010-08-22 17:36:02Z AppEvent.Evt JAN-DF663B3DBF1 S-70-1912632064 COM+     4156     Info      'First attempt to CoCreateInstance(CLSID_ComSystemAppEventData) failed!'
2010-08-22 17:36:02Z AppEvent.Evt JAN-DF663B3DBF1 S-82-1828744960 COM+     4156     Info      'Remove old EventClass(CLSID_ComSystemAppEventData) from event system!.'
```

Sockets

Much like Volatility, Rekall has the ability to parse the memory image for network connections. The Rekall plugin sockets allow analysts to view any active connections.

```
[1] stuxnet.vmem 18:39:07> sockets
                        > sockets()
 offset_v     pid    port   proto    protocol      address          create_time
------------ ------ ------ ------- ------------ ---------------- ---------------
0x81dc2008    680    500     17 UDP           0.0.0.0          2010-10-29 17:09:05Z
0x82061c08      4    445      6 TCP           0.0.0.0          2010-10-29 17:08:53Z
0x82294aa8    940    135      6 TCP           0.0.0.0          2010-10-29 17:08:55Z
0x821a5008    188   1025      6 TCP           127.0.0.1        2010-10-29 17:09:09Z
0x81cb3d70   1080   1141     17 UDP           0.0.0.0          2010-10-31 16:36:16Z
0x81da4d18    680      0    255 Reserved      0.0.0.0          2010-10-29 17:09:05Z
0x81fdbe98   1032    123     17 UDP           127.0.0.1        2011-06-03 04:25:47Z
0x81c79778   1080   1142     17 UDP           0.0.0.0          2010-10-31 16:36:16Z
0x81c20898   1200   1900     17 UDP           127.0.0.1        2011-06-03 04:25:47Z
0x82060008    680   4500     17 UDP           0.0.0.0          2010-10-29 17:09:05Z
0x81cb9e98   1580   5152      6 TCP           127.0.0.1        2010-10-29 17:09:05Z
0x81da54b0      4    445     17 UDP           0.0.0.0          2010-10-29 17:08:53Z
   18:39:08  Plugin: sockets (Sockets)
```

Malfind

The `malfind` plugin assists analysts with finding injected code or DLLs. To run this plugin on a specific PID, such as the `lsass.exe` process 868, the following command should be run:

```
[1] stuxnet.vmem 18:42:56>malfind proc_regex=lsass.exe
```

The preceding command produces the following abridged output:

```
[1] stuxnet.vmem 18:42:56> malfind proc_regex="lsass.exe"
                        > malfind(proc_regex="lsass.exe")
******************************************* of pid 680
Process: lsass.exe Pid: 868 Address: 0x80000
EXECUTE_READWRITEtection:
Protection: 6

0x80000 4d 5a 90 00 03 00 00 00 04 00 00 00 ff ff 00 00   MZ.............. vad_0x80000
0x80010 b8 00 00 00 00 00 00 00 40 00 00 00 00 00 00 00   ........@.......
0x80020 00 00 00 00 00 00 00 00 00 00 00 00 00 00 00 00   ................
0x80030 00 00 00 00 00 00 00 00 00 00 00 00 08 01 00 00   ................

------ vad_0x80000 ------: 0x80000
  0x80000   0x0 4d              dec ebp
  0x80001   0x1 5a              pop edx
  0x80002   0x2 90              nop
  0x80003   0x3 0003            add byte ptr [ebx], al
  0x80005   0x5 0000            add byte ptr [eax], al
  0x80007   0x7 000400          add byte ptr [eax + eax], al
  0x8000a   0xa 0000            add byte ptr [eax], al
  0x8000c   0xc ff              .byte 0xff
  0x8000d   0xd ff00            inc dword ptr [eax]
  0x8000f   0xf 00b800000000    add byte ptr [eax], bh
  0x80015   0x15 0000           add byte ptr [eax], al
  0x80017   0x17 004000         add byte ptr [eax], al
  0x8001a   0x1a 0000           add byte ptr [eax], al
  0x8001c   0x1c 0000           add byte ptr [eax], al
  0x8001e   0x1e 0000           add byte ptr [eax], al
  0x80020   0x20 0000           add byte ptr [eax], al
  0x80022   0x22 0000           add byte ptr [eax], al
  0x80024   0x24 0000           add byte ptr [eax], al
```

The malfind plugin parses through the associated DLLs and other files. In the preceding example, there is an executable associated with the process starting at the memory segment **0x800000**. This provides analysts with a starting point for evaluating what actions in memory the PID and associated executables are performing.

Summary

Several tools, such as Redline, Rekall, and Volatility, have been explored. In addition to an overview of these tools, several of their features have been explored. This really only scratches the surface of the number of features each of these tools has to offer the incident response analyst. These tools, taken in conjunction with a methodology for analyzing system RAM, can give the analyst a powerful tool for determining if there is a compromise to a system. With malware becoming more advanced, including malware that executes entirely in RAM, it is critical that analysts incorporate memory analysis into their capability. Marrying these techniques with network evidence collection can provide analysts and their organization with a powerful tool to identify and remediate an incident. In Chapter 8, *Analyzing System Storage*, the analysis will move from the volatile evidence captured to examining the system's hard drive. Here, an analyst can gain more insight into the events surrounding an incident.

8
Analyzing System Storage

So far, the evidence that has been analyzed has focused on those elements that are obtained from the network or the system's memory. Even though incident root cause may be ferreted out from these evidence sources, it is also important to understand how to obtain evidentiary material from a system's storage, whether that is removable storage such as USB devices or the larger connected disk drives. In these containers is a good deal of data that may be leveraged by incident response analysts in determining root cause. It should be noted that this chapter will only be able to scratch the surface, as entire volumes have been devoted to the depth of forensic evidence available. Rather, it is hoped that this chapter provides some concrete areas of focus with the understanding that analysts will gain a better sense of some of the tools that can be employed, as well as an understanding of some of the critical data that can be leveraged.

Forensic platforms

Over the past 15 years, there has been an increase in the power of disk forensic platforms. For the incident response analyst, there are options as to what type of platform can be leveraged for conducting an examination of the disk drives. Often, the limiting factor in utilizing these platforms is the cost of more robust systems, when a lower cost alternative will be just as effective for an incident response team.

There are several factors that should be addressed when examining software for disk analysis. First, has the platform been tested? There are several organizations that test platforms for efficacy, such as the National Institute of Standards and Technology Computer Forensic Tools Testing Program (https://www.cftt.nist.gov/). Second is an examination of the tool's use in criminal and civil proceedings. There is no single court-accepted standard but tools should conform to the rules of evidence. The use of a platform that has not been tested or does not conform to the rules of evidence may lead to the evidence being excluded from the legal proceedings. In other, more disastrous consequences, it may lead an analyst to arrive at the wrong conclusion.

An example of an untested and forensically unsound toolset that was used in a criminal proceeding was in the case of **The State of Connecticut** vs. **Amero**. In that case, a law enforcement agency utilized unsound forensic methods and tools to convict a woman for allegedly allowing children to see sexual explicit pop-up ads. A subsequent review of the methods and facts of the case indicated that there were a number of problems with the forensic examination. An excellent examination of this case is available from the Journal of Digital Forensics, Security and Law at http://ojs.jdfsl.org/index.php/jdfsl/article/viewFile/120/5.

One final consideration is how the tool fits into the overall incident response plan at the organization. For example, commercial disk forensic tools are excellent at locating images and web artifacts. They are also excellent at carving out data from the suspect drive. This is often due to the fact that forensic software is utilized by law enforcement agencies as a tool to investigate child exploitation cases. As a result, this capability is paramount to bringing a criminal case against such suspects. While these are excellent capabilities to have, incident response analysts may be more interested in tools that can be utilized for keyword searches and timeline analysis, so that they can reconstruct a series of events prior to, during, and after, an incident.

While most commercial and free forensic platforms have a variety features, there are several common ones that can be of use to incident response analysts:

- **File structure view**: It is often very important to be able to view the file structure of the disk under examination. Forensic platforms should have the ability to view the file structure and allow for analysts to quickly review files with known locations on a suspect system.
- **Hex viewer**: Having the ability to view files in hexadecimal allows analysts to have a granular look at the files under examination. This may be beneficial in cases involving malware or other custom exploits.

- **Web artifacts**: With a great deal of data stored on the drive associated with web searching, forensic platforms should have the ability to examine these pieces of data. This is very handy when examining social engineering attacks where users navigate to a malicious website.

- **Email carving**: Incident responders may be called into cases where malicious employees are involved in illegal activities or have committed policy violations. Often, evidence of this type of conduct is contained within emails on the suspect system.Having a platform that can pull this data out for immediate view, assists the analyst to view communications between the suspect system and others.

- **Image viewer**: Often it is necessary to view the images saved on systems. As was stated previously, law enforcement utilizes this feature to determine if there is evidence of child exploitation on a system. Incident response analysts can utilize these features to determine if there has been a policy violation.

- **Metadata**: Key pieces of data about files such as date and time created, file hashes and location of a suspect file on the disk are useful when examining a system associated with an incident. For example, the time an application is run, taken in conjunction with a piece of malware, may be correlated with network activity allowing the analyst to determine the actual executable run.

In terms of commercial options, the following three platforms are generally accepted as sound and are in use by commercial and government entities all over the world. Each of these have the features described among other more specialized tools.

- **EnCase guidance software**: Arguably the preeminent forensics platform, EnCase has a long history with the platform being used in major criminal investigations such as the BTK Killer. EnCase is a feature-rich platform that makes it a powerful tool in the hands of a trained analyst.In addition to disk forensics, EnCase also has integrated features for mobile devices. This is a powerful capability for organizations that may have to analyze not only disks, but also mobile devices, in connection with an incident.

- **Forensic Took Kit by Access Data**: In `Chapter 5`, *Understanding Forensic Imaging,* the FTK Imager tool was utilized to acquire disk and memory evidence. This tool is part of a suite of tools provided by Access Data specifically tailored to disk forensics.In addition to the imager, Access Data has a fully featured forensic platform that allows analysts to perform the range of tasks associated with an incident. FTK is in use by law enforcement agencies such as the **Federal Bureau of Investigation** and has proven to be more than effective in assisting analysts with incident investigations.

- **X-Ways Forensics**: One drawback of FTK and EnCase is cost. These platforms can cost several thousands of dollars per year. For larger organizations such as government agencies and large enterprises, the trade-off of cost versus features may not be an issue. For smaller organizations, these platforms may be cost prohibitive. An alternative, feature rich forensic platform is X-Ways.This platform has the ability to perform the variety of tasks necessary, but at a fraction of the cost.Another great benefit of X-Ways is that it is less resource-intensive and can be run off a USB device, making it an alternative platform, especially for incident response.

Each of these platforms has a rich feature set and provides analysts with a powerful tool for conducting a wide range of forensic tasks. The specific tools in each of these platforms are outside the scope of this book.As such, it is recommended that analysts are trained on the platform in use to ensure that they fully understand the tool's capability.

Autopsy

One alternative to the commercial forensics programs is Autopsy.Autopsy is a GUI-based forensic platform based upon the open source SleuthKit toolset. This open sourced platform has features commonly found in commercial platforms. This includes timeline analysis, keyword searching, web and email artifacts and the ability to filter results on known bad file hashes.One of the key features is its ease of use. This allows incident responders to have a light platform that focuses on critical tasks and obtain the critical evidence needed.

Installing Autopsy

Several of the Linux distributions previously discussed have Autopsy pre-installed. It is a good practice that analysts ensure that the platform they are using is up to date. For the Windows operating system, download the Microsoft self-installer file located at `https://www.sleuthkit.org/autopsy/download.php`. Once downloaded, execute the MSI file and choose the install location. Once finished, the application is ready to use.

Opening a case

Once Autopsy is installed the analyst can open a case with very little pre-configuration. The following process will discuss the process for opening a new case:

1. To begin an analysis, first ensure that the entire disk image is located in a single directory.This enables the entire image to be utilized during the analysis.

Name	Date modified	Type	Size
Laptop_Acc09567_Image.E01	6/13/2017 6:32 PM	E01 File	2,097,133 KB
Laptop_Acc09567_Image.E02	6/13/2017 6:38 PM	E02 File	2,097,123 KB
Laptop_Acc09567_Image.E03	6/13/2017 6:46 PM	E03 File	2,097,138 KB
Laptop_Acc09567_Image.E04	6/13/2017 6:44 PM	E04 File	1,350,414 KB

In the preceding screenshot, is an image file taken from a suspect system. The image has been divided into four 2 GB files. Autopsy will be able to take the four files and reconstruct the entire volume that has been imaged.

> During this chapter, a memory image from the Computer Forensic Reference Data Sets is utilized. The entire memory image can be downloaded from
> `https://www.cfreds.nist.gov/data_leakage_case/data-leakage-case.html`. This chapter makes use of the EnCase image.

2. Open Autopsy. The following window will appear. Choose **Create New Case**:

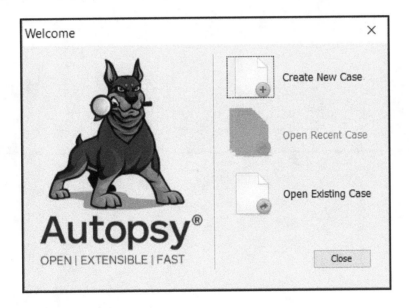

3. A second window will appear where the analyst will input the case title. In addition, the path to Autopsy that will store files associated with the case can also be set. This is useful where circumstances dictate that the analyst has to place the files in a secure container.Once finished, click **Next**:

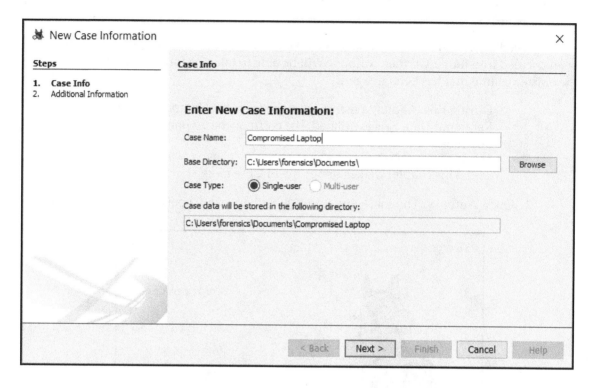

4. In the next window, the analysts should input the case number and their name. Click **Finish**:

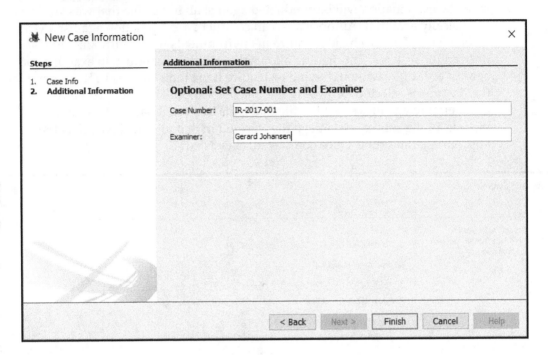

5. Once the case details have been entered, the analyst will need to load the image file that was previously created. Select the appropriate data source type. In this case, the examination will be conducted against an image file that was forensically acquired. Autopsy also can conduct an examination against a virtual machine file. This is a handy feature in environments where virtualization is utilized for systems. This feature allows the analyst to conduct an examination against a VM file, without having to acquire it via tools such as FTK Imager. Once the file type is selected, browse to the image location. The folder contains a number of image files;select the file that ends in `.E01`. Loading this file will include all the subsequent image files located in that folder. Next, select the appropriate time zone. Once completed, click **Next**:

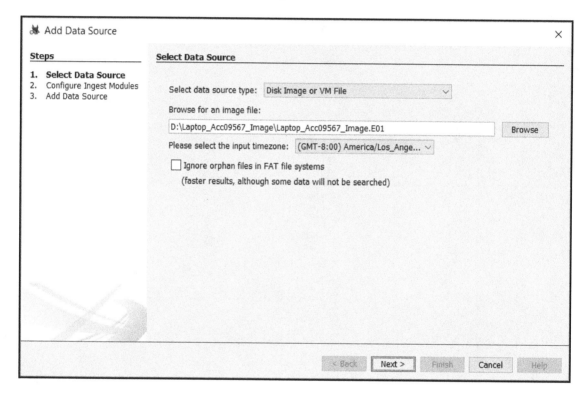

6. The next screen allows the analyst to tailor the modules in use. Depending on the type of investigation, some of these options can go unchecked. In the beginning though, the analyst should select all to ensure that all the necessary information is available for examination. One other option that is important, is to select **Process Unallocated Space**. This captures all information in the space not currently allocated on the hard drive for data. There are methods where unallocated space can be utilized to hide information. Once that is completed, click **Next**:

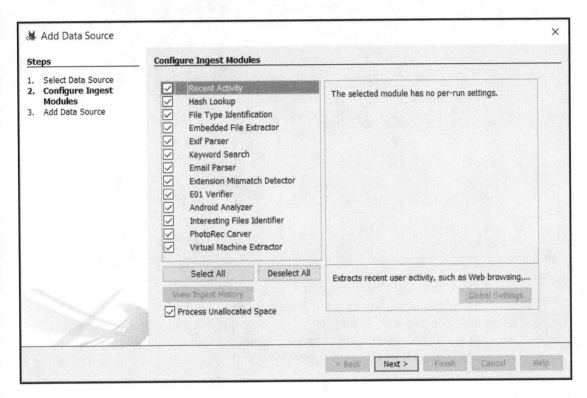

7. On the next screen, verify that the data source has been loaded and click **Finish**:

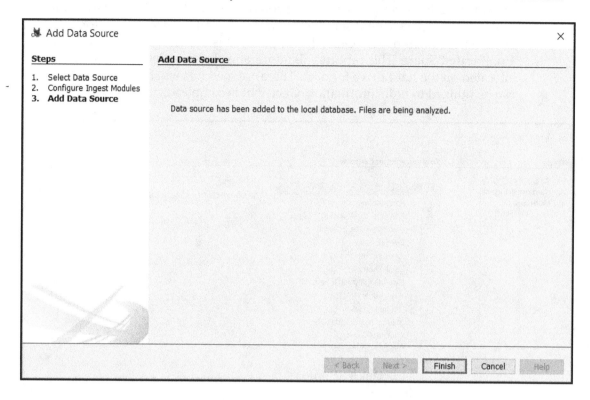

8. Autopsy will now go through the process of analyzing the files from the image. Depending on the size of the image, this may take several minutes to hours. The process bar at the lower right corner of the screen will show the progress. How long this process takes is often dependent on the processing speed as well as the size of the image file(s).

Navigating Autopsy

The Autopsy GUI is divided into three main sections. These sections display details relating to both the system and specific files. When Autopsy has completed processing a new case or opening an existing case, the analyst will see the following window:

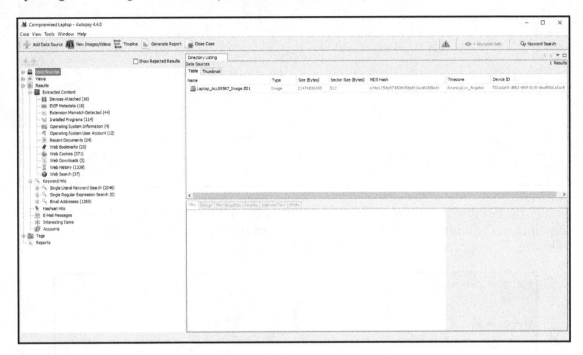

As the previous screenshot shows, Autopsy is divided into three main panes. The first of these is the left pane, which contains the data sources and file structure, as well as search results. Clicking on the plus sign expands the results and clicking on the minus sign collapses them. This allows the analyst to access the system at a high level, as well as drilling down to specific elements.

The center pane contains directory listings or results from searches. For example, the following screenshot shows web cookies that were located on the system:

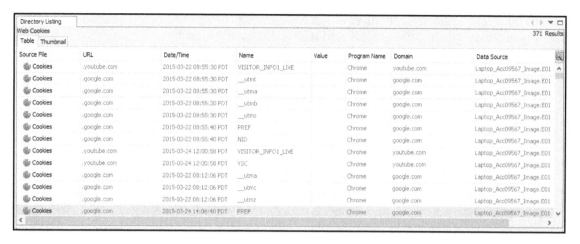

Finally, the bottom pane contains the metadata and other information about individual files contained in the center pane. For example, if the .**youtube.com** cookie is selected, the following data appears when the **Results** tab is selected:

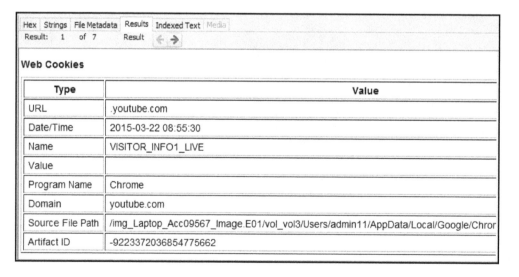

Clicking the **File Metadata** tab will produce information specific to the file. This includes the timestamps for the file as well as an MD5 Hash:

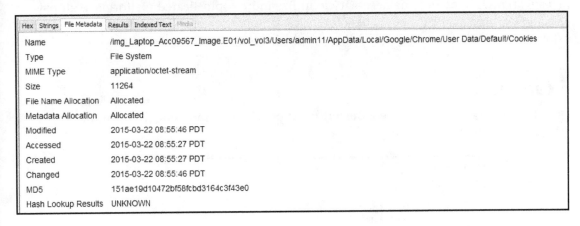

Finally, the file's hexadecimal content can be viewed by clicking on the **Hex** tab:

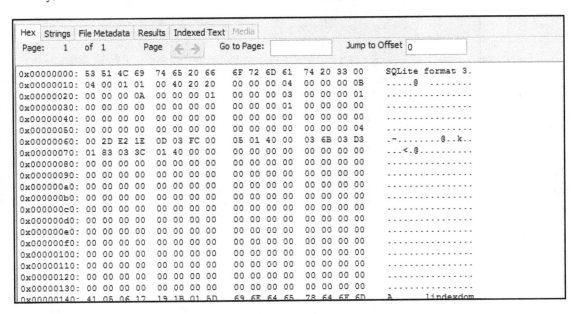

This view is excellent if an analyst wants to inspect an application or other file that is suspected of being malware.

What Autopsy offers is the ability to perform some of the actions and analysis that is found in other commercial platforms. It should be noted though, that in the case of more complex investigations, it may become necessary to utilize more sophisticated platforms. Autopsy also allows those analysts new to disk forensics, a more user-friendly platform to gain experience with, before moving to a more sophisticated commercial solution.

Examining a Case

Once the case has been processed, the left-hand pane will populate with the number of artifacts located on the system:

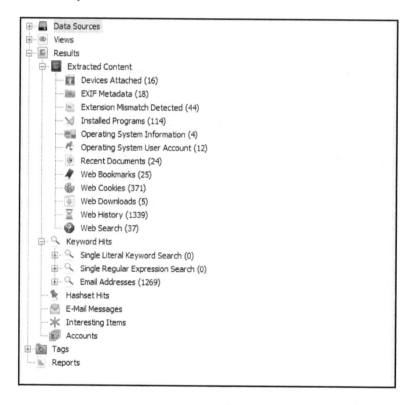

In the previous screenshot, there are several items listed under the **Extracted Content** portion. These include looking at programs that have been installed, the operating system information, and recent documents. Another key feature of Autopsy is the ability to examine the entire folder structure of the image file.Clicking on the plus sign next to **Data Sources** expands the entire folder structure. This is useful if, through other sources, an analyst is able to identify the location of a suspect file.

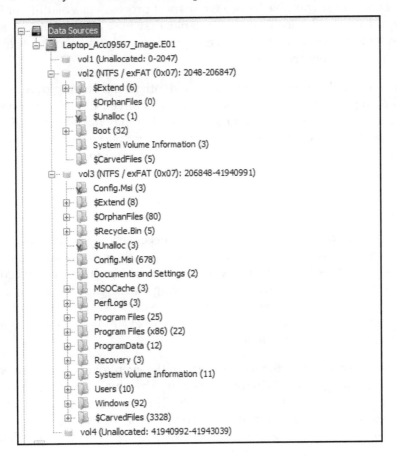

There are different data points that can be examined utilizing Autopsy. What to search for and how to search for it is often dictated by the type of incident or examination under investigation. For example, a malware infection that originates from a compromised website may involve examining the system for URLs that the user may have typed in or otherwise accessed via a browser. Furthermore, the actual file may be located utilizing information obtained via the system memory examination covered in the previous chapter. For example, if an analyst was able to locate a suspect process via Volatility or Redline and was subsequently able to also locate the executable, they may utilize Autopsy to find the last time the executable was launched. This can provide analysts a time to examine other systems for evidence of compromise.

In another scenario, analysts may be tasked with identifying if an employee accessed confidential files to pass onto a competitor. This may involve examining the system for the times and dates files were accessed, email addresses that may have been used, external cloud storage sites that were accessed, or USB storage that was connected to the system. Finally, a full listing of files may provide insight into the confidential documents that were moved.

Web Artifacts

There are several types of incident where it may be necessary to examine a system for evidence of malicious activity conducted by a user. Previously discussed, for example, was the accessing of cloud-based storage where a malicious insider has uploaded confidential documents. In other circumstances, social engineering attacks may have an unsuspecting employee navigate to a compromised website that subsequently downloads malicious software. In either case, Autopsy provides the ability to examine several areas of web artifacts that may be of use to examiners.

The first of these web artifacts is the web history. In the event of a social engineering attack that involves a user navigating to a malware delivery site, this data may provide some insight into the specific URL that was navigated to. This URL can then be extracted and compared with known malicious website lists from internal or external sources. In other cases, where an insider has accessed an external cloud storage site, the web history may provide evidence of this activity. For example,

1. Clicking on the **Web History** section in the left-hand pane opens up the center pane and shows detailed information concerning a URL that was accessed by the system:

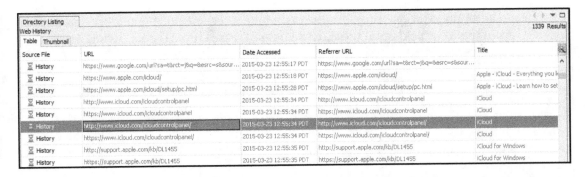

2. In the preceeding screenshot, Autopsy indicates that the iCloud service was accessed by this system. Further information provided by Autopsy allows the analyst to evaluate other information, such as the location of the artifact and what type of browser was used. This information can be accessed via the **Results** tab in the lower pane:

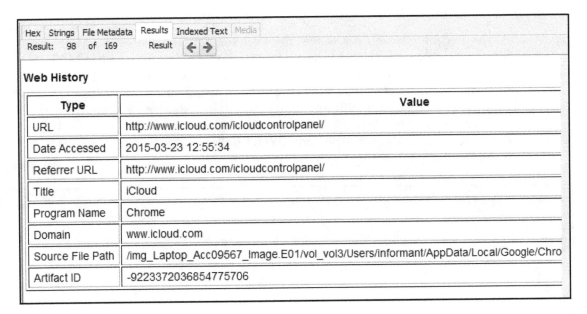

3. In addition, Autopsy provides the metadata of the specific file under examination.Clicking on the **File Metadata** tab produces the following data:

| Hex | Strings | File Metadata | Results | Indexed Text | Media |

Name	/img_Laptop_Acc09567_Image.E01/vol_vol3/Users/informant/AppData/Local/Google/Chrome/User Data/Default/History
Type	File System
MIME Type	application/octet-stream
Size	135168
File Name Allocation	Allocated
Metadata Allocation	Allocated
Modified	2015-03-24 14:07:21 PDT
Accessed	2015-03-22 08:11:53 PDT
Created	2015-03-22 08:11:53 PDT
Changed	2015-03-24 14:07:21 PDT
MD5	db1f9e1a7fb6b9252d903dfafe25f2da
Hash Lookup Results	UNKNOWN
Internal ID	11559

4. As the preceding screenshot shows, there are some more details concerning that file. For example, the analyst has time information, file location, and an MD5 hash that can be utilized to compare any extracted files that are examined further. In some circumstances, a suspect may decide to delete the browsing history from the system in an effort to hide any malicous activity. Another location that may provide evidence of sites accessed by a malicous insider is in web cookies. These can be accessed in the left pane under **Web Cookies**. Clicking on this produces a list of the cookies that are still on the system:

Web Cookies
Table   Thumbnail   371 Results

Source File	URL	△ Date/Time	Name	Value	Program Name	Domain	Data Source
Cookies	.apple.com	2015-03-23 13:43:38 PDT	s_orientation		Chrome	apple.com	Laptop_Acc09567_Image.E01
Cookies	.apple.com	2015-03-23 13:43:38 PDT	s_vnum_n2_us		Chrome	apple.com	Laptop_Acc09567_Image.E01
Cookies	.apple.com	2015-03-23 13:43:38 PDT	POD		Chrome	apple.com	Laptop_Acc09567_Image.E01
Cookies	.apple.com	2015-03-23 13:43:38 PDT	s_orientationHeight		Chrome	apple.com	Laptop_Acc09567_Image.E01
Cookies	.apple.com	2015-03-23 13:43:38 PDT	ac_history		Chrome	apple.com	Laptop_Acc09567_Image.E01
Cookies	.apple.com	2015-03-23 13:43:38 PDT	s_fid		Chrome	apple.com	Laptop_Acc09567_Image.E01
Cookies	.apple.com	2015-03-23 13:43:38 PDT	s_sq		Chrome	apple.com	Laptop_Acc09567_Image.E01
Cookies	.apple.com	2015-03-23 13:43:38 PDT	s_vi		Chrome	apple.com	Laptop_Acc09567_Image.E01
J62NMA2T.txt	taboola.com/	2015-03-23 13:44:21 PDT	t_gid	fd2d9f54-...	Internet Explo...	taboola.com/	Laptop_Acc09567_Image.E01
M7J9OB0R.txt	adtech.de/	2015-03-23 13:44:21 PDT	JEB2	551070EC...	Internet Explo...	adtech.de/	Laptop_Acc09567_Image.E01
NSFKS8HL.txt	www.entertainmentwise.co...	2015-03-23 13:44:23 PDT	UTDP	4	Internet Explo...	entertainmentwise.com/new...	Laptop_Acc09567_Image.E01
1IAP10PB.txt	sitescout.com/	2015-03-23 13:44:24 PDT	ssi	fb5dd921-...	Internet Explo...	sitescout.com/	Laptop_Acc09567_Image.E01
C2KCJMWC.txt	adtechus.com/	2015-03-23 13:44:24 PDT	JEB2	551070EC...	Internet Explo...	adtechus.com/	Laptop_Acc09567_Image.E01
KFTAPQ25.txt	ads.undertone.com/	2015-03-23 13:44:24 PDT	UTID	592502e7...	Internet Explo...	undertone.com/	Laptop_Acc09567_Image.E01
HCFJU4PZ.txt	chango.com/	2015-03-23 13:44:24 PDT	_t	644b4916...	Internet Explo...	chango.com/	Laptop_Acc09567_Image.E01
HMYQY9IZ.txt	mathtag.com/	2015-03-23 13:44:24 PDT	uuid	15365510...	Internet Explo...	mathtag.com/	Laptop_Acc09567_Image.E01
DL6J2U8H.txt	a.scorecardresearch.com/	2015-03-23 13:44:24 PDT	CP4	CP4	Internet Explo...	scorecardresearch.com/	Laptop_Acc09567_Image.E01
CYUVM0L4.txt	w55c.net/	2015-03-23 13:44:25 PDT	wfivefivec	3fOIBvn8...	Internet Explo...	w55c.net/	Laptop_Acc09567_Image.E01

Depending on the type of incident, web artifacts can play an important role. Autopsy has some functionality but analysts may find that other commercial solutions provide a much more robust platform. Tools such as Evidence Finder by Magnet Forensics (`www.magnetforensics.com`) scours the entire system for Internet artifacts and then presents it in a way that is easy for the analyst to view. Another key advantage to commercial solutions such as this is the continued updating of functionality. Depending on the frequency of Internet and web artifact searching, the inclusion of tools such as this may be beneficial.

Email

Locating suspect emails continues to be a task that incident response analysts often engage in. This can include externally caused incidents such as social engineering, where analysts may be tasked with locating a suspect email that had malware attached. In other circumstances, malicious insiders may have sent or received communication that was inappropriate or violated company policy. In those cases, analysts may be tasked with recovering those emails to include in termination proceedings or in legal action.

Autopsy has the ability to locate emails contained on the system. From these emails, they may be able to identify one or more suspicious emails and domains that can be further researched to see if they are associated with social engineering or other malicious activity. Simply click on the **Email Addresses** in the left-hand pane. From there, the analyst can see the email addresses that are located on the system:

Directory Listing `(?=.{8})[a-z0-9%+_-]+(?:\.[a-z0-9%+_-]+)*@(?:[a-z0-9](?:[a-z0-9-]*[a-z0-9])?\.)+[a-z]{2,4}(?<!\.txt|\.exe|\.dll|\.jpg|\.xml)`	
Table Thumbnail	
List Name	Files with Hits
🔍 universidad@example.mx (2)	460
🔍 unknown@gravatar.com (1)	460
🔍 upSVh@S.dVV (2)	460
🔍 uporabnik@contoso.onmicrosoft.com (1)	460
🔍 urcesServer-Help-CHM.na@p.Reso (1)	460
🔍 user1@example.com (2)	460
🔍 user@contoso.com (13)	460
🔍 user@contoso.onmicrosoft.com (3)	460
🔍 user@smartftp.com (1)	460
🔍 user_emailvalueiaman.informant.personal@gmail.com (5)	460
🔍 usuario@contoso.com.No (1)	460

Attached Devices

Another key piece of evidence that may be useful to an analyst is data about when specific devices were attached to the system. In the scenario of a malicious insider attempting to steal confidential documents, knowing whether they utilized a USB device would be helpful. Autopsy utilizes the Registry settings located on the system to identify the types of devices attached and the last time that they were used. In this case, the output of clicking **Devices Attached** in the left pane produces the following results:

Source File	Date/Time	Device Make	Device Model	Device ID	Data Source	Tags
SYSTEM	2015-03-25 06:05:35 PDT		ROOT_HUB	5&3bb57b8&0	Laptop_Acc09567_Image.E01	
SYSTEM	2015-03-25 06:05:35 PDT		ROOT_HUB20	5&299e1c9f&0	Laptop_Acc09567_Image.E01	
SYSTEM	2015-03-24 06:38:00 PDT	SanDisk Corp.	Cruzer Fit	4C530012450531101593	Laptop_Acc09567_Image.E01	
SYSTEM	2015-03-24 12:38:09 PDT	SanDisk Corp.	Cruzer Fit	4C530012550531106501	Laptop_Acc09567_Image.E01	
SYSTEM	2015-03-25 06:05:36 PDT	VMware, Inc.	Virtual USB Hub	6&b77da928&0&2	Laptop_Acc09567_Image.E01	
SYSTEM	2015-03-25 06:05:36 PDT	VMware, Inc.	Virtual Mouse	6&b77da928&0&1	Laptop_Acc09567_Image.E01	
SYSTEM	2015-03-25 06:05:36 PDT	VMware, Inc.	Virtual Mouse	7&2a7d30098&0&0000	Laptop_Acc09567_Image.E01	
SYSTEM	2015-03-25 06:05:36 PDT	VMware, Inc.	Virtual Mouse	7&2a7d30098&0&0001	Laptop_Acc09567_Image.E01	
SYSTEM	2015-03-25 06:05:35 PDT		ROOT_HUB	5&3bb57b8&0	Laptop_Acc09567_Image.E01	
SYSTEM	2015-03-25 06:05:35 PDT		ROOT_HUB20	5&299e1c9f&0	Laptop_Acc09567_Image.E01	
SYSTEM	2015-03-24 06:38:00 PDT	SanDisk Corp.	Cruzer Fit	4C530012450531101593	Laptop_Acc09567_Image.E01	
SYSTEM	2015-03-24 12:38:09 PDT	SanDisk Corp.	Cruzer Fit	4C530012550531106501	Laptop_Acc09567_Image.E01	
SYSTEM	2015-03-25 06:05:36 PDT	VMware, Inc.	Virtual USB Hub	6&b77da928&0&2	Laptop_Acc09567_Image.E01	
SYSTEM	2015-03-25 06:05:36 PDT	VMware, Inc.	Virtual Mouse	6&b77da928&0&1	Laptop_Acc09567_Image.E01	
SYSTEM	2015-03-25 06:05:36 PDT	VMware, Inc.	Virtual Mouse	7&2a7d30098&0&0000	Laptop_Acc09567_Image.E01	
SYSTEM	2015-03-25 06:05:36 PDT	VMware, Inc.	Virtual Mouse	7&2a7d30098&0&0001	Laptop_Acc09567_Image.E01	

Drilling down into the **Results** tab, the analyst would be able to identify the type of device, and the date and time that the USB device was attached:

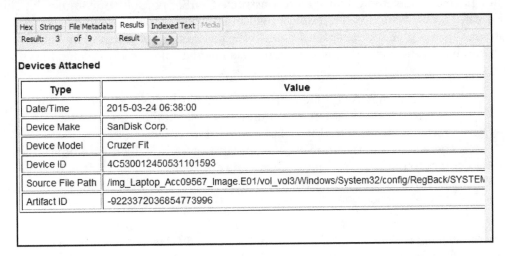

Finally, a more detailed examination of the **File Metadata** contains a good deal of additional data that can be utilized to reconstruct the time that the USB device was accessed on the system:

Name	/img_Laptop_Acc09567_Image.E01/vol_vol3/Windows/System32/config/RegBack/SYSTEM
Type	File System
MIME Type	application/octet-stream
Size	12419072
File Name Allocation	Allocated
Metadata Allocation	Allocated
Modified	2015-03-25 06:24:16 PDT
Accessed	2015-03-25 06:24:10 PDT
Created	2015-03-25 03:15:18 PDT
Changed	2015-03-25 06:24:16 PDT
MD5	a26cbec95c053ca113b9bef2fdfd4878
Hash Lookup Results	UNKNOWN
Internal ID	76153

Deleted Files

Files that have been deleted can also be reconstructed, either partially or completely. The Windows operating system will not delete files when the user selects deletion. The operating system will mark the space a deleted file takes up in the Master File Table as available to write new files to. As a result, analysts may be able to view deleted files that have not been overwritten.

One challenge that is facing forensic analysts is the use of Solid State Drives (SSDs) in tablets and computers.Deleted files can often be recoverable from traditional platter hard drives even after a system is powered down.With SSDs, the operating system will often remove deleted files to make the storage of files more efficient.For more information on this challenge, the following website has an excellent breakdown: `https://www.forensicmag.com/article/2013/05/forensic-insight-solid-state-drives`

To view the deleted files on a system, click on the **Deleted Files** in the left pane.From here, the analyst can see all of the files that are marked for deletion:

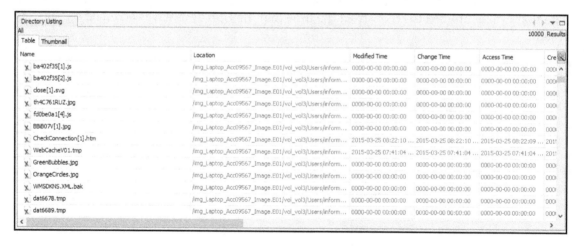

From here, the analyst can search through deleted files.These files may hold evidentiary value. For example, in the case of malicious insider activity, if several sensitive files are found in the deleted files, all deleted within the same time period, it may be indicative of the insider attempting to cover their tracks by deleting suspicious files.

Keyword Searches

One key advantage that forensic applications have is the ability to perform keyword searches. This is especially advantageous as disk drives have gotten larger and analysts would have to parse through an overwhelming quantity of data. Keywords are often derived from other elements of the investigation, or by using external sources. For example, if an analyst is investigating a malware incident, they may use a suspicious DLL or executable name from the analysis of the memory image.In other instances, such as a malicious insider being suspected of accessing confidential information, keywords in those documents, such as secret or confidential, can be used to see if the suspect had used the system to access those files.

Autopsy has the ability to perform keyword searches utilizing an exact or substring match. For example, an analyst is tasked with determining if a system was used to access a particular file titled `pricing decision(16)`. The analyst is tasked with locating any trace evidence that would indicate that the system accessed it and to determine which user accessed the file. The analyst would navigate to the top-right corner and input the following text `pricing decision` in the field. In this case, an exact match will be utilized. Once selected, click the **Search** button. The left pane will indicate if there were any *hits* on that keyword.In this case, **pricing decision** has 16 hits:

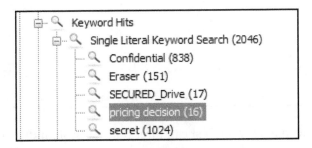

In the center pane will be a list of the files that contained the hits. The first file that stands out is the Master File Table entry. This indicates that there was at least an entry on the MFT:

| 🔍 $MFT | desktop.ini$I30«pricing decision«PRICIN~1progress | pricing decision |

Further review of the results indicates that there are two link files associated with the **pricing decision** spreadsheet:

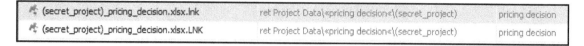

By selecting the first link file in the upper pane, additional details can be uncovered in the lower pane. For instance, if the analyst clicks on **Indexed Data**, there is a good deal of information concerning the access of the file.

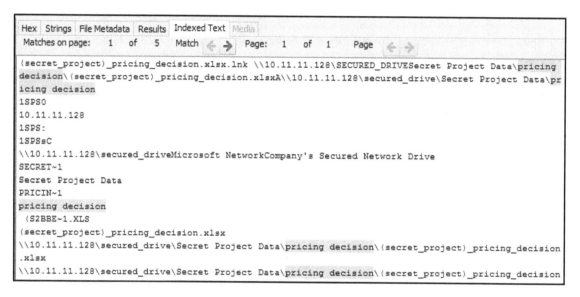

From an analysis of this data, the analyst can infer that the system did in fact access a shared computer at 10.11.11.128 and accessed the pricing decision spreadsheet. Further details are also available by clicking on the **File Metadata** tab:

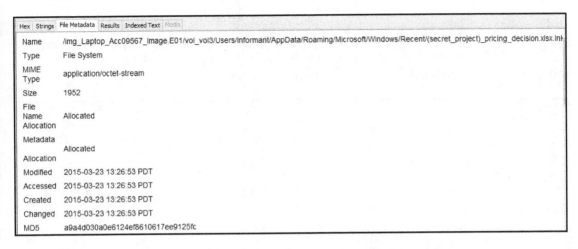

This data indicates not only the time that the file was accessed, but also that the user **informant** is clearly the account accessing the file. By clicking **Operating System User Account** in the left pane, the analyst would then be able to find data concerning the suspect user account:

Username	informant
User ID	S-1-5-21-2425377081-3129163575-2985601102-1000

The ability to search keywords is one aspect of disk forensic platforms that truly make it worth the investment. With the ability to zero in on specific aspects of the incident, analysts can quickly sift through the mountains of data to the key pieces of data they need to reconstruct the sequence of events.

Timeline Analysis

When investigating an incident, it is critical to have an idea of when applications or files were executed. Date and timestamps can sometimes be found in other aspects of the investigation, such as when examining memory images. Also, identifying specific DLL files or executable files in the memory image can be compared to the date and time they were accessed, to correlate other activity observed on the system.

Autopsy has functionality specifically for timeline analysis. Simply click on the **Timeline** button at the top of the window and Autopsy will begin the process of parsing out timeline data. Depending on the size of the image file being analyzed, it may take a few minutes.Once completed, the following window will open:

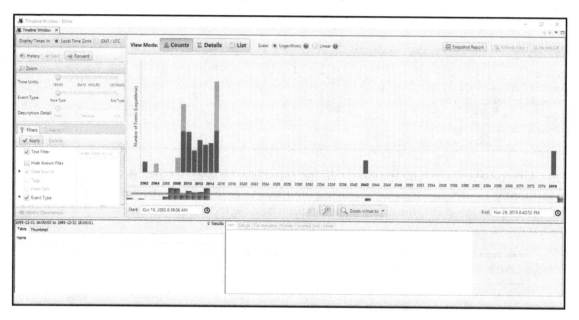

From here, the analyst can utilize several features. First is the text filter in the left-hand side of the screen. From here, the analyst can search for specific text in files. For example, the analyst has already identified that the spreadsheet **pricing decision** had been accessed by the system under investigation.If the analyst would like to know whether that file was accessed at any other times,entering `pricing` into the `Text Filter` box and clicking **Apply** produces the following results:

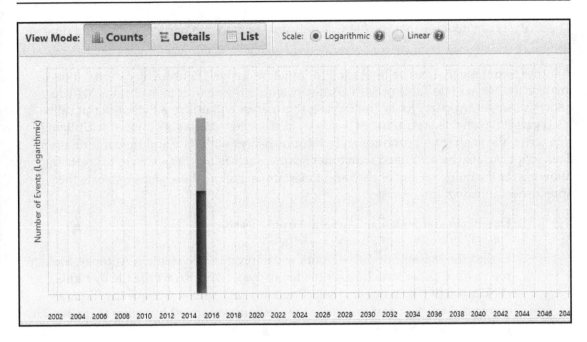

From this graph, the analyst can further drill down into the specific times the file was accessed by clicking on the colored bars. The following window appears in the lower left-hand corner:

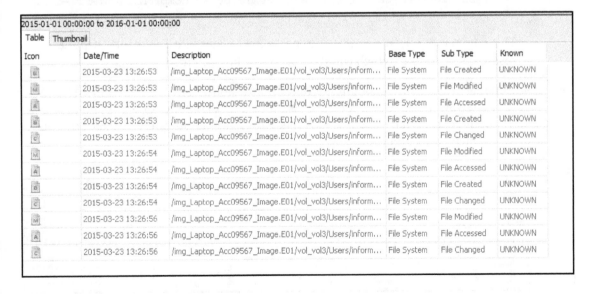

The analysts can now see that the file was only accessed on one particular date and time from this system.

Another technique that can be leveraged for timeline analysis is utilizing external tools to analyze the Master File Table or MFT. Autopsy allows the analyst to export the MFT for analysis using third-party tools. In this case, the analyst will utilize a Python script called `analyzeMFT` available on GitHub at `https://github.com/dkovar/analyzeMFT`. Utilizing this script, the analyst will produce an Excel spreadsheet with date and time information. This script can also be combined with other scripts, such as `Log2Timeline`, to create files allowing for the quick review of date and timestamps. Follow these steps to create the spreadsheet utilizing `analyzeMFT`:

1. Download and install `analyzeMFT` from this site:
   `https://github.com/dkovar/analyzeMFT`

2. Extract the Master File Table from the compromised system. In Autopsy, look in the `Volume 3` file structure for the file named `$MFT`. Extract the file by right-clicking on the file name and selecting `Extract File(s)`. Save the file to a storage folder. It is best to change the file name to something other than `$MFT`. In this case, the name `CompromisedLTMFT` is used.

3. Once the file is saved, navigate to the folder containing the extracted file and type the following command:

   root@DESKTOP-DPQF2KP:/mnt/d# analyzeMFT.py -f CompromisedLTMFT -c CompromisedLaptop

   This command tells `analyzeMFT` to parse the Master File Table and output the results to a CSV file, which can then be viewed by Microsoft Excel.

4. Navigate to the folder containing the MFT file and the CSV file should be there. The analyst may have to add the extension `.csv` to the file for it to open properly. From there, they can view a spreadsheet utilizing the program of choice (in this case, Microsoft Excel is utilized):

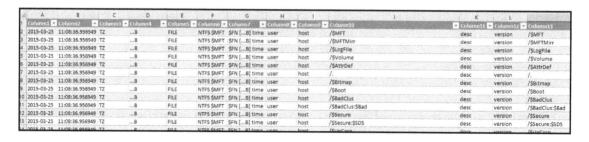

From here, the analyst can review the entire timeline, as well as using any of the searching tools available in the spreadsheet program. There are other scripts and tools available to analysts to further parse out this information. One such example is the use of **Log2Timeline** and **analyzeMFT**, which can be found on GitHub at

`https://github.com/log2timeline/plaso/wiki/Tips-and-Tricks.`

Registry analysis

There is a great deal of activity that occurs under the hood with the Windows operating system. One place that this activity occurs is in the Windows Registry. The Windows Registry is a database that stores the low-level system settings for the Windows operating system. This includes settings for devices, security, services, and the storage of user account security settings in the **Security Accounts Manager(SAM)**.

The registry is made up of two elements. The first is the **key**. The key is a container that holds the second element, the **values**. These values hold the specific settings information. The highest-level key is called the root key and the Windows operating system has six root keys or **registry hives**, which are located in the `\system32\ folder` on the Windows file structure. The following are the six registry hives and their associated locations in the Windows file structure:

- **HKEY_LOCAL_MACHINE \SYSTEM** :`\system32\config\system`
- **HKEY_LOCAL_MACHINE \SAM** : `\system32\config\sam`
- **HKEY_LOCAL_MACHINE \SECURITY** :`\system32\config\security`
- **HKEY_LOCAL_MACHINE \SOFTWARE** :`\system32\config\software`
- **HKEY_USERS \UserProfile** :`\winnt\profiles\username`
- **HKEY_USERS.DEFAULT** :`\system32\config\default`

Analysts can access the various registry hives using Autopsy. Simply navigate to the `vol3/Windows/System32/config` folder in the file structure in the left-hand pane:

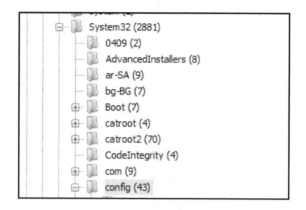

In the center pane, the SAM registry file is located:

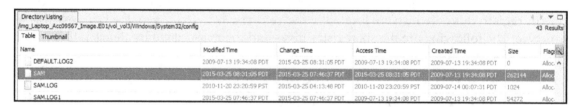

The actual examination and evidentiary value of registry key settings is, like many of the aspects of digital forensics, very detailed. While it is impossible to cover all of the aspects of registry forensics in this chapter, or even in this book, it is important for analysts to first be able to acquire the registry keys for evaluation, as well as to have some familiarity with tools that can allow analysts to gain some hands-on experience with evaluating registry settings.

In this case, the system, SAM, security, and software registry keys will be acquired for analysis. For this, the analyst can use Autopsy to acquire the proper keys and then examine them with a third-party tool:

1. First, navigate to the proper folder, `/System32/config`, on the third volume of the system image.
2. Next, select the four registry keys using the right mouse button and *Ctrl* key. Right-click on one of the files and select `Export File(s)`.

3. Select a folder to output the registry keys. In this case, a separate file folder was created to contain the keys. Select Save.
4. Verify that the registry keys have been saved:

Name	Date modified	Type	Size
76156-SAM	6/25/2017 11:26 A...	File	256 KB
76162-SECURITY	6/25/2017 11:26 A...	File	256 KB
76168-SOFTWARE	6/25/2017 11:26 A...	File	47,360 KB
76173-SYSTEM	6/25/2017 11:26 A...	File	12,288 KB

The preceding screenshot shows the four registry files that have been acquired.

Now that the suspect image's registry files have been saved, the analyst can then use a third-party tool to examine the registry. In this case, the **Registry Explorer/RECmd Version .0.9.0.0** tool developed by Eric Zimmerman will be used to analyze the registry keys.This freeware application can be downloaded from https://ericzimmerman.github.io/. Unzip the file to a location and the application is ready to execute.

As the analysis of the image has progressed, the analyst has identified that a potential data loss has occurred via a USB device that was attached to the system at some point. While Autopsy has provided us some information, it may be necessary to find out what registry key settings have been changed as a result of the USB being connected. The best location for additional information is contained within the system registry hive.

The Windows operating system records and maintains artifacts of when USB devices such as mass storage, iOS devices, digital cameras, and other USB devices are connected. This is due to the Plug and Play manager, which is part of the Windows operating system. The PnP receives notification that a USB has been connected and queries the device for information so that it can load the proper device driver. Upon completion, the Windows operating system will make an entry for the device within the registry settings.

To determine what USB devices were connected, follow these steps:

1. Open Registry Explorer.
2. Click **File** and then **Load Offline Hive**.
3. Navigate to the **system registry hive**.

4. Once loaded, the following window appears:

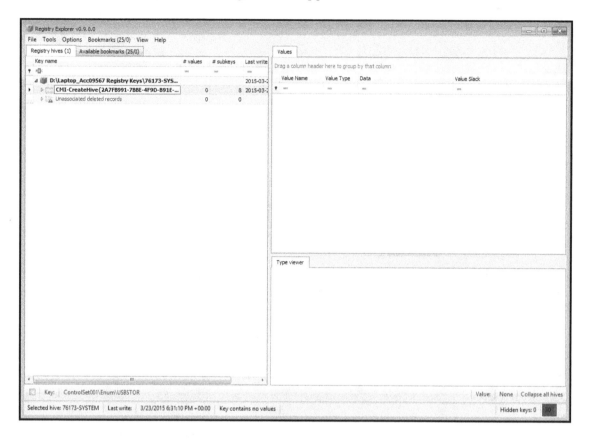

From here, navigate down to the proper USB registry location at `CurrentControlSet\Enum\USBSTOR\`:

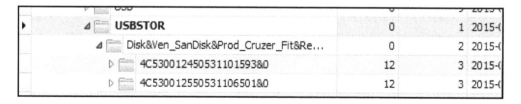

5. Click on the first registry value, **4C530012450531101593&0**. The following information will appear in the upper right-hand pane:

Values			
Drag a column header here to group by that column			
Value Name	Value Type	Data	Value Slack
ᴀʙc	ᴀʙc	ᴀʙc	ᴀʙc
▶ DeviceDesc	RegSz	@disk.inf,%disk_devdesc%;Disk drive	22-00-00-00
Capabilities	RegDword	16	
HardwareID	RegMultiSz	USBSTOR\DiskSanDisk_Cruzer_Fit__...	00-00-00-00
CompatibleIDs	RegMultiSz	USBSTOR\Disk USBSTOR\RAW	
ContainerID	RegSz	{4933888a-6002-5a33-95a4-bad21ec...	00-00-00-00-00-00
ConfigFlags	RegDword	0	
ClassGUID	RegSz	{4d36e967-e325-11ce-bfc1-08002be...	00-00-00-00-00-00
Driver	RegSz	{4d36e967-e325-11ce-bfc1-08002be...	00-00-00-00
Class	RegSz	DiskDrive	
Mfg	RegSz	@disk.inf,%genmanufacturer%;(Sta...	B7-DA-00-00-00-00
Service	RegSz	disk	50-00
FriendlyName	RegSz	SanDisk Cruzer Fit USB Device	

From here, the analyst has a good deal of information that can be reviewed. Of particular importance is the **HardwareID**. Clicking on that section of the output produces the following in the lower right window:

Type viewer	Slack viewer
Value name	HardwareID
Value type	RegMultiSz
Value	USBSTOR\DiskSanDisk_Cruzer_Fit_____2.01 USBSTOR\DiskSanDisk_Cruzer_Fit_____USBSTOR \DiskSanDisk_ USBSTOR\SanDisk_Cruzer_Fit_____2 SanDisk_Cruzer_Fit_____2 USBSTOR\GenDisk GenDisk
Raw value	55-00-53-00-42-00-53-00-54-00-4F-00-52-00-5C-00-44-00-69-00-73-00-6B-00-53-00-61-00-6E-00-44-00- ⌃ 69-00-73-00-6B-00-5F-00-43-00-72-00-75-00-7A-00-65-00-72-00-5F-00-46-00-69-00-74-00-5F-00-5F-00- 5F-00-5F-00-5F-00-5F-00-32-00-2E-00-30-00-31-00-00-00-55-00-53-00-42-00-53-00-54-00-4F-00-52-00- ⌄
Slack	00-00-00-00

What the analyst has been able to uncover by evaluating the date and timeis that a **SanDisk Cruzer Fit** was first connected to the system. The analyst was able to ascertain that it was connected at 13:38:00 on 03/24/2015. This is critical when compared to the date and time that the confidential files were accessed.

As was previously stated, registry analysis is a deep subset of digital forensics in and of itself. Whole volumes have been written on the evidentiary value present in the settings and entries in registry hives. At a minimum, analysts should be prepared to at least acquire this evidence for others for further examination. Having said that, as analysts gain more and more experience and skill, the registry should be an area that can be leveraged for evidence when examining a disk image.

Summary

In many ways, this chapter just scratches the surface of what information can be found by leveraging disk forensic tools. Specific tools and techniques are largely dependent on the tool utilized. What is important to understand is that modern operating systems leave traces of their activity all over the disk, from file change evidence in the Master File Table to registry key settings when new user accounts are added.Incident response analysts should have expertise in understanding how modern operating systems store data and how to leverage commercial or freeware tools to find this data. Taken in concert with other pieces of evidence obtained from network sources and in memory, disk evidence may provide more clarity on an incident and aid in determining its root cause. One critical piece that is addressed in the next chapter is how analysts need to record and report their findings. The previous chapters have discussed a good deal of technical work that unless it is documented will not be useful.

9
Forensic Reporting

An incident response team functions in much the same way a fire department does. Both teams take time to prepare themselves with training on their respective techniques, tools, and practices, and can respond at a moment's notice to a fire or incident. During their response to the fire, the firefighters take notes and record their actions, ensure that critical decisions are documented, and that individual contributions are noted. Once the fire is out, they sift through the debris to determine what the cause and origin were. Once the proper documentation has been prepared, the fire department conducts an after-action review to critique their performance and to find avenues of improvement. Other reports allow fire departments and safety experts to update building codes and improve the survival of structures should a fire break out.

Incident response teams utilize much the same workflow. During an incident, notes are taken and actions recorded. Evidence is obtained from systems and maintained in a forensically sound manner. A root cause analysis is conducted utilizing the notes, observations, and evidence obtained during the incident. This root cause analysis is utilized by information technology personnel to patch up vulnerabilities and further harden systems. Finally, the team conducts their own after-action review where the series of events is laid out and critiqued so that the team may improve their processes, their tools, and techniques, as well as make any corrections to the incident response plan.

To maximize the benefits of the root cause analysis and after-action brief, incident responders will need to ensure that all their actions are recorded in the proper fashion. They will also be required to prepare several documents that senior leaders and decision makers will use when considering the future state of the IT infrastructure. For this and other reasons that will be covered in this chapter, incident responders need to be able to record their actions either within an automated system or in a simple report.

Documentation overview

The documentation associated with an incident takes several forms. The length of any documentation is often dictated by the type of incident. Simple incidents that take very little time to investigate and have a limited impact may be documented informally in an existing ticketing system. In more complex incident investigations, such as a data breach that has led to the disclosure of confidential information (such as medical records or credit card information), may require extensive written reports and supporting evidence.

What to document

When looking at documenting an incident, it is not very difficult to ascertain what should be documented. Following the five W's, and sometimes *How*, is an excellent foundation when considering what to document during an incident. Another good piece of wisdom when discussing documentation, especially when discussing the legal implications of security incidents, is the axiom *if you didn't write it down, it didn't happen*. This statement is used to drive home the point that proper documentation is often comprised of as much detail that the incident response analyst can bring. Analysts may be involved in an incident that ends up in a civil proceeding. The wheels of justice often move slowly, and an analyst may be called to the witness stand after 18 months, during which 10 other incidents have transpired. Having as much detail available in the incident reporting will allow analysts to reconstruct the events in the proper manner.

An excellent example of using this five W (and one H) structure to document is when looking at a digital forensics task, such as imaging a hard drive. In `Chapter 5`, *Understanding Forensic Imaging*, proper documentation was partially addressed when we looked at the practice of taking photos of the suspect drive. The following is a more detailed record of the event:

- **Who**: This is the easiest detail to make a note of. Simply, who was involved in the process? For example, the person involved was Analyst Jane Smith.
- **When**: Record the date and time that the imaging began and when it ended.For example, the imaging process was started at 21:08 UTC on April 16, 2017 and ended at 22:15 UTC on April 16, 2017. Times are critical, and you should ensure that a standard time zone is utilized and indicated in the report.
- **Where**: This should be a detailed location, such as an office.
- **What**: The action that was performed,for example, acquiring memory or firewall logs or imaging a drive.

- **Why**: Having a justification for the action helps in understanding the reason why the action was performed.
- **How**: A description of how an action is performed should be included. Also, if an incident response team utilizes playbooks or standard operating procedures as part of their plan, this should be included. Any departure from the standard operating procedures should also be similarly recorded.

Putting all this information together, the following sample language can be entered into the report:

> *On April 16, 2017, Analyst Jane Smith arrived at office 217 of the Corporate Office Park located at 123 Maple St., Anytown, US as part of the investigation. Upon arrival, Smith took control of the Dell laptop, asset tag #AccLT009, serial #7895693-862. An alert from the firewall IDS/OPS indicated that the laptop had communicated with a known Command and Control server. The laptop was to be imaged in an attempt to ascertain if it had been infected with malware. At 21:08, Smith imaged the drive utilizing the live imaging technique in accordance with the Standard Operating Procedure IR-002. The process was completed at 22:15 UTC on April 16, 2017.*

This entry provides sufficient detail to reconstruct the events that transpired. Taken together with other documentation, such as photographs and the chain of custody, the analyst has a clear picture of the process and the outcome.

Types of documentation

There is no one standard that dictates how an incident is documented, but there are a few distinct categories. As was previously stated, the depth of the documentation will often depend on the type, scale, and scope of an incident, but in general the following categories apply:

- **Trouble ticketing system**: Most enterprise organizations have an existing ticketing system utilized to track system outages and other problems that normally arise in today's network infrastructure. These systems capture a good deal of data associated with an incident. An entry usually captures the start and stop date and time, the original reporting person, and the action performed, and also provides an area for notes. The one major drawback to ticketing systems is that they were originally designed to support the general operations of enterprise infrastructures. As a result, more complex incidents will require much more documentation than is possible in these systems. Due to this, they are often reserved for minor incidents, such as isolated malware infections or other such minor incidents that are disposed of quickly.

- **Incident response orchestration**: Some organizations have seen the need for a dedicated incident response platform and have come up with applications and other types of infrastructure that support incident response teams. These incident response orchestration platforms allow analysts to input data, attach evidence files, and collaborate with other team members, as well as pull in outside resources, such as malware reverse-engineering and threat intelligence feeds.

- There are several of these platforms available both commercially and as freeware. The main advantage to these platforms is that they automate the capture of information, such as date, time, and analyst actions. Another distinct advantage is that they can limit who sees the information to a select group. With ticketing systems, there is the possibility that someone without authorization will observe details that the organization may want to keep confidential. Having an orchestration system can provide a certain level of confidentiality. Another key advantage is the ability for team members to see what actions are taken and what information is obtained. This cuts down on the number of calls made and the possibility of miscommunication.

- **Written reports**: Even with automated platforms in use, some incidents require extensive written reporting. In general, these written reports can be divided into three main types. Each of the following types will be expanded on later in this chapter:

- **Executive summary**: The executive summary is a one- to two-page report that is meant to outline the high-level bullet points of the incident for the senior management. A brief synopsis of the events, a root cause, if it can be determined, and remediation recommendations are often sufficient for this list.

- **Incident report**: This is the detailed report that is seen by a variety of individuals within the organization. This report includes the details of the investigation, a detailed root cause analysis, and thorough recommendations on preventing the incident from occurring again.

- **Forensic report**: The most detailed report that is created is the forensics report. This report is generated when forensic examination is conducted against log files, captured memory, or disk images. These reports can be very technical, as they are often reviewed by other forensic personnel. These reports can be lengthy, as outputs from tools and portions of evidence, such as log files, are often included.

Sources

When preparing reports, there are several sources of data that are included within the documentation, whether the incident is small, requiring only a single entry into a ticketing system, all the way to a complex data breach that requires extensive incident and forensic reporting. Some sources include:

- **Personal observations**: Users may have some information that is pertinent to the case. For example, they might have clicked on a file in an email that appeared to come from a legitimate address. Other times, analysts may observe behavior in a system and make a note of it.
- **Applications**: Some applications produce log files or other data that may be necessary to include in a report.
- **Network/host devices**: A great deal of this book deals with acquiring and analyzing evidence from a host of systems in an enterprise environment. Many of these systems also allow for outputting reports that can be included with the overall incident or forensic reporting.
- **Forensic tools**: Forensic tools often have automated reporting functions. This can be as simple as an overview of some of the actions, as was addressed in the previous chapters, or the actual outputs, such as file hashes, that can be included within a forensic report.

Wherever the material comes from, a good rule to follow is to capture and include as much as possible in the report. It is better to have more information than less.

Audience

One final consideration when preparing documentation is who will read an incident report versus a detailed forensic report. In general, the following are some of the personnel both internal and external to an organization that may read the reports associated with an incident:

- **Executives**: High-profile incidents may bring the attention of the CEO or CFO, especially if they involve the media. The executive summary may suffice, but do not be surprised if the senior leadership requires a more detailed report and briefing during and at the conclusion of an incident.
- **Information technology personnel**: These individuals may be the most interested in what the incident response analysts have found. Most likely, they will review the root cause analysis and remediation recommendations very seriously.

- **Legal**: In the event that a lawsuit or other legal action is anticipated, the legal department will be examining the incident report to determine if there are any gaps in security or the relevant procedures for clarification. Do not be surprised if revisions have to be made.
- **Marketing**: Marketing may need to review either the executive summary or the incident report to craft a message to customers in the event of an external data breach.
- **Regulators**: In regulated industries, such as healthcare and financial institutions, regulators will often review an incident report to determine if there is potential liability on the part of the organization. Fines may be assessed based upon the number of confidential records that have been breached, or if it appears that the organization was negligent.
- **Law enforcement**: Some incidents require law enforcement to become involved. In these cases, law enforcement agencies may require copies of incident and forensics reports for review.
- **Outside support**: There are some instances where the need to bring in outside forensics or incident response support becomes necessary. The existing reports would go a long way in bringing these individuals up to speed.

Understanding the audience gives incident response analysts an idea of who will be reading them. Understand that the report needs to be clear and concise. In addition, technical details may require some clarification for those in the audience that do not have the requisite knowledge or experience.

Incident tracking

Many organizations utilize an IT trouble ticket tracking system for incidents. While tracking incidents in this manner works when there are few incidents and there is no need to automate incident response processes, organizations that have a more robust incident response capability that is in use a great deal may need to utilize an incident response platform to track and assist with the proper execution and documentation of the incident response process.

There are several commercial solutions available for tracking incidents. Some of these solutions can integrate with other toolsets so that a good deal of the process is automated. They may also incorporate playbooks into the platform so that incident response teams have immediate access and can work through the process, all the while recording their actions on the platform itself. One of the most significant advantages of a dedicated platform is the ability to track incidents over time and gain a sense of what types of attacks the organization is dealing with.

Fast incident response

The Societe Generale CERT has put together a platform titled **Fast Incident Response** (**FIR**) as a freeware tool to aid incident response teams with the creation, tracking, and reporting of incidents. This web application can allow anyone within the organization to create incidents, make notes, and track incidents to completion. This tool provides a good deal of features that may make it a very handy tool for incident response teams that have budgetary considerations.

The tool utilizes a MySQL backend database and a combination of Python, Django, and Bootstrap to create a web application environment where analysts and other users can input data, as well as perform queries. Another key feature of the FIR application is the ability to customize fields to fit the organization. FIR can be installed either in a Docker container or installed on a Linux system, such as Ubuntu.

FIR is available for both a development and production environment. Installation of either option is based on the size of the organization and how often data will be put into the system. A complete build guide is available at:
`https://github.com/certsocietegenerale/FIR/wiki/Installation-on-a-production-en vironment`.

For the purposes of this book, we will give a review of how to customize the platform and how to record an incident. There are other options that can be utilized to tailor the FIR platform for a particular CSIRT. The FIR site at
`https://github.com/certsocietegenerale/FIR/wiki/User-manual` has additional information that is useful.

To create a new incident without any modification, go through the following steps:

1. Once FIR is installed, navigate to the login screen by entering
   `http://localhost:8000` in the URL bar in a web browser. The sign in form
   will appear. For the development environment, sign in using admin/admin:

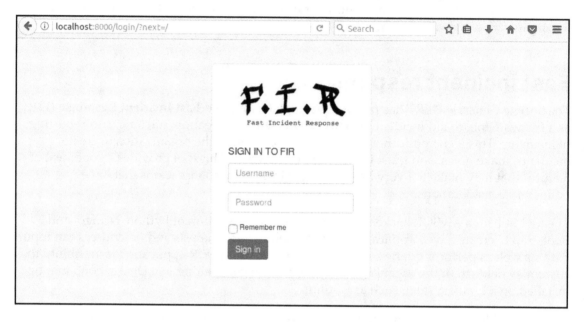

2. Once logged in, the dashboard will be empty as there are no incidents to record.
   Click on the **New event** button in the upper left-hand corner. The following
   window will appear:

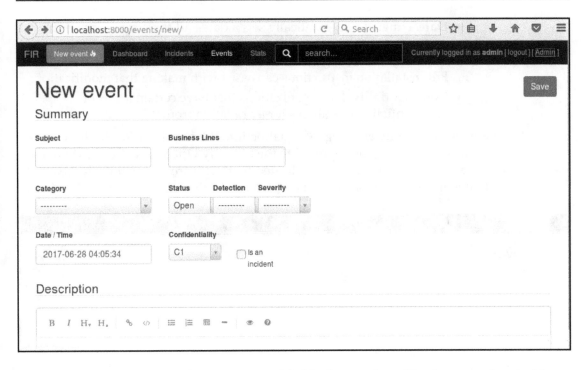

3. Within the form, there are several fields that can be utilized to record an incident:

- **Subject**: This is a free text field that can take any plain text. For best practices, this would best be utilized for the individual incident number.
- **Business lines**: This is one of the pre-configured fields that can be modified. Depending on the size of the organization, separating out incidents by business line may show decision makers the security vulnerabilities within that department.
- **Category**: FIR has a good deal of incident categories pre-configured that cover the wide range of attacks that an incident response team would see. There is also the ability to add additional categories.
- **Status**: This indicates if the incident is still open.
- **Detection**: This shows who or what the first entity to detect the incident was.
- **Severity**: FIR comes pre-configured with severity levels set from 1-4.

- **Date/Time**: FIR automatically sets a date and time stamp for actions performed within the application. During configuration, you may need to modify the settings within the platform to change the time zone. The FIR installation instructions can assist with making that modification.
- **Confidentiality**: For organizations that have certain levels of confidentiality, this allows for a gradation from 0-3.

4. Create the incident by entering information into the specific fields. In this case, a laptop has been stolen and reported to the **Security Operations Center** (**SOC**). In this case, the reporting party has indicated that there are approximately 2,000 confidential files stored on an unencrypted hard drive:

5. When the box for an incident is checked, two additional fields, **Actor** and **Plan**, appear. These are selections that can be modified to fit the organization. In this case, the actor is the CERT team and the plan will be the Data Loss Playbook. Once the fields are completed, click **Save**.

6. FIR then opens another window with the incident information. Click on **Add** and **To-Do** in the lower portion of the window. This will open up the following:

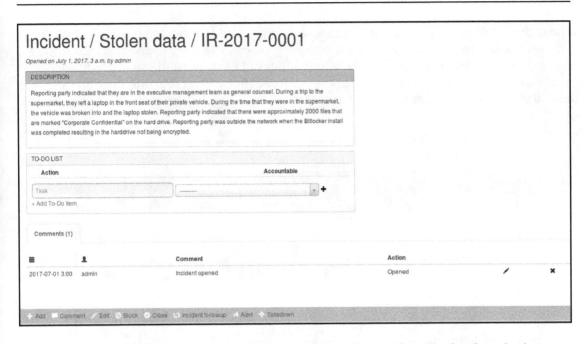

7. In the **Task** field, enter in **Execute Data Loss Prevention Playbook** and select **CERT** under **Accountable**. Once done, click the **plus** icon. This adds a task into the FIR system for follow-up. Click on **Dashboard** and the incident will appear.

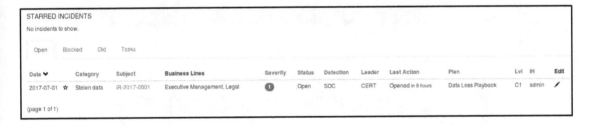

8. Click on **Tasks** and the task that was assigned to the CERT can be seen:

Through the use of the FIR platform, an incident response team can have a single repository for the incident data, as well as the ability to assign specific tasks to individuals. To further enhance this capability, FIR allows the administrator of the system the ability to make modifications to fields such as the business units or actions. To access this, click on the **admin** icon in the top right-hand corner of the window. This will open the configuration menu:

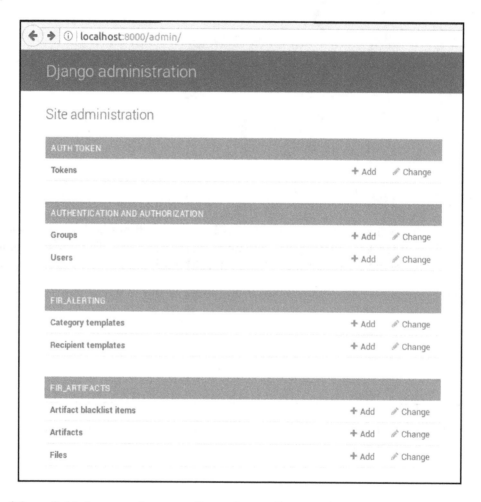

Many of these fields have not been configured yet, allowing the administrator to set specific types of alerting and artifacts. One area that the administrator may want to configure prior to utilizing is the incident information. Scrolling down, the following fields for incidents can be modified by the administrator:

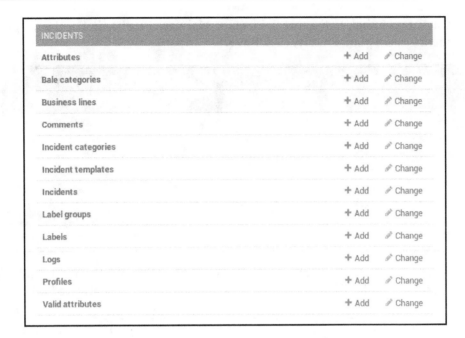

For example, suppose the administrator wants to add a malware playbook to the Plan drop-down menu. This addition would immediately alert other CSIRT personnel that the playbook should be executed:

1. Click on **Labels** and the following window will appear:

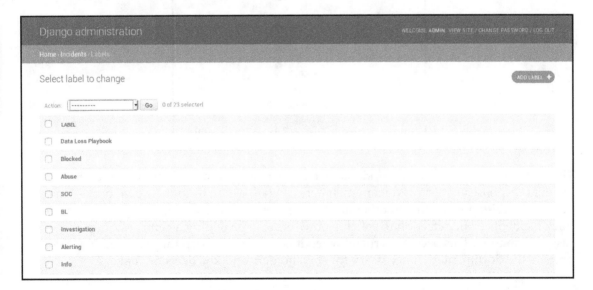

2. Click **Add Label**. In the text field, enter **Malware Playbook**. For the drop-down menu, select **plan**. Finally, click **Save**.

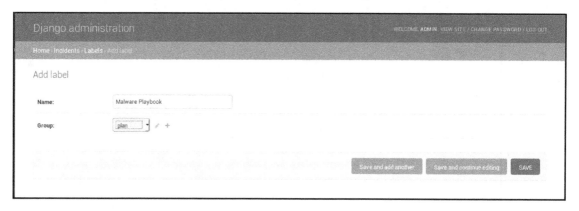

3. Navigate back to the home screen and click **New Event**. Click the **Is an incident** checkbox. Under **Plan**, there should be a selection titled **Malware Playbook**.

This is an example of the many options that are available for modification so that the incident response analysts and team members can tailor the FIR to their own operational needs. The FIR application and other applications like it allow incident response teams to track incidents from detection to conclusion while also providing a central storage place for case information. This becomes crucial when it is time to wrap up the investigation and prepare the documentation necessary for stakeholders and key decision makers.

Written reports

How the written report is structured is often dictated by several factors. There are many aspects of an incident response, such as the personnel involved, the type and depth of the investigation conducted, the amount of resources involved, and how many individuals from the organization were involved not only in investigating the incident, but who also have a stake in the outcome. As a result, some organizations may combine the core elements of the incident report, executive summary, and the forensic report into a single document. Others may find that separating out the documentation may better serve those with differing involvement and stakes in the incident investigation. The following are some of the key pieces of information that should be captured and reported during an investigation.

Executive summary

As was previously discussed, the executive summary captures the macro-level view of the incident. This includes a summary of the events, a description of the root cause, and what recommendations are being made to remediate and prevent such an occurrence from happening again. In regulated industries, such as financial institutions or hospitals that have mandatory reporting requirements, it is good practice to state whether notification was necessary, and, if it was necessary, how many confidential records were exposed. This allows senior management to understand the depth of the incident and ensure that the appropriate legal and customer communication steps are addressed.

Incident report

The incident report has perhaps the widest audience within and external to the organization. Even though there are individuals with limited technical skills that will be reviewing this report, it is important to have the proper terminology and associated data. There will always be time to explain technical details to those that may be confused.

The following are some of the key pieces of data that should be captured and incorporated into the report:

- **Background**: The background is the overview of the incident from detection to final disposition. A background of the incident should include how the CSIRT first became aware of the incident and what initial information was made available. Next, it should draw conclusions about the type and extent of the incident. The report should also include the impact on systems and what confidential information may have been compromised. Finally, it should include an overview of what containment strategy was utilized and how systems were brought back to normal operation.

- **Events timeline**: As the report moves from the background section to the events timeline, there is an increased focus on detail. The events timeline is best configured in a table format. For each action performed, an entry should be made in the timeline. The following table shows the level of detail that should be included:

Date	Time	Description	Performed by
6/17/17	19:08	SOC alerted CSIRT on-call about attempted C2 traffic from internal host.	John Smith
6/17/17	19:10	Examined firewall log and determined that host 10.25.4.5 had connected to known malware C2 server.	John Smith
6/17/17	19:14	Contacted the network security CSIRT member to administratively down the port connecting host 10.25.4.5 on switch 009.	John Smith
6/17/17	19:25	Removed connectivity to the internal network from host 10.25.4.5 from the network switch 009.	Dale Mitchell

- This log may include several pages of entries, but it is critical to understand the sequence of events and how long it took to perform certain actions. This information can be utilized both to recreate the sequence of events, but it can also be utilized to improve the incident response process by examining response and process times.

- **Network infrastructure overview**: In the event an incident has occurred that involves multiple systems across a network, it is good practice to include both a network diagram of the impacted systems and an overview of how systems are connected and how they communicate with each other. Other information, such as firewall rules that have a direct bearing on the incident, should also be included.

- **Forensic analysis overview**: Incidents that include forensic analysis of logs, memory or disk drives, an overview of the process, and the results should be included in the incident report. This allows stakeholders to understand what types of analysis were performed, as well as the results of that analysis, without having to navigate the very technical aspects of digital forensics. Analysts should ensure that conclusions reached via forensic analysis are included within this section. If the incident response team made extensive use of forensic techniques, these can be recorded in a separate report covered later in this chapter.

- **Containment actions**: One of the key tasks of an incident response team is to limit the amount of damage to other systems when an incident has been detected. This portion of the report will state what types of containment actions were undertaken, such as powering off a system, removing its connectivity to the network, or limiting its access to the internet. Analysts should also ensure that the effectiveness of these measures is incorporated into the report. If, for example, it was difficult to administratively remove network access via accessing the switch, and a manual process had to be undertaken, knowledge of this fact will help the CSIRT create new processes that streamline this action and limit the ability of a compromised host to access the other portions of the network.

- **Findings/root cause analysis**: The meat of the report that is of the most use to senior leadership and information technology personnel is both the finding and, if it has been discovered, the root cause. This portion of the report should be comprehensive and incorporate elements of the timeline of events. Specific factors within hosts, software, hardware, and users that contributed to either a negative or positive outcome within the incident should be called out. If the specific exploit used by the attacker, or a vulnerability that was exploited, has been determined, then this should also be included. The overall goal with this portion of the report is to describe how the threat was able to compromise the infrastructure, and to lend credence to the remediation and recommendations that follow.

- **Remediation**: If steps were taken during the incident to remediate vulnerabilities or other deficiencies, they should be included. This allows the CSIRT to fully brief other IT personnel as to what changes were made to limit damage to the rest of the network so that they can then be placed into the normal change control procedures and vetted. This ensures that these changes do not have an adverse impact on other systems in the future.
- **Final recommendations**: Any recommendations of improvements to the infrastructure, patching of vulnerabilities, or addition controls should be included in this section of the report. However, any recommendations should be based upon observations and a thorough analysis of the root cause.
- **Definitions**: Any specific definitions that would aid technical personnel in understanding the incident should be included within the report. Technical terms, such as **Server Message Block** (**SMB**), should be included if, in particular, an exploit was made against vulnerabilities within the SMB protocol on a specific system.

It is critical to understand that this report is the most likely to make its way to various entities within and external to the organization. The report should also make its way through at least one quality control review to make sure that it is free of errors and omissions, and can be read by the target audience.

Forensic report

Forensic reports are the most technically complex of the three main report types. Analysts should be free to be as technically accurate as possible and to not dumb down the reporting for those that may be nontechnical. Analysts should also be aware that the forensic report will be critical to the overall incident reporting if it was able to determine a specific individual, such as a malicious insider.

In cases where a perpetrator has been identified or where the incident may incur legal ramifications, the forensic report will undergo a good deal of scrutiny. It therefore behooves the analyst to take great pains to complete it accurately and thoroughly:

- **Examiner bio/background**: For audience members such as legal or external auditors, it is critical to have an idea of the background and qualifications of the forensic analysts. This background should include formal education, training, experience, and an overview of an analyst's courtroom experience, which should include if they were identified as an expert witness. Often times, a complete CV can be attached to the forensic report, especially if it is anticipated that the report will be used as part of a court case.
- **Tools utilized**: The report should include a complete list of hardware and software tools that were utilized in the analysis of evidence. This information should include the **make**, **model**, and **serial number** of hardware, such as a physical write blocker, or the software name and version utilized for any software used. A further detail that can be included in the report is that all tools were up to date prior to use.
- **Evidence items**: A comprehensive list of the evidence items should include any disk images, memory captures, or log files that were acquired by the analysts during the incident. The date, time, location, and analyst who acquired the evidence should also be included. It may be necessary to include as an attachment the chain of custody forms for physical pieces of evidence. If there are a number of evidence items, this portion of the report can be included as an addendum to allow for better flow of reading for the reader.
- **Forensic analysis**: This is where analysts will be very specific with the actions that were taken during the investigation. Details such as dates and times are critical, as well as detailed descriptions of the types of actions that were taken.

- **Tool output**: During the previous chapters, there have been a great many tools that have been leveraged for investigating an incident. Some of these tools, such as Volatility or Rekall, do not have the ability to generate reports. It is therefore incumbent upon the analyst to capture the output of these tools. Analysts can include screen captures or text output from these command-line tools and should incorporate them within the report. This is critical if these tools produce an output that is pertinent to the incident. Other tools, such as Autopsy, have the capability to output reports for inclusion in the forensic analysis report. For example, to run the report from the analysis conducted in the previous chapter, open the case in Autopsy. Navigate to **Tools** and then to **Generate Report**. Select **Results - HTML**. Click **Next** and then **All Results**. This produces an HTML report that will open in the default browser:

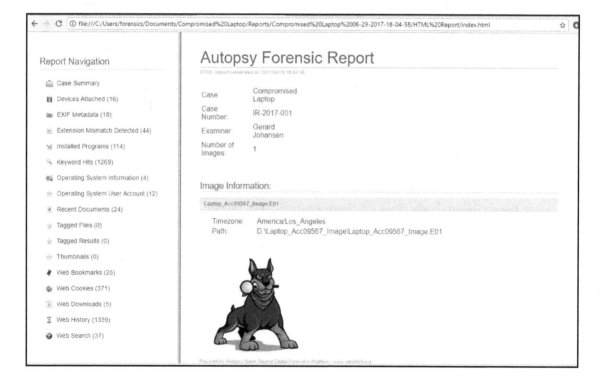

- From here, the analyst can review the information. Other techniques, such as printing to a PDF file, allow analysts to attach the output directly to the report. Analysts should become familiar with their toolset, as having the ability to export a report directly from the tool will reduce errors, and can stand up better under scrutiny.
- **Conclusions**: Conclusions that are derived from the evidence can be included in the report. For example, if an analyst determines that a specific executable is malware by matching the hash with a known strain, and that this malware steals credentials, they are well within their bounds to make that conclusion. However, analysts should be cautious about supposition and making conclusions without the proper evidence to support it.
- **Definitions**: As the forensic report is very technical, it is important to include the necessary definitions. Internal stakeholders, such as legal representatives, will often review the report in the event that legal action is anticipated. They may need further clarification on technical details.
- **Exhibits**: Output from tools that are too long to include within the body of the report can be included as an addendum. For example, if the output of a Volatility command is several pages long, but the most pertinent data is a single line, the analyst can pull that single line out and include it in the forensic analysis portion while making it clear that the entire output is located as an addendum. It is important to include the entire output of a tool as part of this report to ensure that it will stand up to scrutiny.

One of the key factors of the forensic report is to have a peer review process before it is issued as part of the incident documentation. This is to ensure that the actions that have been performed, the analysis, and the conclusions match the evidence. This is one of the reasons that analysts should include as much data as possible from the output of tools or through the review. In the event that a forensic report does go to court, understand that an equally or even more qualified forensic analyst may be reviewing the report and critiquing the work. Knowing this may make analysts more focused on preparing their report.

Whether or not an organization chooses to separate the documentation or prepare a master report, there is certain data that should be captured within the report. Having an idea of what this data is comprised of allows incident response personnel to ensure that they take the proper notes and record their observations while the incident investigation is in progress. Failure to do so may mean that actions taken or observations made are not captured in the report. Furthermore, if the case is going to see the inside of a court room, evidence may be excluded. It is better to over document than under document.

Summary

Incident response teams put a great deal of effort into preparing for and executing the tasks necessary to properly handle an incident. Of equal importance is properly documenting the incident so that decision makers and the incident response team itself have a clear understanding of the actions taken and how the incident occurred. It is through the use of this documentation and analyzing a root cause that organizations can improve their security and reduce the risk of similar events in the future. One area of major concern to incident responders and forensic analysts is the role that malware plays in incidents. The next chapter will discuss some of the techniques available to analysts in addressing these types of incidents

10
Malware Analysis

Malicious Software continues to be an ever-evolving scourge on enterprise and consumer systems. As soon as defenses are created, malware coders create a new strain that has the power to corrupt or destroy a system. Malware is even being utilized as a weapon against nation states and global organizations. A great many of the data breaches that have made the news have some component, either in whole or in part, that involves the use of malware to achieve some goal. Organizations in every sector of the economy have faced malware. With the addition of ransomware attacks such as WannaCry and Petya, organizations have had to spring into action to address these attacks.

With malware an ever-present risk, it is critical that incident response analysts have some knowledge of the methods and tools utilized in the analysis of malicious code. It would be impossible to address the complexities of malware analysis in a single chapter. Therefore, this chapter will focus on the foundation elements of malware analysis while examining some of the tools that are utilized. This will give the analyst a solid understanding of these methods who will then be better able to see the results of such an analysis in the context of an incident.

In this discussion of malware analysis, the following topics will be addressed:

- Malware overview
- Static malware analysis
- Dynamic malware analysis
- Tools for analysis
- Sandbox tools and techniques.

Malware overview

Malicious software or malware is an all-encompassing term for any software that has been created to damage, disable or produce an unwanted condition within a computer system. This definition, while functional is also very broad in its categorization of malware. There is malware that is coded specifically to steal credit card numbers from payment systems while other malware is utilized to take control of a system allowing an attacker to remotely control that system. Analysts who observe these specific behaviours, such as how a compromised system sends communications out to the internet after infection, or what actions are taken on an infected system, may be able to determine what type the malware is, and what the end goal of the attacker may be.

In general, when discussing malware, the following are some of the more specific categories:

- **Virus**: For a time, the term *virus* was used as the term for any malicious code that had a determinantal impact on a computer system. As the types of malware increased, the term *virus* was relegated to mean any code that has an intentional malicious impact on a system.
- **Worm**: Often part of a virus, a worm can not only have an impact on a system, but is able to self-replicate and impact other systems connected to it. One of the most famous worms was the Morris Worm that spread worldwide causing denial of service attacks across the internet in 1988.
- **Trojan**: The Trojan horse of mythology is the inspiration for this class of malware. Trojan malware is often hidden within a legitimate application or file. When an unsuspecting user opens the file, the malware infects the system. This type of malware often leverages a social engineering attack to infect a system.
- **Keylogger**: This specific malware hides in the background of a running system and captures the keystrokes of the user. It then takes this information and sends it to a controller for review. Coders who write keyloggers are often interested in obtaining credentials.
- **Root Kit**: Rootkits are utilized to conceal other malicious code such as a Remote Access Trojan (RAT), which allows for an attacker to take remote command of an infected system.
- **Information Stealing Malware**: Often coded for a single purpose, this type of malware is used to capture information such as credit card numbers or banking credentials such as the Shylock malware which was created specifically to capture banking logins.

- **Backdoor**: Another variation of remote access, this type of malware infects a system and then allows the attacker to take control of the infected system.
- **Downloader**: As defensive have gotten more sophisticated, so have the malware writers. A downloader is part of a *multi-stage* malware program. The downloader often infects a system and then reaches out to a remote server for the rest of the code. This method is often utilized to by-pass security controls and is useful for malware coders to utilize larger and more sophisticated malware.
- **Botnet**: A botnet is a series of computers all controlled through a central system on the internet called a *botnet controller*. First, the botnet malware infects a system. As the number of infected systems grows, the malware writers can then utilize this botnet to conduct Distributed **Denial of Service** (**DOS**) attacks against a single target.
- **Ransomware**: A relatively new type of malware, ransomware encrypts a victim's files. The malware then solicits a payment, often in the form of a crypto currency such as Bitcoin from the victim for the decryption key.
- **File Wipers**: A file wiper either destroys the files or is able to infect the Master Boot Record and modify records so that files are no longer accessible to the system.

Many of the variants are used together in a chain. For example, a malware coder may conduct an initial infection of a system with a Remote Access Trojan disguised as a legitimate application. When an unsuspecting user opens the application, code executes itself. It then downloads a second payload and further infects the system, allowing the coder remote access. Finally, with remote access, the attack continues with the attacker identifying a payment system. From there, they load a second piece of malware onto the payment system and capture clear text credit card numbers.

Another key aspect to malware is how it has evolved over time. There has been an explosion in how many variants of malware there are and the sheer number of malicious codes there are currently in the wild. Malware is evolving every day with new techniques of encoding and delivery as well as execution, changing rapidly. Analysts will be well advised to make a point to keep abreast of these changes as they are happening, so that they are prepared for the latest and more damaging code.

Malware analysis overview

Malware Analysis or malware reverse engineering is a highly technical and specialized field in forensics. Anti-Virus and Threat Intelligence utilizes a highly trained cadre of programmers and forensic personnel that acquire malware from the wild and then rip it open to determine what it does, how it does it, and who may be responsible for it. This is done utilizing two types of analysis, Static and Dynamic. Like much of digital forensics, each type of analysis affords some advantages and incident response analysts should be familiar with both.

 An excellent treatment of malware analysis conducted against actual malware found in the wild is Kim Zetter's book Countdown to Zero Day. Comprehensively researched, this book delves deep into the Stuxnet virus as various research teams attempt to understand what the malware is doing.

An excellent malware analysis methodology was created by Lenny Zeltser, a malware analysis professional who has an excellent array of resources on his website at https://Zeltser.com. This methodology is comprised of seven steps that aid the analysts in their process.

1. Create a controlled laboratory environment where examinations can be conducted.
2. Examine the behavior of the suspected malware as it interacts with the operating system environment.
3. Examine the suspicious application's code to gain a sense of the inner workings.
4. Perform a Dynamic Analysis to determine what actions are taken that could not be identified in the Static Analysis.
5. Determine if the malware is *packed* and unpack as necessary.
6. Continue the process until the analysis objectives have been completed.
7. Prepare a supplement to the forensics reporting and return the laboratory to the state prior to the analysis.

Static analysis

Static Analysis is an examination of the actual malware code without executing it on a system. For malware researches, the code may be obtained from systems that are left out to be deliberately infected or from production systems that have been impacted by the malware.

In this case, incident response analysts can obtain the actual source code or executable through a combination of memory analysis and acquiring the actual executable during an analysis of the hard drive. Static analysis is often comprised of several different techniques:

- **Fingerprinting**: One of the most basic techniques is obtaining a cryptographical hash of the code.These hashes can then be compared to other known hashes to determine if the code has been seen before.

- **Anti-Virus Scanning**: Anti-Virus vendors often do not catch every virus. For example, some vendors may have done an analysis of the code and deployed a signature for their own product. Other vendors may not have had access to the code or deployed their own signature. A good step is to use multiple different anti-virus vendors to scan a file.

- **String Extraction**: Malware coders will often include IP Addresses, error messages or other data encoded within the malware in clear text. Finding these strings may allow the analysts to identify a Command and Control (C2) server or other data that may indicate the purpose of the malware.

- **File Format**: With any executable, legitimate or not, there is metadata associated with it.Malware analysts can view the compilation time, functions, strings, menus and icons of Portable Executable format applications.

- **Packer Analysis**: To bypass Anti-Virus programs, malware coders make use of packers.These packers use compression or encryption so that they do not leave a tell-tale file hash.There are some tools available but, often, conducting a static analysis against packed malware is difficult.

- **Disassembly**: Reversing the code through the use of specialized software allows malware analysts to view the assembly code.From here, the analyst may be able to determine what actions the malware is attempting to perform.

When compared to Dynamic Analysis, Static Analysis may seem a bit more laborious. While there is a lot of searching and analysis done by hand, there are some advantages. First, it is safer to examine the code without having to execute it. This is especially true in organizations where a comprehensive sandbox solution is not in place. Also, it provides a more comprehensive analysis and better understanding of what the malware coder's intention might be.

There are several disadvantages to static analysis as well. This technique requires the malware code in its entirety for the best results. Another key disadvantage is the time necessary. With malware becoming increasingly more complex, the time required for a static analysis may be longer than an organization can afford.

This is even more an issue during an incident where the incident response team may be better off with an analysis that covers most of their issues now rather than having to wait for the most comprehensive analysis.

Dynamic analysis

In static analysis, the focus was on examining the potential malware in a controlled environment. The focus was on examining the actual code or to look for specific file attributes that could be compared to other sources. In dynamic analysis, the focus is on allowing the potential malware to execute within a controlled environment and to observe the behaviors that the program exhibits.

There are several advantages that Dynamic Analysis affords malware researchers and incident responders. First, allowing the code to execute fully will remove the barriers such as encryption or other obfuscation techniques that are utilized by malware coders. Second, there are several automated tools that can be leveraged for Dynamic Analysis. This removes the manual process which can be very labor intensive as malware continues to increase in complexity. Finally, dynamic analysis is often much faster. As the researcher can monitor in real time how a piece of potential malware works on a system.

There are two broad categories of dynamic malware analysis that can be utilized.

- **Defined point analysis**: In this method, a test operating system such as Windows 7 is configured in a live production state. Analysts make a recording of various registry key settings, processes and network connections. Once these are recorded, the suspected malware is executed on the system. Once the analysts are confident that the malware is executed completely, they will then compare the two points of the system such as comparing the running processes or identify changes. This type of analysis can make use of some of the forensic techniques addressed in previous chapters. For example, analysts can take a freshly installed operating system and perform a memory capture. This memory capture and a subsequent one that is taken from the infected machine gives the analysts a point of comparison to identify specific behaviors of the malware.
- **Runtime behavior analysis**: In this method, analysts utilize tools such as Process Explorer and other utilities to observe the behavior of the suspected malware while it is executing. There are also tools that automate a good deal of this process to give analysts a good understanding of how the malware is executing.

While there are distinct advantages to dynamic analysis, incident responders should understand some of the concerns that need to be addressed prior to detonating suspected malware on a system. First, a controlled environment must be configured.

Suspected malware should never be executed on a production environment.Researchers and incident responders should ensure that any test or analysis environment is completely separated from the production environment.

Another concern is the amount of resources that are required to create a proper environment for dynamic analysis. Malware researches and incident responders make use of a sandbox environment for the analysis of malware. A Sandbox is simply a controlled environment where suspect malware is executed and the associated analysis can take place. For organizations that research malware, this Sandbox can become quite large as copies of the various operating systems and their patch levels should be maintained. For example, for an organization to test a malware sample that impacts the Windows operating system, they will often have to have instances of Windows XP, Windows 7, Windows 8 and finally Windows 10 with the various patch levels. This allows them to zero in on the specific operating systems that are impacted by the malware. In addition to the operating systems, analysts will also have to have images of the memory.

Analyzing malware

The tools for analysing malware range from simple hex editors and Interactive Disassemblers to GUI based tools that integrate online searching and analysis. Each incident will often dictate the specific tools or techniques utilized. A possible infection through a social engineering email that is in the process of infecting network systems may require analysts to work rapidly to identify the malware's behaviour and craft a solution to remove it.In other circumstances, a security control may have identified a file that it deems suspicious.With no active incident at hand, the incident response analysts may want to completely rip apart the code to determine if it had a specific purpose. In either case, the following tools are useful in assisting in the process but, by no means, it is the list all inclusive.

There are several sites that provide sample malware for training and research. For example, in this chapter, two such samples were taken from malware-traffic-analysis.net. These files can be downloaded in ZIP format. As a general rule, any malware sample will be password protected with the word *infected*.

Before taking on the task of analyzing, ensure that the system utilized is properly isolated from the network and anti-virus is turned off. One technique is to utilize a virtual machine that can be snapshotted before use and returned to that state after analysis.

Static analysis

There are several tools that can be leveraged for static analysis. The combination of automated and manual tools allows an analyst to identify components of the malware that should have additional focus as well as identifying specific elements within the application that is indicative of malware.

Pestudio

A good place to begin a Static Analysis is with Pestudio. Chapter 7, *Analysing System Memory* introduced this application when examining suspect malicious software obtained through the analysis of a memory image. In this case, an actual piece of malware will be analysed using the Pestudio. This tool allows analysts to focus on specific attributes of the malware for further analysis.

In this scenario, a live piece of malware will be examined. The malware sample is a **Loki Bot Malspamtrojan**. This sample was taken from http://www.malware-traffic-analysis.net/2017/06/12/index.html. Ensure that the proper pre-configuration is done as any anti-virus program will quarantine the malware making any analysis impossible. Once downloaded into a folder, the file is ready for analysis.

1. Open Pestudio. Click the folder icon in the upper left-hand corner and navigate to the malware sample.

2. Once loaded, the following window will appear. In the pane to the left are several elements that Pestudio examines against the malware. Several of these elements (in red) indicate that the code is suspected of containing malware.

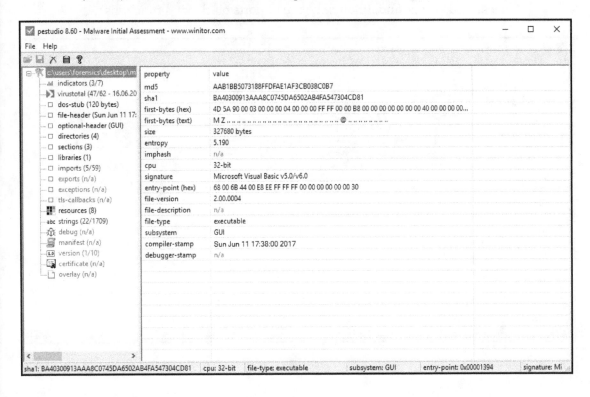

3. Click on **indicators** first to get an overview of the specific components of the malware that have been identified as malicious. Pestudio has identified three specific indicators--the file has 47/62 hits on VirusTotal, there are several blacklisted strings and, finally, the file imports blacklisted functions.

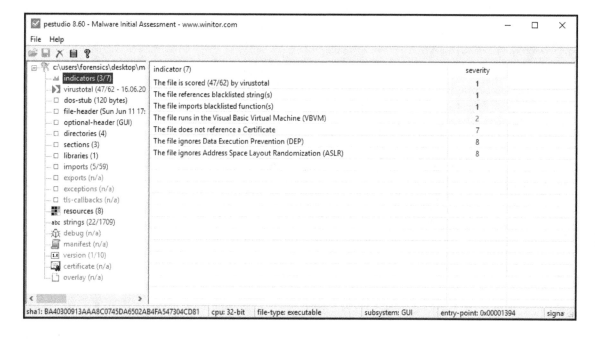

4. Click on **imports**. From here, the analyst can see the imported library files that are blacklisted.

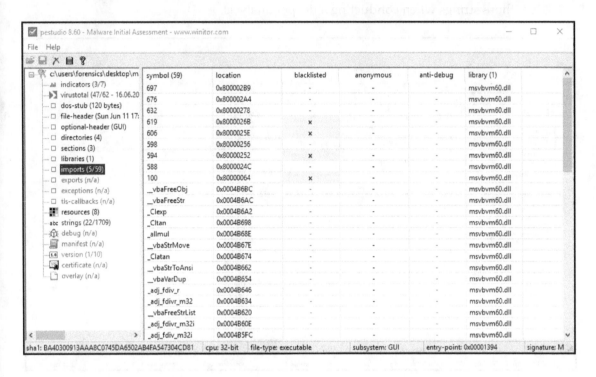

5. Click on **strings**. This gives the analysts a clear understanding of the various strings within the malware that are suspect. From here, the analyst can focus on those strings when conducting a deeper analysis.

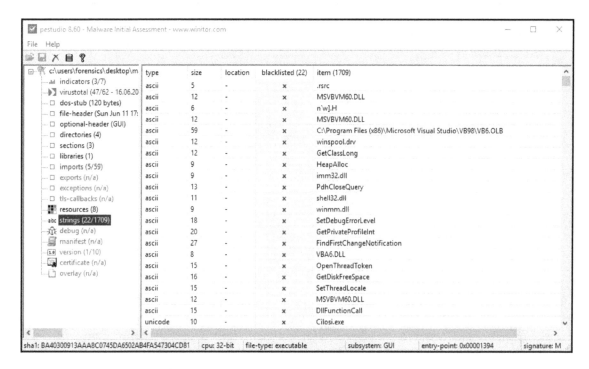

Pestudio allows an analysts to get a 10,000 foot overview over suspected malware. Often, this may be enough for incident responders to work off in terms of identifying other infections. In other incidents, it may be necessary to perform a deeper analysis. This is where other tools come into play.

Remnux

Remnux is a freeware commandline based utility for conducting malware analysis. Developed and maintained by Lenny Zeltser, Remnux has a variety of tools that allow analysts to examine suspicious documents, JavaScript, and other artifacts associated with malware. Further, there are tools such as Wireshark that can be utilized to not only analyze the malware but to identify network connections or traffic.

Remnux can be downloaded in a OVA file format from:
`https://docs.google.com/uc?id=0B6fULLT_NpxMampUWlBCQXVJZzA&export=download`.

Once downloaded, the file can be converted by the analyst's select virtualization software. On the desktop are two links to .html files and a PDF document that contains all of the necessary information for an analyst to conduct an examination. To start an examination, click on the terminal icon and an icon window will appear. For most commands, the convention is:

```
remnux@remnux:~$ <Command><Malware File>
```

In the following example, a malware executable will be analyzed. This particular file, `rad7DAC6.tmp.exe` is available from `http://www.malware-traffic-analysis.net/2017/04/28/index.html`. Again, ensure that proper precautions are taken when working with malware. One advantage to Remnux as a Linux platform, is that there is little risk in downloading a Windows based malware sample directly onto that system.

Once the file is properly situated, the following basic check, *pescanner* will be run against the file. Pescanner is a tool that statically examines a PE formatted file. To run the tool, the following command is used:

```
remnux@remnux:~$ pescanner rad7DAC.tmp.exe
```

The command produces a good deal of information. It first provides, the metadata including a file hash and the type of file packer, in this case **Armadillo v1.71.**

```
remnux@remnux:~$ pescanner rad7DAC6.tmp.exe
################################################################################
[0] File: rad7DAC6.tmp.exe
################################################################################

Meta-data
================================================================================
Size           : 366434 bytes
Type           : PE32 executable (GUI) Intel 80386, for MS Windows
Architecture   : 32 Bits binary
MD5            : b71d80ba5c8467471def36580a98bcfd
SHA1           : 9f104ffe6f6817235d1da0947b601c5f9bf014af
ssdeep         : 6144:C1qqPp4J+q3BYHbxYRa39tfuhIVx4+TGVHsKaxWjNDr+vy:C1qs4JybmIt3v4rsK1DAy
imphash        : af218f9056bae4ea1b75733252e39cd7
Date           : 0x58FA3088 [Fri Apr 21 16:17:12 2017 UTC]
Language       : []
CRC:   (Claimed) : 0x0, (Actual): 0x5c990 [SUSPICIOUS]
Packers        : Armadillo v1.71
Entry Point    : 0x2013806 .text 0/6
==================
```

Another key focus point is that Remnux identified that the CRC does not match, indicating suspicious behavior. Other information includes the instructions that the malware is programmed to perform.

```
Offset | Instructions
- - - - - - - - - - - - - - - - - - - - - - - - - - - - - - - - - - - - - - - - -
0           push ebp
1           mov ebp,esp
3           push byte 0xffffffff
5           push dword 0x2016938
10          push dword 0x20139b0
15          mov eax,fs:[0x0]
21          push eax
22          mov fs:[0x0],esp
29          sub esp,0x68
32          push ebx
33          push esi
34          push edi
35          mov [ebp-0x18],esp
38          xor ebx,ebx
40          mov [ebp-0x4],ebx
43          push byte 0x2
45          call [0x201891c]
51          pop ecx
52          or dword [0x2017900],0xffffffff
59          or dword [0x2017910],0xffffffff
66          call [0x2018918]
72          mov ecx,[0x20178ec]
78          mov [eax],ecx
80          call [0x2018914]
86          mov ecx,[0x20178e8]
92          mov [eax],ecx
94          mov eax,[0x2018910]
99          mov eax,[eax]
```

Next, Pescanner has identified the sections of memory in use by the piece of malware. There is also a section that details the **Entropy** of specific sections. Higher entropy indicates that a file is compressed or encrypted. In this case, Pescanner has indicated that a specific memory section is suspicious, due, most likely, to its being outside the norm for entropy.

```
Sections
=======================================================================================
Name       VirtAddr    VirtSize    RawSize    MD5                                Entropy
- - - - - - - - - - - - - - - - - - - - - - - - - - - - - - - - - - - - - - - - - - - - -
.text      0x1000      0x14c73     0x15000    a0d7ef7c53bbbe8e1c6d275b109b518b  4.153114
.rdata     0x16000     0xd3e       0x1000     0682992734f6e229b163ca7279674ead  3.102434
.data      0x17000     0x914       0x1000     563a9fb35965513bdca569e6fac6f107  0.327826   [SUSPICIOUS]
.idata     0x18000     0xc99       0x1000     a152968547de25453afb9f36fe4ec24d  3.459574
.rsrc      0x19000     0x6344      0x7000     1b4ed2bf8a886624845c747027dee275  5.812523
.reloc     0x20000     0x7ad       0x1000     e3c9891dba773a9a15bcbcca0d0d6d75  2.956748
```

Moving down the results, Pescanner indicates what DLL files are imported as part of this malware. From here, the analyst can possibly determine more of the malicious file's behavior by examining these files.

```
Imports
=========================================================================================
[1] MFC42
[2] MSVCRT.dll
[3] KERNEL32.dll
[4] USER32.dll
```

Finally, Pescanner will indicate what suspicious **Import Address Table** (**IAT**) entries are being called by the malicious software. This allows analysts to determine what behavior the malicious code is exhibiting and possibly what actions it is performing on the infected system by examining these entries.

```
Suspicious IAT alerts
=========================================================================================
[1] CreateFileW
[2] FindWindowW
[3] GetModuleFileNameW
[4] GetModuleHandleA
[5] GetStartupInfoA
```

Boasting a wide range of tools, Remnux is an excellent resource to conduct a wide range of tasks associated with examination. Further, Remnux includes other tools like Rekall and Volatility so that analysts can perform the panoply of tasks from memory image analysis, in conjunction with malware analysis.

Dynamic analysis

Dynamic Analysis is often facilitated using a sandbox. One method is to have a virtual appliance with the proper operating system installed. From here, the analyst can monitor network traffic, examine processes and compare them to normal baseline behavior. Deviations from this baseline can be examined in more detail to determine if they are legitimate or tied to a malicious executable.

In addition to utilizing virtual machines, there are several automated tools that re-create the sandbox environment for analysts to execute live applications that are suspected of containing malicious code. These tools can be configured and deployed within the enterprise environment, or there is the ability to upload the potential malware to a cloud-based service that can perform the functions of a malware sandbox.

Process Explorer

One of the key tools that allows for detailed examination of malware as it is executing is the Process Explorer. This tool is made as part of the Windows Sysinternal suite of tools and provides a no cost platform for analysts to gain a sense of what each process is running, their parent process as well as examining CPU usage. Simply download the application from the following site:

`https://technet.microsoft.com/en-us/sysinternals/processexplorer.aspx`. Extract the contents and then double-click the version of **Process Explorer** (32-bit or 64-bit version) that is applicable. The following window will appear:

As can be seen, there are several key pieces of information available to the analyst. The major advantage of this tool is the visual representation. As opposed to attempting to utilize either native Windows tools or other memory analysis tools after capture, analysts can quickly see if any processes look suspicious.

Analysts have the ability to send a process and associated data to `VirusTotal.com` for analysis. If a suspicious process is identified, **Process Explorer** will send the information off to the site for analysis and comparison. If a process is identified, click on it in the window. Navigate to **Process** and then Check VirusTotal. The results will be indicated by a number over 62.

WavesSvc64.exe	0.66	16,780 K	7,016 K	9280 Waves MaxxAudio Service ...	Waves Audio Ltd.	
quickset.exe	< 0.01	6,512 K	8,960 K	9328 QuickSet	Dell Inc.	0/62
OneDrive.exe	< 0.01	88,032 K	81,304 K	9396 Microsoft OneDrive	Microsoft Corporation	

Another key feature that **Process Explorer** can provide is the ability to dump the process contents in much the same way that Volatility is able to. The major difference is that the analyst is able to conduct the dump without having to acquire a memory image. To dump the memory, click on the process and navigate to **Process** and then **Create Dump**. The analyst has the option to choose from a *Mini-Dump* or a *Full Dump*. As a standard practice, it is advisable to capture a *Full Dump*. This dump can then be saved to a directory of choice.

One technique that can be used is to create a virtual machine with the appropriate Windows Operating System. It is best to start with a bare-bones operating system with the Microsoft Office Suite installed. Other third-party programs can be installed later if it appears that the malicious code leverages a vulnerability in those applications. Start **Process Explorer** and let run for a few minutes. Next, execute the suspected malware. Observe what new processes are created. From here, the analysts can compare these processes and associated DLL files with VirusTotal and then dump any of those processes for later static analysis.

Cuckoo sandbox

The Cuckoo Sandbox is a malware analysis system that automates many of the tasks associated with malware analysis. This open source application has the ability to analyse a variety of suspected malicious files such as Windows executables, documents and Java applets all within a virtualized environment. This analysis includes network traffic and memory analysis utilizing Volatility.

Installing the Cuckoo Sandbox can take some time and effort.An excellent resource on installing the local sandbox can be found at `https://bdavis-cybersecurity.blogspot.com/2016/11/cuckoo-sandbox-installation-part-1-of-4.html`

In addition to a local version of Cuckoo Sandbox, analysts can make use of a web-based version. The site `https://malwr.com/` is a free service that allows analysts to upload a copy of the malware and have the site conduct a dynamic analysis. From here, the site will produce a report that can be reviewed. In the following example, `malwr.com` will be utilized to conduct a review of the Loki Bot Malspam that was previously analyzed with Pestudio.

1. Navigate to the site `http://malwr.com`and click **Submit** in the upper left hand corner. This will open the following window:

2. Click **Select File** and then navigate to the malware file to be analyzed. `Malwr.com` allows the analyst to share the sample of malware with the community or not. In this case, as the malware being tested is known, this is not selected. Finally, complete the equation and click **Analyze**. The following window will appear.

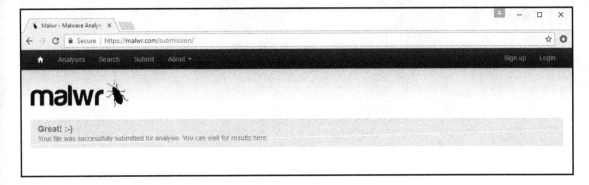

3. Depending on the type of malware and its size, it may take a few minutes for Malwr to analyze. During that time, the following window will appear:

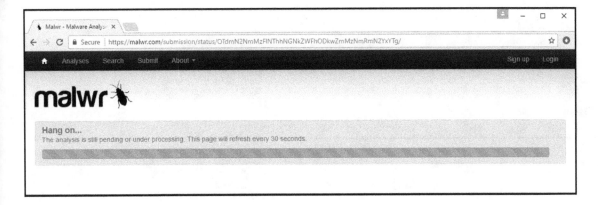

4. Once the analysis is complete, a window will open with the analysis results. The analysis results include static and dynamic analysis elements such as behavioral and network elements for review.

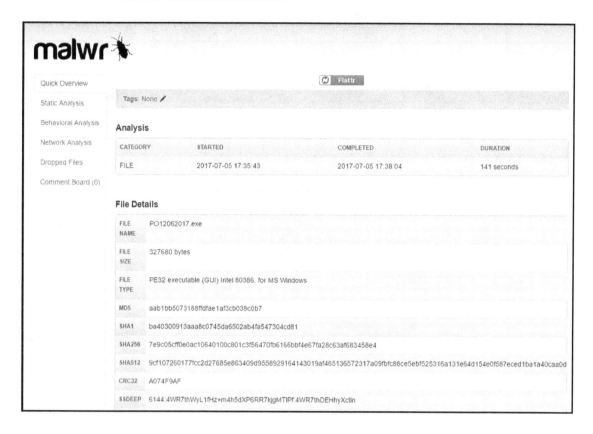

5. Click on **Static Analysis**. From here, the analyst can view specific elements including strings and what elements are imported as part of the DLL file which, in this case is the MSVBVM60.dll.

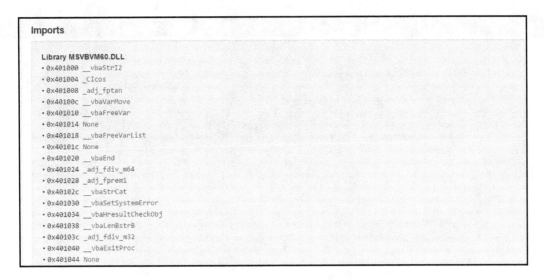

6. While in the **Static Analysis** section, click on **Antivirus**. This provides the analysts with a breakdown of VirusTotal results for the sample uploaded.

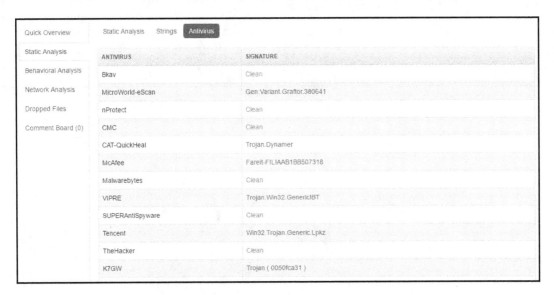

7. Next, click **Behavioral Analysis**. From here, specific file behaviors are outlined. There are charts that break down the sequence of events that transpired after the malware was executed. This allows analysts to view the specific elements in greater detail.

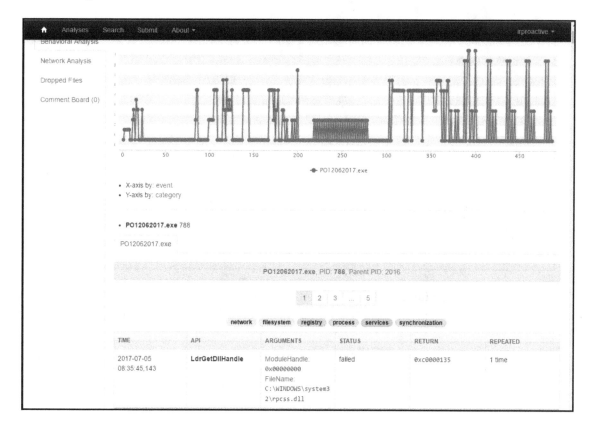

8. Often malware drops other files as part of the infection. Malwr also allows the analyst to see these files as well. Click on **Dropped Files**. Malwr indicates that there were two files that were dropped via this malware.

FILE NAME	filename.vbs
FILE SIZE	384 bytes
FILE TYPE	ASCII text, with CRLF line terminators
MD5	899dbb13af252b6cd89a6de23048cf8c
SHA1	857745ec21332c7e3a2f6f44af1113ecd9ec3f6a
SHA256	bf01560f94fd75d02a21b8cd133cab3d6e181f7eb4d41b6d415b65fe63665e96
CRC32	DA5FB4F1
SSDEEP	3:j+qAHmFEm86oQ/FERMQsNC2xA+KdIH1MARm5iRMQbm34MkWJJFHrLL:j+q9Nht6G9KdEARm5Mm34M9
YARA	• embedded_win_api - A non-Windows executable contains win32 API functions names

FILE NAME	filename.exe
FILE SIZE	327680 bytes
FILE TYPE	PE32 executable (GUI) Intel 80386, for MS Windows
MD5	1f54f93c28df730aa1c13d0090c7eeb5
SHA1	c152e04d928a5397943d9285af8373813affed25
SHA256	75d49db3c12349a5be3da567ed9ca169e05d0ced8e6a15846bf9b884ed954f0c
CRC32	9E4A0D9D
SSDEEP	6144:9WR7thWyL1fHz+m4h5dXP6RR7kjgMTIPv:9WR7thDEHhyXctIX
YARA	None matched

There is good deal more information that can be obtained via Malwr including examining network activity and comments provided by the Malwr community. One key consideration does need to be made when examining this platform against a local solution. Malware coders do pay attention to community boards and VirusTotal to see if a hash or the actual file has been uploaded. If the malware is specific to a single organization such as government entity or large retailer, they will know that incident response analysts have discovered their creation.Incident response teams need to balance the speed and ease of this technique with the possibility that their efforts might be discovered.

Summary

In many ways, this chapter has merely scratched the surface in regards to malware analysis. It should become apparent that, even with tools for static and dynamic analysis, incident response analysts still have a great deal of skill building ahead of them if they want to master this highly specialized subset of digital forensics. Although it may be difficult, it is important to have at least a functional knowledge of this type of analysis as the cyber criminals and nation states continue to utilize more sophisticated malware. This chapter delved into malware analysis by examining the types of malware currently being seen. An overview of the two primary methods of analysis; static and dynamic gave some context to the tools available. The tools discussed allow an analyst to identify behaviors in malware that can be used to identify them. Finally, actually executing malware can provide further details. The next chapter will tie in the use of threat intelligence into malware analysis and allow analysts an opportunity to tie in their observations to what is happening to other organizations.

11
Threat Intelligence

One area of incident response that has had a significant impact on an organization's ability to respond to cyber-attacks is the use of cyber threat intelligence or simply threat intelligence. The term *cyber threat intelligence* covers a wide range of information, data points, and techniques that allows analysts to identify attack types in their network, and adequately respond to them and prepare for future attacks. To be able to properly leverage this capability, information security analysts should have a solid foundation of the various terminologies, methodologies, and tools that can be utilized in conjunction with threat intelligence. If analysts are able to utilize this data, they will be in a better positioned to take pro-active security measures and in the event of a security incident, be more efficient in their response.

Threat intelligence overview

Like some terms in information security and incident response, threat intelligence is a bit nebulous. Various organizations such as government and academics produce information and data that is often touted as threat intelligence. Various commercial providers also have information available either through free or paid subscriptions that is touted as threat intelligence. This often results in difficulty to determine what threat intelligence is and what is simply data or information.

A good starting point to determining what comprises threat intelligence is to utilize a definition. The Gartner research company's definition of threat intelligence: *Threat intelligence is evidence-based knowledge, including context, mechanisms, indicators, implications and actionable advice, about an existing or emerging menace or hazard to assets that can be used to inform decisions regarding the subject's response to that menace or hazard.*

When examining this definition, there are several key elements that need to be present for data or information to be considered threat intelligence:

- **Evidence based**: This chapter will examine how evidence obtained through other processes, such as malware analysis, produces threat intelligence. For any intelligence product to be useful, it first must be obtained through proper evidence collection methods. In this way, analysts that rely on it can be sure of its validity.
- **Utility**: For threat intelligence to have a positive impact on a security incident's outcome or an organization's security posture, it has to have some utility. The intelligence must provide clarity in terms of context and data about specific behaviors or methods to determine an analyst is evaluating an incident against other incidents of a similar nature.
- **Actionable**: The key element that separates data or information from threat intelligence is action. Intelligence should drive action, whether that is a specific sequence of events or a specific focus area of an incident or whether or not a specific security control is implemented in the face of intelligence about what cyber threats the organization is most likely to face.

To see how this plays together, imagine a scenario where an incident response team at a healthcare institution is attempting to ascertain what types of attacks are most likely to occur against their infrastructure. Vagaries about cyber criminals wanting to steal data is not useful. There is no specific context or information in that dataset and the end result is the organization cannot put that information into action.

On the other hand, say that the incident response team leverages a third-party threat intelligence provider. This third party outlines specific criminal groups by name. The provider also indicates that these groups are currently utilizing PDF files sent via email to hospital employees. The PDF files contain a Remote Access Trojan that is controlled from C2 servers that are spread out in Europe. The third party also provides the team with MD5 file hashes of malware, the IP and domain addresses of the C2 servers, and finally, the file names most associated with the PDF document.

With this information, the incident response team can align their security controls to prevent PDF attachments from opening in emails. They can also utilize tools to search their infrastructure to determine if an infection has already occurred. Finally, they may be able to configure their event management solution to alert the team if any host within the network attempts to communicate with the C2 server. The major difference between these two scenarios is that the latter scenario drives actions within the organization. In the first scenario, the information was so vague and useless that the organization was left no better off.In the second scenario, the team could execute specific actions to either prevent an adverse condition or be better prepared to respond to one.

Threat intelligence is a response to the increased complexity and technical skill of cyber threat actors. The focus of threat intelligence is on the following threat actor groups:

- **Cyber criminals**: Organized and technically skilled, cyber criminals have been responsible for a variety of financial crimes against banking, retail, and other organizations. The motive for these groups is purely mercenary and their ultimate goal is to acquire data that can be monetized. For example, attacks against retailers such as Home Depot and Target involved the theft of credit card data with the intent of selling numbers on the Dark Web or other black markets.
- **Hacktivism**: Groups such as **Anonymous** and the **Idlib Martyrs' Brigade** are hacker groups that take on large businesses, government, and even religious institutions to further a political cause. Penetrating networks to obtain confidential data for disclosure or conducting denial of service attacks are done as part of an overall political versus a monetary objective.
- **Cyber-espionage**: Nation states such as the United States, Russia, China, Iran, and North Korea continually engage in espionage activities involving penetrating networks and obtaining intelligence. One of the most well-known cyber-attacks, the Stuxnet virus, was reportedly perpetrated by the United States and Israel.

Another key element to understanding threat intelligence is the concept of the **Advanced Persistent Threat** (APT). The term APT has been around for approximately a decade and is used to describe a cyber threat actor whose capability and motivation go far beyond that of a cyber-criminal or cyber-vandal. APT groups often target organizations for an intended purpose with a clear objective in mind and over a long period of time. As the term Advanced Persistent Threat describes, these groups have the following characteristics:

- **Advanced**: APT threat actors have advanced skills. These skills often involve intelligence gathering skills that exceed what can be obtained through open sourced methods. This includes such sources as **Imagery Intelligence** (**IMINT**), telephone or **Signals Intelligence** (**SIGINT**), and the ability to leverage **Human Intelligence** (**HUMINT**). Further, these groups can not only utilize advanced network penetration tools, but they are also adept at finding zero-day vulnerabilities and crafting custom malware and exploits that specifically target these vulnerabilities.

- **Persistent**: APT threat actors are focused on a clearly defined objective and will often forgo other opportunities to get closer to achieving their objective. APT threat actors will often go months or even years to achieve an objective through the intelligent leveraging of vulnerabilities and continuing a pace that allows them to bypass detection mechanisms. One of the key differentiators between APT threat actors and others is the intention to stay within the target network for a long period of time. Whereas a cyber-criminal group will stay long enough to download a database full of credit card numbers, an APT group will maintain access within a network as long as possible.

- **Threat**: To organizations that face APT groups, they are most definitely a threat.APT threat actors conduct their attacks with a specific objective and have the necessary infrastructure and skill set to attack targets such as large corporations, military, and government organizations.

Threat intelligence is a wide field of study with many elements that are tied together. In the end, threat intelligence should drive action within an organization. What that action may be is often decided after careful evaluation of the threat intelligence. This involves understanding the type of threat intelligence being reviewed and what advantage each of those types provides the organization.

Threat intelligence types

When discussing the wide variety of information types and datasets that constitute threat intelligence, they often fall into one of three main categories:

- **Tactical threat intelligence**: This is the most granular of the three threat intelligence categories. Information in this category involves either **Indicators of Compromise** (**IOCs**) or Tactics, techniques, or procedures.

  - **Indicators of Compromise**: An IOC is an artifact observed on a system that is indicative of a compromise of some sort. For example, a C2 IP address or an MD5 hash of a malicious file are IOCs.

  - **Tactics, techniques, and procedures**: Humans are creatures of habit and as a result, cyber attackers often develop a unique methodology to how they attack a network. For example, a cyber-criminal group may favour a social engineering email that has an Excel spreadsheet that executes a Remote Access Trojan. From there, they may attempt to access the credit card Point of Sale device and infect it with another piece of malware. How this group executes such an attack is considered as their TTPs.

- **Operational threat intelligence**: The past decade has seen more and more coordinated attacks that do not just target one organization but may target an entire industry, region, or country. Operational threat intelligence is data and information about the wider goal of cyber-attacks and cyber threat actors. This often involves not just examining the incident response team's own organization but examining how cyber threat actors are attacking the larger industry. For example, in returning to a previous example where incident responders at a healthcare institution were preparing for an attack, a wider knowledge of what types of attacks are occurring at similar sized and staffed healthcare institutions would be helpful in aligning their own security controls to the prevalent threats.

- **Strategic threat intelligence**: Senior leadership such as the CIO or CISO often must concern themselves with the strategic goals of the organization alongside the necessary controls to ensure that the organization is addressing the cyber threat landscape. Strategic threat intelligence examines trends in cyber-attacks, what cyber threat actors are prevalent, and what industries are major targets. Other key data points are changes in technology that a threat actor or group may leverage in an attack.

The best use of threat intelligence is to understand that each one of these types can be integrated into an overall strategy. Leveraging internal and external threat intelligence of all three types provides key decision makers with an understanding of the threat landscape; managers with the ability to implement appropriate security controls and procedures and analysts the ability to search for ongoing security issues or to prepare their own response to a cyber-attack.

Threat intelligence methodology

Threat intelligence goes through a feedback cycle in order to keep pace with an ever-changing environment. While there are several methodologies that can place context around this challenge, one that is often utilized is the cycle of intelligence that is used by the US Department of Defense.

This cycle provides the framework and a starting point for organizations to incorporate threat intelligence into their operations:

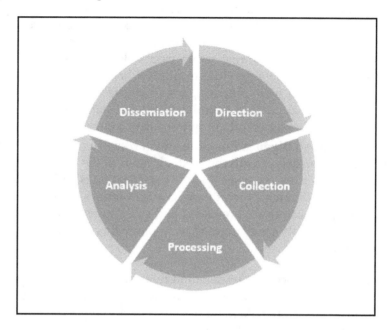

- **Direction**: Decision makers such as the CISO, information security personnel or incident response analysts set down what threat intelligence is required. In determining the requirements for intelligence, it is a good practice to identify the users of each of the types of threat intelligence previously discussed. For example, a CISO might want threat intelligence about what trends in cyber-attacks against hospitals are anticipated in the next year. An incident response analyst may require intelligence on what the individual IOCs of malware are being seen in other healthcare institutions. The organization may also start by looking at what critical systems and applications are in use as well as critical data they are trying to protect. Another good starting point is if an organization already has some information about what types of cyber threats they may face.

- **Collection**: In the collection stage, the organization obtains the data and information from their sources. In terms of cyber threat intelligence, this can come from government organizations such as government sponsored CERTs or through third-party organizations that sell threat intelligence. Finally, there are a great many **Open Source Intelligence** (**OSINT**) feeds that an organization can leverage.
- **Processing**: The sheer amount of intelligence that an organization may obtain can be staggering. During the processing stage, the organization takes the raw data and evaluates it and determines the relevance and reliability of the data and then collates it for the next step.
- **Analysis**: During the analysis stage, the organization evaluates the data that has been processed and combines it with other data from other sources. From here, it is interpreted and the finished product can be deemed *curated* or properly evaluated threat intelligence.
- **Dissemination**: The newly curated threat intelligence is then sent to the various users within the organization for use.

The cyclical nature of this methodology ensures that feedback is part of the process. Those analysts involved in the collection and processing should make sure that they receive feedback on the relevancy and veracity of the intelligence that is disseminated. From here, they would be able to tune the intelligence product over time. This ensures the highest level of relevancy and fidelity of intelligence consumed by the end users.

Threat intelligence direction

There is a great deal of information and data points available to an organization in terms of threat intelligence. One of the major hurdles that organizations will have to jump is in determining what their threat intelligence requirements are. With the depth of threat intelligence available, it is necessary to sift out the noise and focus on only threat intelligence that drives action within the organization.

In determining an organization's threat intelligence requirements, it is advisable to examine what actors pose a threat to the organization and how those threat actors would conduct an attack against the organization's network. To determine this, there are resources such as the **MITRE ATTACK** methodology, the cyber-kill chain and diamond method that can aid an organization in determining what their threat landscape is like and better align their threat intelligence utilization to meet that threat.

Cyber kill chain

The cyber kill chain is a concept first authored by three researchers at Lockheed-Martin. (`https://www.lockheedmartin.com/content/dam/lockheed/data/corporate/documents/LM-White-Paper-Intel-Driven-Defense.pdf`). The cyber kill chain outlines the stages of a network penetration that an attacker would have to go through to reach their ultimate goal. From here, organizations can extrapolate the various methods and IOCs that the organization may observe using detection capabilities enhanced with threat intelligence.

The cyber kill chain breaks down a network attack into seven steps that the attacker will progress through:

1. **Reconnaissance**: Attackers often spend a considerable amount of time reviewing open source intelligence such as social media, corporate websites, and domain registration to map the externally facing network of a target organization. Other reconnaissance methods include using network mapping and scanning tools such as NMAP and NETCAT to determine open ports or enabled services. Reconnaissance activities are often very difficult to detect as threat actors can conduct such attacks with no direct action or tune scanning so as to hide their efforts behind normal network traffic.

2. **Weaponization**: After conducting their reconnaissance, threat actors will then craft their tools for the actual penetration. For example, this can be a multi-stage malware payload that compromises a system. From an examination of the tools utilized in an attack, specific data points such as how the malware is packed or what exploits are used, can be combined to create a mosaic which is unique to the adversary, creating almost a DNA profile to compare against.

3. **Delivery**: Threat actors need a vector to deliver their malware or exploit payload. They may make use of VPN connections or deliver malware attached to a Word document emailed to an employee of the target organization.

4. **Exploitation**: In this stage, a threat actor either leverages a vulnerability within the target network or a functionality of tool sets such as PowerShell.

5. **Installation**: To gain more than a temporary foothold in the target organization, the threat actor will install their exploit or malware. This can even include the modification of settings or other functions on a compromised system.

6. **Command and Control (C2)**: To control the system once installation has been successful, the threat actor has to configure a remote C2 channel back to a central server. From here, they are able to maintain control, load additional exploits or malware, and observe the target organization's actions.

7. **Actions on objective**: Once the previous six steps have been completed, the threat actor moves onto accomplishing the objective of the penetration. For retail targets, this may mean infecting **Point of Sale** (**POS**) devices with malware and obtaining credit card numbers. In government, it may be acquiring a database of confidential data to sell.

By working through these various steps, an organization can see where individual IOCs and more general TTPs about threat actors can be obtained. One technique that is often utilized is to determine what threats are applicable to an organization and map them out at each stage to the individual IOCs that they will need specific threat intelligence to address. For example, they may have a report about a cyber-criminal group that targets POS devices. From here, they realize that they would need to understand what the IOCs would be for the initial tools configured in the weaponization stage. Next, they would examine the TTPs surrounding how the threat actor delivers the exploit or malware. The organization would then need to understand how the threat actor exploits the network either through vulnerabilities or utilizing native utilities. The installation of an exploit or malware will produce IOCs in running memory and the registry settings of a compromised system. Having access to the specific IOCs in those areas would assist the organization with developing additional detective capabilities or the ability to find these IOCs during an incident investigation.

Diamond model

The diamond model of intrusion analysis is a methodology to describe the process for differentiating APT threats and their specific attributes. The diamond is comprised of four components: **Adversary**, **Infrastructure**, **Capabilities**, and **Victim**.

The model attempts to determine the interplay between each of these four groups.

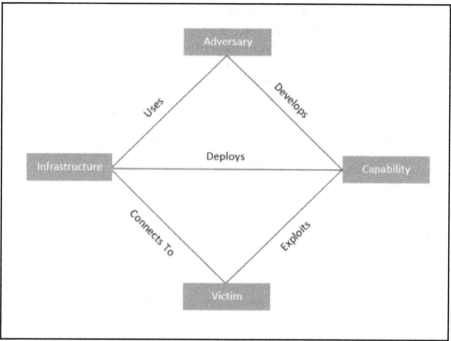

For example, take a simple malware attack. The **Adversary** is going to use a custom piece of malware. They develop the malware which feeds into their **Capability**. The **Adversary** then utilizes their capability to deploy the malware via a compromised web server or infrastructure. This connects to the **Victim** where the capability exploits a social engineering vulnerability.

This simple example highlights just a small sliver of how the diamond model can be utilized to categorize attacks. Therefore, it is recommended that a deeper exploration be undertaken by reviewing the diamond model paper, which can be downloaded at `http://www.dtic.mil/dtic/tr/fulltext/u2/a586960.pdf`. By integrating this model, an organization can have a better understanding of the threats they face and how those threats interact during an attack against their infrastructure. From here, they will be able to align their threat intelligence requirements to better fit their unique challenges.

One key reference in determining threat intelligence requirements is the MITRE ATT&CK wiki located at `https://attack.mitre.org/wiki/Main_Page`. The **Adversarial Tactics, Techniques & Common Knowledge (ATT&CK)** is an extensive collection of tactics and techniques in use by adversaries. The tactics include each stage of the *kill chain* and includes in-depth analysis of each technique.

ATT&CK also includes detailed information on the various APT groups that have been identified by various information security and incident response research organizations. Entries in the ATT&CK platform are also thoroughly documented and footnoted to allow analysts to view both a digest and a comprehensive report.

The value of the ATT&CK wiki is that it allows analysts to have detailed information on threat groups, their techniques, and tactics. This can better inform the other models such as the cyber kill chain and the diamond model. This allows organizations to fully understand what threats they face and align their threat intelligence requirements to fulfill that need.

Threat intelligence sources

There are three primary sources of threat intelligence that an organization can leverage. Threat intelligence can be produced by the organization in an internal process, acquired through open source methods, or finally, through third-party threat intelligence vendors. Each organization can utilize their own internal processes to determine what their needs are and what sources to leverage.

Internally developed sources

The most complex threat intelligence sources are those that an organization internally develops. This is due to the infrastructure that is needed to obtain the individual IOCs from malware campaigns and TTPs from threat actors. To obtain IOCs, the organization can make use of honeypots or other deliberately vulnerable systems to acquire unique malware samples. They will also need to have the expertise and systems available to not only evaluate suspected malware but reverse engineer it. From there, they would be able to extract the individual IOCs that can then be utilized.

Other systems such as SIEM platforms can be utilized to track an attacker's TTPs as they attempt to penetrate a network. From here, a **Security Operations Center (SOC)** analyst can record how different attackers go about their penetration attempt. With this information, the organization can build a profile of specific groups. This can aid in the alignment of security controls to better prevent or detect network intrusions.

Developing threat intelligence internally requires expertise in areas such as malware analysis, network, and host-based forensics. Further, the infrastructure required is often cost prohibitive. As a result, organizations are often forced to rely on third-party providers on what is shared openly among other organizations.

Commercial sourcing

An alternative to internal sourcing is to contract with a threat intelligence vendor. These organizations utilize their own personnel and infrastructure to acquire malware, analyze attacks, and conduct research on various threat groups. Commercial threat intelligence providers will often process the threat intelligence so that it is tailored to the individual client organization.

Often, commercial vendors provide SIEM and SOC services for a variety of clients utilizing a common SIEM platform. From here, they can aggregate samples of malware and attacks across various enterprises that span the entire world. This allows them to offer a comprehensive product to their clients. This is one of the distinct advantages to utilizing a commercial service. This is in addition to the cost savings that comes from transferring the cost to a third party.

Open source

One sourcing area that has become quite popular with organizations of every size are OSINT providers. Community groups and even commercial enterprises make threat intelligence available to the general public free of charge. Groups such SANS and US-CERT provide specific information on threats and vulnerabilities. Commercial providers such as Alien Vault provide an **Open Threat Exchange** (**OTX**) that allows a user community to share threat intelligence such as IOCs and TTPs. Other commercial organizations will provide whitepapers and reports on APT groups or strategic threat intelligence on emerging trends within the information security industry. Depending on the organization, OSINT is often very useful and provides a low-cost alternative to commercial services.

The widespread use of OSINT has led to various organizations creating methods to share threat intelligence across organizations. Depending on the source, the actual way that an organization can obtain threat intelligence is dependent on how it is configured.

While not a completely exhaustive list, the following are some of the formats that OSINT will be make available:

- **OpenIOC**: OpenIOC was first developed so that Mandiant products, such as the Redline application utilized in `Chapter 5`, *Forensic Imaging*, could ingest threat intelligence and utilize it to search for evidence of compromise on the systems analyzed. It has evolved into an XML schema that describes the technical IOCs that can be said an incident response analyst in determining if a system has been compromised.
- **STIX**: The **Structured Threat Information Exchange** (**STIX**) is a product of the OASIS consortium. This machine-readable format allows organizations to share threat intelligence across various commercial and freeware threat intelligence aggregation platforms.
- **TAXII**: The **Trusted Automated Exchange of Intelligence Information** (**TAXII**) is an application layer protocol that shares threat intelligence over HTTPS. TAXII defines an API that can be utilized to share threat intelligence in the STIX format.
- **Veris**: The **Vocabulary for Event Recording and Incident Sharing** (**VERIS**) is a comprehensive schema for standardizing the language of a cyber security incidents. The one key problem that the VERIS schema is attempting to solve is the lack of a standard way to document security incidents. VERIS provides a structure in which organizations have a defined way to categorize the variety of attacks that may occur. The VERIS schema also serves as the collection point of data provided by organizations that is incorporated into the Verizon Data Breach Study.

Threat intelligence platforms

As organizations begin to aggregate threat intelligence, whether it is created internally or externally sourced, they will need a platform in which to aggregate it. Any platform should be able to store threat intelligence indicators as well as provide analysts with an easily searchable database that allows them to connect IOCs from an incident to the intelligence available. There are several commercial platforms available as well as freeware versions that provide analysts with this capability. It is up to the individual organization to determine which platform fits their needs.

MISP threat sharing

One freeware platform available is the **Malware Information Sharing Platform** (**MISP**). This community project has produced a software platform that can be used by analysts to store data about malware and other exploits. From here, they can share this intelligence within their team or other personnel. MISP is a feature-rich application with such functionality as searching, a correlation engine, the ability to export and import IOCs, and community support where users can share data.

Installing MISP is dependent on the type of operating system platform in use. Complete directions are available at: `https://github.com/MISP/MISP/tree/2.4/INSTALL`. The creators of MISP also have provided users with a complete installation on an OVA Virtual Machine that can be downloaded for testing. The OVA file is available at: `https://www.circl.lu/assets/files/misp-training/MISP_v2.4.77.ova`. This is a good option as it allows analysts to test the functionality of the application without having to populate the database.

For the following demonstration, the training version of MISP will be utilized. Once logged in, the following window will appear:

The window contains all of the *Events* that the MISP database has on file. There is a good deal of data on this page, including *Tags* which identify the classifications of events, the date that they were added, and basic information that allows analysts to quickly sort through the various entries.

Clicking on an **Event ID** or the **View** icon to the far right of an event brings up another window:

In this window, analysts will be provided with a good deal of intelligence on the specific event. First off is the event data which is an overview of the attributes about the IOCs contained within the event:

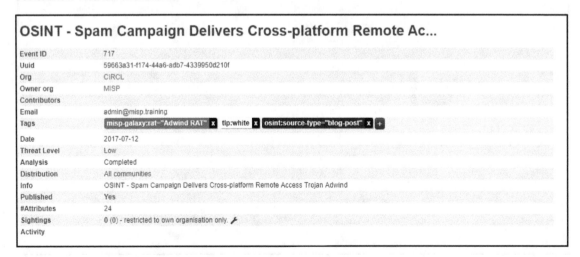

This data gives the analysts an overview of the event information that was available in the overall home window. Further down, the window reveals the specific elements of the event:

Here, the specific Trojan indicated in the background information has been evaluated by VirusTotal and following the link indicates that **45/59** anti-virus providers have detected that this event is linked with a Trojan virus:

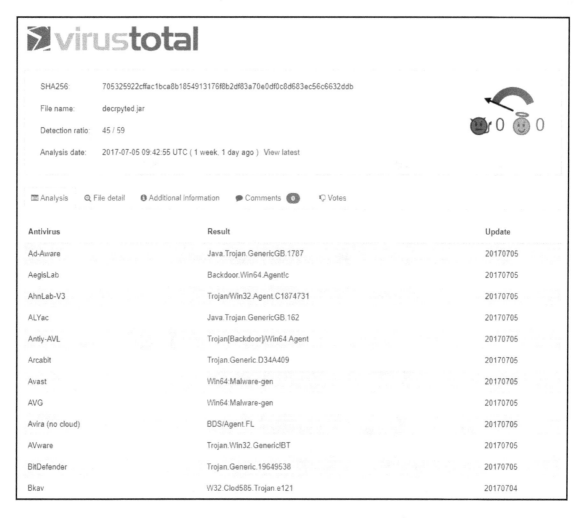

The real value of the MISP platform is the IOCs that are associated with this event. Navigating down the window, the analyst can then view the individual IOCs associated with this malware addressed in this event:

From here, the analyst is able to identify specific URLs that are associated with either C2 communications or if the malware is part of a multi-staged attack. The analyst can then either correlate these URLs with logs on the firewall or block those URLs through a web proxy to contain a possible malware outbreak.

Further down the window is more specific network information:

This intelligence allows analysts to drill down to a specific IP address and either block or craft an alert on the network exit point to determine if there are any additional systems that have been compromised.

MISP also allows analysts to see specific files associated with the event:

From here, analysts can utilize memory or disk images and search for matching hashes. This allows response analysts to drill down on the specific files that need to be addressed by any analysis and recover activity.

Threat intelligence needs to be timely in order for it to be effective. In the realm of cyber attacks, intelligence goes stale very quickly. Any platform that aggregates threat intelligence should have the ability to be updated. MISP has the ability to integrate various threat intelligence feeds and add those records to the event view. To demonstrate, navigate to the **Sync Actions** tab and then click **List Feeds**.

The following window will open:

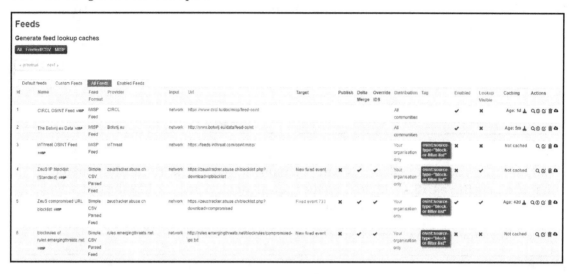

From here, navigate to the far right-hand corner to the down arrow surrounded by a circle. This will fetch all of the events from that source. For example, click on the button for source number five. After syncing, an additional entry is made within the events window:

Depending on the type of threat intelligence feed that the organization utilizes, MISP is able to enrich its dataset utilizing a connection from those sites. This allows analysts to keep their own dataset from various providers in one searchable location. From here, they can utilize this data as part of their proactive detection capability or to assist during an incident investigation.

Using threat intelligence

There are two distinct advantages to integrating threat intelligence into an organization's security methodology and response capability. From the proactive approach, organizations can utilize this data to increase the effectiveness of their detective and preventive controls. This allows organizations to enhance their ability to either block attacks through such mechanisms as blacklisting known malware sites or their detective capability through alerting on specific host behavior indicative of a compromise. On a reactive stance, organizations can integrate threat intelligence into their existing toolset and bring those to an investigation. This allows them to find evidentiary items that may have gone undetected with traditional information.

Proactive threat intelligence

Threat intelligence providers will often provide CSIRT and SOC teams with threat intelligence that can be easily fed into their SIEM of choice. This allows these teams to enhance their detective capability with intelligence that is timely, possible allowing them to keep pace with the current threats and increase the probability that they will detect one or more of these threats before damage can be done.

In the MISP platform, events with specific IOCs can have those IOCs converted into several different types of detective rules. For example, an organization is concerned about ransomware impacting the organization and wants to enhance their detective capability. Event number 711 in the MISP platform is associated with the *Locky* ransomware campaign. Clicking on the event number produces the following screen:

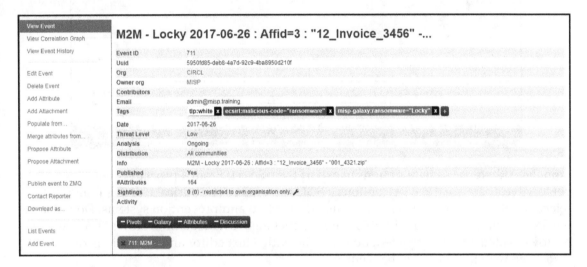

Navigate to the left-hand column and click on **Download as...** . This produces the following window:

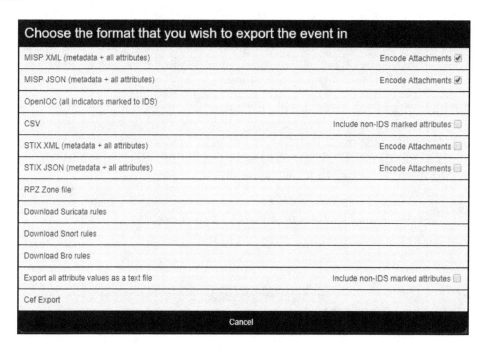

From here, there are several options to export the rule set. From a proactive/detective perspective, there are three key options a SOC can utilize. The Suricata, SNORT, and BRO selections all feed into open source intrusion detection and prevention systems. Download the SNORT rule associated with this event by clicking **Download Snort rules**. The file will be downloaded. Once completed, open the file with a text editor and the various rules associated with the event can be seen:

```
1  #This part might still contain bugs, use and your own risk and report any issues.
2  #
3  # MISP export of IDS rules - optimized for snort
4  #
5  # These NIDS rules contain some variables that need to exist in your configuration.
6  # Make sure you have set:
7  #
8  # $HOME_NET - Your internal network range
9  # $EXTERNAL_NET - The network considered as outside
10 # $SMTP_SERVERS - All your internal SMTP servers
11 # $HTTP_PORTS   - The ports used to contain HTTP traffic (not required with suricata export)
12 #
13 alert tcp $HOME_NET any -> $EXTERNAL_NET $HTTP_PORTS (msg: "MISP e711 [] Outgoing HTTP URL: http
14 alert udp any any -> any 53 (msg: "MISP e711 [] Hostname: 1010technologies.com"; content:"|01 00
15 alert tcp any any -> any 53 (msg: "MISP e711 [] Hostname: 1010technologies.com"; content:"|01 00
```

There are a number of rules that can be set with this download. Examining line 14, for example, indicates that the particular rule is setting Snort to alert if there is any attempted connection over UDP port 53 to the host `101otechnologies.com`. This host is in some fashion associated with this ransomware campaign. If this rule is incorporated, an organization would be alerted to this type of connection and be able to respond much quicker than finding out about ransomware activity when a user contacts the helpdesk indicating that their files have been encrypted.

One advantage that Snort rules have is that a good deal of commercial IDS/IPS vendors have the capability to ingest Snort rules into their own proprietary platform. This allows SOC and CSIRT personnel to load these rules from various sources, thereby enhancing their capability without having to have several different platforms to maintain.

Reactive threat intelligence

During an investigation, the CSIRT or analysts may come across a situation where an incident investigation seems to have stalled. This could be due to the fact that the analysts know something is wrong or have indicators of a compromise but no concrete evidence to point in a specific direction. Threat intelligence can be leveraged by analysts to enhance their ability to discover previously undiscovered evidence.

Autopsy

A good deal of tools that can ingest threat intelligence are available to incident response analysts. For example, disk forensic platforms discussed in Chapter 8, *Analyzing System Memory,* have the ability to ingest hashes from threat intelligence feeds to search for IOCs. In addition to commercial disk forensic tools, the Autopsy platform can conduct searches against a hash set. Navigating back to the export format in MISP, there is the ability to download a `.csv` file of the event indicators. For event 711, download the CSV file. Next, filter the data and select on hash values in the *type* column. This produces the following list:

uuid	event_i	category	type	value	comme	to_ids	date
5950fd86-	711	Artifacts dropped	md5	8cd9f803947badddbfafc584edfdeebb		1	20170627
5950fd87-	711	Artifacts dropped	md5	a0d81f0bffb0e20a34191385031cf17a		1	20170627
59520c6b-	711	Artifacts dropped	sha1	f5fce485a72ab82a5e5b48b98befd5e0568a83e1	#NAME?	1	20170627
59520c6b-	711	Artifacts dropped	sha256	83b366204ef60cca5468c2db1baadeb7590f97493c451fa005f9b583ce691133	- Xcheckec	1	20170627
59520c6b-	711	Artifacts dropped	sha1	3e19f754ea0fef9e62d91dfd4f22e6c73240bcbc	- Xcheckec	1	20170627
59520c6b-	711	Artifacts dropped	sha256	8015133c16d41fdfbeb5f86f5d82ffb124a131ed012375d3cf70babe2f440ac8	#NAME?	1	20170627

From here, the hash values can be loaded into Autopsy. First, in Autopsy, click *Tools* and then *Options*. Then click *Hash Databases* and then *New database*. The following window will appear:

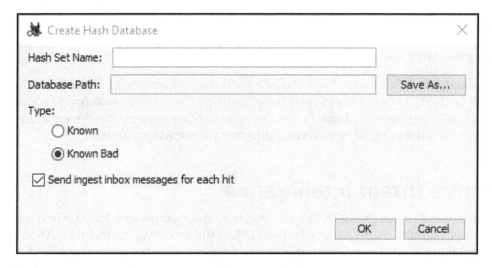

Enter in a name for the hash set. A suggestion is to use a title and the MISP event number 711. Click *Save As* and navigate to where the database will be saved. Leave the default settings in place. This will indicate a hit on any of the hash files located. Click **OK**. In the next window, click **Add Hashes to Database**. Copy the hashes to the clipboard from the CSV file and then right click in the blank space and select **Paste**. The hashes are now loaded. Click **Add Hashes to Database**.

This capability allows analysts to search through disk images for matching hashes. This is a much more efficient way to search for evidence than attempting to find the files through other methods. Autopsy also allows for different databases depending on the incident. This ability to continually feed updated information allows analysts to find evidence on a new type of compromise on that event a week or two ago that would have gone undetected with traditional searching.

Redline

Threat intelligence can also be utilized with Redline. Redline allows for searching for IOCs through a collector or IOCs can be loaded and searched in an existing memory capture. For example, if analysts would like to search for matching IOCs in a memory image, they would first open the memory image. In the lower left-hand corner, click on the tab **IOC Reports**. This will create a new button titled **Create a New IOC Report**.

The following window will appear:

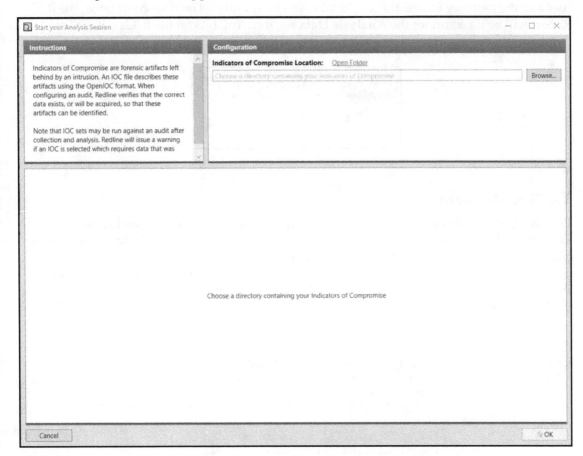

Redline has the ability to ingest IOCs within the OpenIOC format. Analysts should create a folder on their system where the IOC files can be placed, as Redline will not read a single file but all IOC files within the folder. Click on **Browse** and navigate to the IOC folder. Then IOCs are loaded and specific information is loaded into the Redline platform.

Name:	STUXNET VIRUS (METHODOLOGY)
Author:	Mandiant **Created:** 1/1/0001 12:00:00 AM
Path:	D:\IOCs\iocbucket_d9c807f2ee2822e0349ead3c6965130b6c6c64ff_stuxnet.ioc
Description:	Generic indicator for the stuxnet virus. When loaded, stuxnet spawns lsass.exe in a suspended state. The malware then maps in its own executable section and fixes up the CONTEXT to point to the newly mapped in section. This is a common task performed by malware and allows the malware to execute under the pretense of a known and trusted process.

Clicking **OK** runs the IOCs against the memory capture. Depending on the amount of IOC files and the memory image, this could take several minutes. The once completed, the IOC Report will be listed under the **Analysis Data** section. Any hits on the IOCs will be listed there.

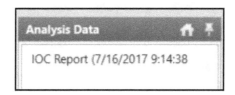

Yara and Loki

Two integrated tools that allow for leveraging threat intelligence during an incident are Yara and Loki. Yara is often referred to as the *Swiss Army Knife* of pattern matching. It was created to assist malware researches with classifying malware.(https://github.com/virustotal/yara). Through the use of Boolean expressions and strings, a malware sample can be classified. For example, the Yara rule for a variation of the PoisoIvy RAT looks like this:

```
rule PoisonIvy_Generic_3 {
    meta:
            description = "PoisonIvy RAT Generic Rule"
            author = "Florian Roth"
            date = "2015-05-14"
            hash = "e1cbdf740785f97c93a0a7a01ef2614be792afcd"
    strings:
            $k1 = "Tiger324{" fullword ascii
            $s2 = "WININET.dll" fullword ascii
            $s3 = "mscoree.dll" fullword wide
            $s4 = "WS2_32.dll" fullword
            $s5 = "Explorer.exe" fullword wide
            $s6 = "USER32.DLL"
            $s7 = "CONOUT$"
            $s8 = "login.asp"
            $h1 = "HTTP/1.0"
            $h2 = "POST"
            $h3 = "login.asp"
            $h4 = "check.asp"
            $h5 = "result.asp"
            $h6 = "upload.asp"
    condition:
            uint16(0) == 0x5a4d and filesize < 500KB and
                (
```

```
            $k1 or all of ($s*) or all of ($h*)
      )
  }
```

The preceding rule configures Yara to alert to any of the strings found as the PosionIvy RAT generic.

Yara is available as a tool for use in malware research but one of the features is the ability to integrate the Yara functionality into other tools. One such tool is Loki - a simple IOC scanner (`https://github.com/Neo23x0/Loki`). This lightweight platform allows incident response analysts to scan folders, files, or even entire volumes for IOCs such as Yara rules, known bad file hashes, filename IOCs, and known C2 servers. Out of the box, Loki has an extensive library of IOCs that are updated regularly.

To check a system volume for specific IOCs, download and extract Loki to a USB device. Open the `Loki` folder and the following files are found:

config	7/16/2017 9:21 AM	File folder	
docs	7/16/2017 9:21 AM	File folder	
loki	6/17/2017 2:12 PM	Application	7,794 KB
loki-upgrader	6/17/2017 2:13 PM	Application	7,709 KB
README.md	9/18/2016 12:54 PM	MD File	14 KB
requirements	5/16/2016 2:04 PM	Text Document	1 KB
run_loki	3/10/2015 3:42 PM	Windows Batch File	0 KB

Loki has to be updated with the most current IOCs so right click on **loki-upgrader**. The upgrader will run, updating both the executable and the signature files. Once completed, the updater will close. Navigate back to the Loki file and a new file called **signature-base** will have been added:

config	7/16/2017 9:52 AM	File folder	
docs	7/16/2017 9:52 AM	File folder	
signature-base	7/16/2017 9:53 AM	File folder	
loki	7/16/2017 9:53 AM	Application	7,794 KB
loki-upgrade	7/16/2017 9:53 AM	Text Document	23 KB
loki-upgrader	6/17/2017 2:13 PM	Application	7,709 KB
README.md	7/16/2017 9:53 AM	MD File	14 KB
requirements	7/16/2017 9:53 AM	Text Document	1 KB
run_loki	7/16/2017 9:53 AM	Windows Batch File	0 KB

This folder contains all of the IOCs that Loki can search a volume against. This also allows analysts who create their own Yara rules to load them into the file as well, giving them the ability to customize the solution. To run a scan of a system, right click on the **loki** application and run it as an administrator. This will start the executable and open the following window:

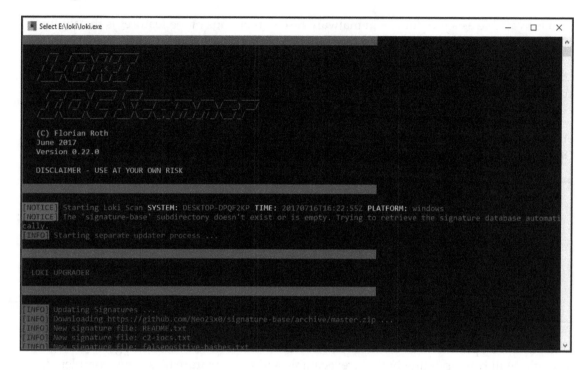

From here, Loki will begin to update its ruleset:

After the ruleset is updated, Loki will then begin searching the volume for any matching patterns or IOCs:

From here, the analyst can make note of any hits and conduct an examination later. Another key feature is that Loki can be deployed on multiple systems as part of a triage of systems that have possibly been infected with a new strain of malware. For example, an incident response analyst may be able to search for the IOC of the Petya ransomware attack using Yara rules taken from a threat intelligence provider, such as Kaspersky's SecureList, which includes a download of the Yara rules.

Yara rules

Download Yara rule expetr.yara as a ZIP archive.

```
rule ransomware_exPetr {
meta:

copyright = "Kaspersky Lab"
description = "Rule to detect PetrWrap ransomware samples"
last_modified = "2017-06-27"
author = "Kaspersky Lab"
hash = "71B6A493388E7D0B40C83CE903BC6B04"
version = "1.0"

strings:

$a1 =
"MIIBCgKCAQEAxP/VqKc0yLe9JhVqFMQGwUITO6WpXWnKSNQAYT0O65Cr8PjIQInTeHkXEjfO2n2JmURWV/uHB0ZrlQ/wc
YJBwLhQ9EqJ3iDqmN19Oo7NtyEUmbYmopcq+YLIBZzQ2ZTK0A2DtX4GRKxEEFLCy7vP12EYOPXknVy/+mf0JFWixz29QiTf
5oLu15wVLONCuEibGaNNpgq+CXsPwflTDbDDmdrRliUEUw6o3pt5pNOskfOJbMan2TZu" fullword wide
$a2 =
".3ds.7z.accdb.ai.asp.aspx.avhd.back.bak.c.cfg.conf.cpp.cs.ctl.dbf.disk.djvu.doc.docx.dwg.eml.fdb.gz.h.hdd.kdbx.mail.mdb.
msg.nrg.ora.ost.ova.ovf.pdf.php.pmf.ppt.pptx.pst.pvi.py.pyc.rar.rtf.sln.sql.tar.vbox.vbs.vcb.vdi.vfd.vmc.vmdk.vmsd.vmx.vsdx.v
sv.work.xls" fullword wide
$a3 = "DESTROY ALL OF YOUR DATA! PLEASE ENSURE THAT YOUR POWER CABLE IS PLUGGED" fullword ascii
$a4 = "1Mz7153HMuxXTuR2R1t78mGSdzaAtNbBWX" fullword ascii
$a5 = "wowsmith123456@posteo.net." fullword wide

condition:

(uint16(0) == 0x5A4D) and
(filesize<1000000) and
(any of them)
}
```

From here, the Yara rules can then be fed into Loki or another platform and utilized to triage suspected systems.

The number of tools that an incident response analyst can bring to bear is increasing every day. These include commercial tools and freeware tools that integrate a variety of threat intelligence feeds and functionality. These tools can be used proactively to detect and alert as well as investigate an incident in progress. CSIRTs should make a concerted effort to examine these tools and integrate them into their processes. Doing so will aid them in detecting and efficiently investigating an incident.

Summary

Sun Tzu's Art of War includes the strategic concept of knowing your adversary and knowing yourself. Through this, one can be confident in your ability to prevail in the contest. Threat intelligence has quickly become a critical component of an organization's proactive security controls as well as an important factor in its ability to respond to an incident. For organizations to leverage the advantages that threat intelligence provides, they first must understand the threat. From here they can define their requirements and begin the intelligence process. Finally, by integrating their toolset to utilize threat intelligence, they can position themselves to have more effective proactive controls and the ability to respond efficiently. While threat intelligence may not remove the fear of an adversary entirely, it allows organizations a good deal more ammunition to combat today's threats.

Index

CPSIA information can be obtained
at www.ICGtesting.com
Printed in the USA
FSHW011323111119
63978FS

9 781787 288683